# Rimsky-Korsakov's Harmonic Theory

# Rimsky-Korsakov's Harmonic Theory

## The *Practical Manual of Harmony*, Its Sources, History, and Traditions

Larisa Petrushkevich Jackson

University of North Texas Press
Denton, Texas

Printed in the United States of America.

10 9 8 7 6 5 4 3 2 1

Permissions:
University of North Texas Press
1155 Union Circle #311336
Denton, TX 76203-5017

The paper used in this book meets the minimum requirements of the American National Standard for Permanence of Paper for Printed Library Materials, z39.48.1984. Binding materials have been chosen for durability.

Library of Congress Cataloging-in-Publication Data

Jackson, Larisa Petrushkevich, author.
Rimsky-Korsakov's harmonic theory : the Practical manual of harmony, its sources, history, and traditions / Larisa Petrushkevich Jackson.
pages cm
Includes bibliographical references and index.
ISBN-13 978-1-57441-860-6 (cloth)
ISBN-13 978-1-57441-871-2 (ebook)
1. LCSH: Rimsky-Korsakov, Nikolay, 1844–1908. Prakticheskiĭ uchebnik garmonii. 2. Rimsky-Korsakov, Nikolay, 1844–1908—Harmony. 3. Rimsky-Korsakov, Nikolay, 1844–1908—Criticism and interpretation. 4. Rimsky-Korsakov, Nikolay, 1844–1908—Influence. 5. Harmony. 6. Modulation (Music) 7. Music theory—Germany—History—19th century. 8. Music theory—Russia—History—19th century.

ML410.R52 J33 2022
781.2/5–dc23

2022005564

The electronic edition of this book was made possible by the support of the Vick Family Foundation.

Typeset by vPrompt eServices.

Image on front cover and frontispiece courtesy of www.last.fm/music/Nikolai+Rimsky-Korsakov/+images

# Contents


Acknowledgments vii

Introduction ix

**Part One** **Introduction and Analysis of Rimsky-Korsakov's Harmonic Theory**

Chapter 1 The Background and History of the *Practical Manual of Harmony* 3

Chapter 2 Editions of the *Practical Manual of Harmony* 11

Chapter 3 Introduction to the Theory 15

Chapter 4 Scales and Chords 17

Chapter 5 Modulation and First-Degree Key Relationships 21

Chapter 6 Aspects of Modulation between the First-Degree Keys 23

Chapter 7 Second- and Third-Degree Key Relationships 27

Chapter 8 Deceptive Progressions and Enharmonicism 33

Chapter 9 The Modulatory Plan 37

Chapter 10 Analysis of Rimsky-Korsakov's Harmonic System 43

**Part Two** **Rimsky-Korsakov's Harmonic Theory and the Nineteenth-Century German Theoretical Tradition**

Chapter 11 Channels of German Influence 59

Chapter 12 Modulation and Key Relationships in Nineteenth-Century German Music Theory 65

Moritz Hauptmann 65

Gottfried Weber 74

Adolf Bernhard Marx 78

Siegfried Dehn 85

Johann Christian Lobe 90

Ernst Friedrich Richter 92

Ludwig Bussler 95

Chapter 13 Analysis of German Tonal Models 99

Chapter 14 Rimsky-Korsakov's System in the Context of Nineteenth-Century German Theory 107

**Part Three Rimsky-Korsakov's Harmonic Theory and the Nineteenth-Century Russian Theoretical Tradition**

Chapter 15 Early Treatises 119

Chapter 16 Liadov and Rimsky-Korsakov 125

Chapter 17 Tchaikovsky and Rimsky-Korsakov 129

Chapter 18 Balakirev and Rimsky-Korsakov 145

Conclusions 169

Appendix 1: Table of Editions in Russia and Soviet Union of Rimsky-Korsakov's *Manual of Harmony* and *Practical Manual of Harmony* 171

Appendix 2: List of Translations of Rimsky-Korsakov's *Practical Manual of Harmony* 173

Appendix 3: Table of Contents of Tchaikovsky's *Manual of Harmony* (1872) 174

Appendix 4: Tables of Contents of Rimsky-Korsakov's *Manual of Harmony* (1884/1885) and *Practical Manual of Harmony* (1886) 176

Appendix 5: Balakirev, *Sbornik Russkikh Narodnykh Pesen*, selected songs 183

Appendix 6: Ekmalian, *Pataraq*, selected songs 203

Appendix 7: List of Early Russian Treatises and Translations of Foreign Treatises 208

Endnotes 215

Bibliography 249

Index 263

# Acknowledgments

While most of the material in this book was initially based on my doctoral dissertation, it evolved into its current form after presentations at various institutions and the many fruitful discussions and exchanges that ensued. I am very grateful to the many people who contributed in various ways to the preparation of this final text. In particular, my sincere gratitude goes to Ian Bent, Joseph Dubiel, Richard W. Wortman, Marina Ledkovskaya, Adalyat Issiyeva, Ada Aynbinder, Igor Kornilov, Lydia Ader, William Hussey, Frank Heidlberger, Marla McDaniel, Inessa Bazayev, and Elena Geilikman, for their thoughtful advice, inspirational ideas, and support through the various stages of the manuscript. I am thankful to the staff of numerous libraries and archives, especially the St. Petersburg Conservatory Library and the RGMTR (Russian State Music Television and Radio) Center Archive.

My greatest inspiration for this book came from the prodigious work of Richard Taruskin and his Promethean spirit. I am grateful to Richard not only for the inspiration, but also for his generosity in offering a painstaking reading of the manuscript and enlightening advice.

My thanks to Morgan Gieringer and Adriance Rhoades of UNT Libraries Special Collections for providing archival scans of Balakirev's songs for Appendix 5.

Finally, I am very grateful to Karen DeVinney and Ronald Chrisman of the University of North Texas Press for their outstanding editorial help.

In memory of Richard Taruskin (1945–2022)

# Introduction

The harmonic system Rimsky-Korsakov presented in his *Practical Manual of Harmony* was highly distinctive among European theoretical treatises of its kind. A unique element of his harmonic system was what he called the "harmonic major scale." Rimsky-Korsakov not only first identified this scale but included it among the scales fundamental to his elaborate harmonic system. By doing so, Rimsky-Korsakov rolled out a system that is unlike any other. The etiology of the harmonic major scale was attributed to Rimsky-Korsakov in earlier scholarship.[1] It could nonetheless be closely tied in important ways to the German theoretical tradition and specifically to Moritz Hauptmann, as it manifests elements similar to the idea of harmonic dualism.[2]

One of the most imaginative composers of the nineteenth century, Rimsky-Korsakov is acknowledged to be among its leading figures. In stark contrast to his universally praised treatises on instrumentation, it can come as a complete surprise to many outside Russia to learn that Rimsky-Korsakov wrote a treatise on harmony. Despite translations into several languages, including English in 1930, this treatise has escaped the scrupulous examination it warrants.[3] Rimsky-Korsakov's role as a leading pedagogue is similarly less familiar outside of Russia. These two facets of his creativity, as a composer and as a teacher, intersect in his *Practical Manual of Harmony* of 1884–1886, which was written in response to the need for a definitive text on this subject for his conservatory teaching in composition. Moreover, the study of Rimsky-Korsakov's harmonic theory, as codified in his harmony treatise, sheds light on his compositional practice. It also opens avenues for further research into both the pre- and post-Rimsky musical repertoire of older composers, such as Glinka and Balakirev, as well as the following generations of composers trained in the St. Petersburg school. Finally, studying Rimsky-Korsakov's perspective on tonal relationships and the system they form offers a new instrument for understanding the larger musical landscape known as Russian musical style.

Rimsky-Korsakov's *Practical Manual of Harmony* was one of only two harmony manuals written by a major composer in the nineteenth century.[4] It is therefore even more remarkable that it has been only marginally researched in Russian musicology and has largely escaped meaningful scholarly inquiry outside of Russia, even in such major reference collections as *New Grove Dictionary of Music and Musicians* and *Die Musik in Geschichte und Gegenwart.*[5] In the present study we examine Rimsky-Korsakov's harmonic theory and its most exceptional element, the fully developed system of key relationships, from which we then infer his concept of tonal space and place it in a wider historical context.

Let us briefly glance now at the history of harmonic theory, focusing specifically on the idea of key relationships. It was in the eighteenth century that theorists began to explore the logic of movement within tonal space, or the large-scale coherence of key changes within a movement or a complete composition, by measuring distances of secondary keys from a central key. Their observations resulted in a number of conceptions, beliefs, or models displaying the distances, or proximities, involved. Prompted by Jean-Philippe Rameau's pioneering *Traite de l'harmonie* of 1722, this topic was further tackled by German theorists,[6] with various discussions of key relationships developed by Johann Heinichen,[7] Johann Mattheson,[8] Johann Kirnberger,[9] and Heinrich Koch.[10]

During the nineteenth century, the relationship of keys was revisited in French theory by Charles-Simon Catel, Jérôme-Joseph de Momigny, Antoine Reicha, François-Joseph Fétis, and Marie Gabriel Savard.[11] In Vienna, Emanuel Förster, August Swoboda, and Simon Sechter included some discussion of key relationships in their theoretical works.[12] In German theory, we can find discussion of key relationships, with varying degrees of involvement, in the works of the majority of prominent nineteenth-century theorists: Gottfried Weber, A. B. Marx, Siegfried Dehn, Johann Christian Lobe, Ernst Richter, Mortiz Hauptmann, Arthur von Öttingen, and Hugo Riemann.[13] It is important to note here that Riemann's well-known and widely studied concept of harmonic dualism, which appears in his 1887 writings, not only relies on the concept of the major-minor key from Hauptmann's 1853 seminal work, but also echoes Rimsky-Korsakov's core 1884 concept of the harmonic major scale. Riemann, who was younger than Rimsky by five years and began publishing on harmonic dualism a few years after Rimsky's treatise, has attracted due attention from music theorists. However, neither Riemann's late 1880s harmony studies nor the 1898 *Geschichte der Musiktheorie im IX.–XIX. Jahrhundert*, nor the work of Riemannian or neo-Riemannian scholars showed familiarity with or even acknowledged Rimsky-Korsakov's harmonic theory, let alone examined or considered its implications.[14]

In the twentieth century, tonal relationships were discussed by Viennese theorists Heinrich Schenker[15] and Arnold Schoenberg.[16] It is worth noting that Schoenberg's Chart of Regions bears a strong resemblance to Weber's aforementioned work, including the well-known Table of the Relationships of Keys developed more than a century earlier. In French theory, relationships of keys were discussed in the writings of Vincent d'Indy, Darius Milhaud, and Olivier Messiaen.[17] In Russian theory, tonal relationships were examined by Boris Yavorsky.[18] More recently, the issue of tonal space has served as the main focus of study for a number of North American theorists, including Darius Meyer, Fred Lerdahl, both singly and with Ray Jackendoff, David Lewin, H. Christopher Longuet-Higgins Edward Lisle, and Carol Krumhansl.[19]

Although, as mentioned, the subject of the relationship of keys was discussed by nineteenth19th-century French theorists, including Catel, Momigny, and Savard, it was Fétis who assigned to the term "tonality" the meaning of a "principle regulateur des rapports" (principle regulating the relationships).[20] Fétis extended this concept to describe four different historical stages of musical style: *tonalité ancienne* or *ordre unitonique, tonalité moderne* or *ordre transitonique, ordre pluritonique*, and *ordre omnitonique*.[21] In contrast to his famous predecessor Rameau, Fétis perceived tonality not as being controlled by acoustical or "natural" law but rather as having a "metaphysical nature," a concept he inherited from Momigny, whose forward-looking concept of tonality described tonal space as encompassing twenty-seven notes.[22] The resulting expanded key was then divided into three categories echoing familiar Greek division: diatonic, chromatic, and enharmonic. Nineteenth-century Viennese theory and culture can therefore be described as adhering to the classical ideas.[23] However, the German theory of the period also consistently displayed a forward-looking trend, the vast output and strong influence of which will be considered below in considerable detail.

In this study, in addition to analyzing Rimsky-Korsakov's harmonic ideas, we will also examine the environment in which he created his harmony treatise and its sources. Evidence is lacking of either French or Viennese theoretical treatises having a direct impact on Rimsky-Korsakov's background or immediate environment. Only two theoretical traditions may be clearly documented as relevant and will, therefore, be considered: the Russian and the German. This contextual analysis will also help us to better understand the place of the *Practical Manual of Harmony* in the history of theory.

In part 1 we first consider the history and circumstances surrounding the writing of the treatise. We then offer a detailed account of Rimsky-Korsakov's theory of the relationship of keys and conclude with an analysis of this theory. In part 2 we trace specific sources that may have been available or influenced Rimsky-Korsakov, analyzing the concept of the relationship of keys in these sources and mapping out ties between German theoretical ideas and Rimsky-Korsakov's work. Finally, in part 3, we examine the immediate musical and social environment in which the *Practical Manual of Harmony* was written and place Rimsky-Korsakov's work in the context of Russian theoretical tradition.

With the exception of customary spellings of certain names, such as Tchaikovsky, the US Library of Congress system is used for transliterating Russian words written using the Cyrillic alphabet into the Latin alphabet. Translations from Russian are my own unless specified otherwise.

Both versions of Rimsky-Korsakov's harmony treatise *Uchebnik garmonii*, the lithograph edition of 1884/1885 and *Prakticheskii uchebnik garmonii* of 1886, are reprinted in his Complete Edition of Works and are referenced under the abbreviation *PSS/LPP* (*Polnoe sobranie sochinenii. Literaturnye proizvedeniia i perepiska*) throughout the book.

# Part One

# Introduction and Analysis of Rimsky-Korsakov's Harmonic Theory

# Chapter 1

# The Background and History of the *Practical Manual of Harmony*

Until the nineteenth century, an indigenous secular theoretical tradition was almost nonexistent in Russia.[24] Russian church music theory, with roots extending to the seventeenth century, had remained an isolated field bound to a limited repertory of *a capella* sacred works, since the Russian Orthodox church traditionally prohibited the use of instruments in services. In addition, the church had discouraged any contact with developments in secular music, Russian or Western, for the greater part of its history. Thus, the sacred and secular domains of music and consequently music theory did not intersect in Russia until the nineteenth century.

The beginning of the modern Russian theoretical tradition was stimulated by the creation of conservatories in St. Petersburg in 1862 and Moscow in 1866, as well as by the appearance of two harmony manuals, that of Tchaikovsky in 1872 and Rimsky-Korsakov in 1884–1886.[25] There were no models of superior value in the national tradition, so, when confronted with the need to teach theoretical disciplines in the newly established conservatories, Tchaikovsky and Rimsky-Korsakov each wrote a treatise incorporating his own individual understanding of the subject. These works are as distinct as the two composers' music and will be examined and compared in part 3.

Tracing the sources of Rimsky-Korsakov's distinctive harmonic thinking takes us back to his formative years with Balakirev and the aesthetics of the latter's radical circle, Moguchaya Kuchka, also known as The Five or the New Russian School. Balakirev became a central force in the development of Russian art music in the second half of the century. His volcanic personality and brilliant musical gifts worked together to ignite an outburst of splendid creativity in a group of young composers, whose music later became Russian classics: Musorgsky, Rimsky-Korsakov, and Borodin. One of Balakirev's fundamental inspirations, transmitted to the members of his circle, was a quest for new musical ideas and ways of expression, which led Balakirev to explore the folk traditions of the vast territory of Imperial Russia, particularly Russian folklore and the music of areas then regarded as the Russian Orient.

Rimsky-Korsakov, the youngest member of this progressive circle, became part of The Five in 1861 at the age of seventeen. The ideas and astonishing personality of its leader, Balakirev, left a deep imprint upon Rimsky-Korsakov's mind:

> the spell of his personality was tremendous. Young, with marvelously alert eyes, with handsome beard; unhesitating, authoritative, and straightforward in speech; ready at any moment for beautiful piano improvisation, remembering every bar of music familiar to him, instantly learning by heart the compositions played for him, he was bound to exercise that spell as none else could ... His influence over those around him was boundless, and resembled some magnetic or mesmeric force.[26]

In contrast to Balakirev, Rimsky-Korsakov increasingly felt a need for more comprehensive and systematic training (which Balakirev could not and would not offer to him):

> What did I need? A piano technique, the technique of harmony and counterpoint, and an idea of musical forms. He [Balakirev] should have given me a few lessons in harmony and counterpoint, should have made me write a few fugues and explained the grammar of musical forms to me. He could not do it, as he had not studied systematically himself and considered it unnecessary. Having made me write a symphony after our first meeting, he cut me off from preparatory work and the acquisition of a technique. And I, who did not know the names of all intervals

> and chords, to whom harmony meant but the far-famed prohibition of parallel octaves and fifths, who had no idea as to what a double counterpoint was, or the meaning of cadence, thesis and antithesis, and period, I set out to compose a symphony.[27]

In the 1870s, or in his late twenties, Rimsky-Korsakov finally began to study harmony and counterpoint on his own, a clear sign of alienation from the philosophy of Balakirev's group. Rimsky-Korsakov recalls, Musorgsky's reaction to Rimsky-Korsakov's new preoccupation was typical of The Five: "Musorgsky regarded me with a certain suspicion. My studies in harmony and counterpoint, which began to absorb me, did not please him at all. It looked as though he suspected me of being the conservative professor who might convict him of parallel fifths, and this was unbearable to him."[28] The following remark by Rimsky-Korsakov sums up his new status as a "heretic" in relation to the aesthetics cultivated by The Five: "my studies of harmony and counterpoint made me a suspect in the artistic sense."[29]

If a typical beginner's initiation into the formal discipline of music involves memorizing a new body of material to adopt its logic and principles and acquire new techniques, it was a very different experience for Rimsky-Korsakov, who completed this immersion through writing his own treatise. However, standard portrayals of Rimsky-Korsakov's belated and amateurish musical education are misleading and poorly informed. Rimsky-Korsakov started to compose at age ten, joined Balakirev's group at age seventeen, and was well on his way as a composer at twenty-seven when he unconventionally undertook a concentrated study of harmony and counterpoint upon entering St. Petersburg Conservatory as a professor. This was at about the same age as Tchaikovksy, who followed a traditional path when he took on a Moscow Conservatory professorship following his graduation from the St. Petersburg Conservatory. Before Rimsky even began this music theory tour de force, he had already composed the opera *Pskovitianka* (*The Maid of Pskov*), orchestral works including Symphony no. 1, *Overture on Russian Themes*, *Fantasia on Serbian Themes*, the opera *Sadko*, and Symphony no. 2 (*Antar*), and he was completing his Symphony no. 3, several song sets (including opp. 2, 3, 4, 7, and 8), and some character pieces. By the time of writing his harmony treatise, he had also finished the operas *May Night* and *Snow Maiden*, a piano concerto, numerous choral compositions, various works of chamber music (including two string quartets), a string Sextet in A Major and wind Quintet in B-flat Major. The creation of his own *Manual of Harmony* was one of the major and significant results of years of study and application.

Rimsky-Korsakov's training by Balakirev had been timely—he was seventeen when initially introduced to him—but it was certainly unorthodox and unique. Rimsky-Korsakov's desire for comprehensive knowledge stemmed from a growing realization of the technical limitations which stood in the way of his composing. In other words, rather than a student eager to survey a new landscape, he was a craftsman looking for additional tools. Rimsky-Korsakov rapidly outgrew Balakirev's legacy, as in fact happened to all members of the circle, and this took the form of increasing resentment toward and disillusionment with the New Russian School in general: "O Russian school! O Stasov! O Balakirev ... who began to disappoint me more and more as a musician, as his pupil and as a person!"[30]

Rimsky-Korsakov's disenchantment with his earlier experience and past idol, Balakirev, coincided with a period of artistic stagnation in the mid-1880s. After completing his highly successful opera *The Snow Maiden* in 1881, Rimsky-Korsakov wrote no important compositions until *Capriccio Espagnol* in 1887. This was a time of uncertainty, self-doubt, and searching for new musical ideas: "I have not created any music since autumn because I have no desire, and because nothing comes to mind. ... Such confusions and contradictions have appeared in my musical views and convictions that I see no hope of sorting it all out."[31] This prolonged creative crisis, which lasted about six years, also shaped his first theoretical treatise, the *Practical Manual of Harmony*.

Confronting the task of writing his own harmony manual, Rimsky-Korsakov was at the same time confronting common-practice theoretical tradition. Work on the harmony treatise was one of the ways for Rimsky-Korsakov to resolve certain contradictions within himself, to identify his position in relationship to common-practice theory, and to redefine his artistic position.

During the same critical period, Rimsky-Korsakov also manifested these changes by joining a new group, known as Beliaev's circle, and by surrounding himself with a different environment. As a young composer in the 1860s, Rimsky-Korsakov had been completely immersed in the contagious ideas and atmosphere of The Five and Balakirev's commanding influence. Twenty years later, however, Rimsky-Korsakov was a mature musician and himself became the center of an artistic circle formed in 1883.

Beliaev, an amateur music lover, performed the role of Maecenas in the St. Petersburg music world during the 1880s through his activities as a publisher, impresario, and host, while Rimsky-Korsakov was the artistic leader and adviser of the circle. Rimsky's new role displeased Balakirev, who continued to hold regular musical evenings on Tuesdays in spite of the fact that the most promising young composers and musicians of St. Petersburg were now more interested in Beliaev's Friday events, as we can see from Balakirev's telling remark: "he [Rimsky-Korsakov] sold his talent for 30 pieces of silver to Satan who, disastrously for Russian music, revealed himself in the form of M. P. Beliaev."[32]

Despite its proclaimed new course, Beliaev's circle headed by Rimsky-Korsakov was in many ways a continuation of Balakirev's The Five. Rimsky-Korsakov and Stasov were an important part of the new group, just as they were in Balakirev's circle. Commitment to the advancement of new Russian music was as strong in Beliaev's circle as it was in Balakirev's circle. However, Rimsky-Korsakov's personality and approach created a number of important differences in the atmosphere of Beliaev's circle by comparison with that of Balakirev. The membership of Balakirev's circle was small and exclusive and yielded some of the most prominent composers and critics of the capital's musical society, while Beliaev's circle had far more members, only three of whom were prominent composers: Rimsky-Korsakov, Glazunov, and Liadov. Another important difference may be found in the technical background of the members of the two groups, since Beliaev's circle, unlike Balakirev's, primarily comprised trained professionals, the majority of whom were Rimsky-Korsakov's students. And, finally, Balakirev's group adhered to radical modernist ideas, while Beliaev's was more tolerant and encompassing in its tastes. Rimsky-Korsakov summarized the underlying distinction between the two groups as follows: "Balakirev's circle corresponded to the period of storm and stress in the evolution of Russian music; Beliaev's circle represented the period of calm, onward march."[33]

Another important event signified Rimsky-Korsakov's steady alienation from the *kuchkists'* philosophy as well as his growing independence in general: his acceptance in 1871 of a professorship at the St. Petersburg Conservatory, the decade-long enemy camp to Balakirev and his *kuchkists*.[34] Rimsky-Korsakov's tenure of over thirty years at the conservatory entailed the beginning of a new era and significant irrevocable changes. Initially in charge of only two courses, the theory of composition and orchestration, Rimsky-Korsakov gradually acquired a position of supreme authority at the conservatory and implemented new programs in all departments, including composition and performance. The scope of Rimsky-Korsakov's influence can hardly be overestimated. As one example, the theory content of the composition program underwent a major reform in 1885 on his initiative, eventually producing a generation of musicians in St. Petersburg that was brought up in "the school of Rimsky-Korsakov."[35] Indeed, some of Russia's greatest composers were products of this school, including Stravinsky, Prokofiev, and Shostakovich.

The specific areas upon which Rimsky-Korsakov left his imprint were harmony and orchestration, the two subjects on which the composer wrote treatises. The treatise on harmony was written initially for a course at the Imperial Court Chapel, where Rimsky-Korsakov became an assistant director to Balakirev in 1883. Later his treatise became the main textbook for harmony instruction at the St. Petersburg Conservatory and also in some Moscow circles, as testified by Semen Kruglikov in *Sovremennye Izvestiia* in 1886: "It is, I think, the best of the existing manuals on the subject, and I am happy for the St. Petersburg Conservatory, the Court Chapel, and the Moscow Philharmonic Society that they have adopted it for instruction."[36] In St. Petersburg, Rimsky-Korsakov's treatise remained the primary pedagogical resource for teaching harmony for nearly a century.

The presence of Rimsky-Korsakov was greatly felt in St. Petersburg's rich musical life in the late nineteenth century. By the 1880s, he had become one of the major Russian composers; he had also conducted many concerts, first at the Free Music School and, later, performances of the Russian Symphony in St. Petersburg, Moscow, and abroad. His historic endeavor to complete the unfinished compositions of his deceased friends Dargomyzhsky, Musorgsky, and Borodin made more of their music available to audiences and earned Rimsky-Korsakov great respect in the musical worlds of St. Petersburg as well as Russia at large. His inspiring and thoughtful leadership in Beliaev's circle and his professorship at the two major schools, the St. Petersburg Conservatory and the Imperial Court Chapel, put him in a position of great influence over a large body of young musicians in St. Petersburg.

# Chapter 2

# Editions of the *Practical Manual of Harmony*

Rimsky-Korsakov's *Practical Manual of Harmony* was initially issued by a lithograph method. The manual was copied by hand with a special lithographic ink by Rimsky-Korsakov's assistant at the Imperial Court Chapel, G. V. Ivanitsky,[37] under the title *Uchebnik Garmonii, Kurs Pridvornoi Kapelly. Vypusk pervyi: Garmonizatsiia akkordami v predelakh lada* (Manual of Harmony: A Course at the Court Chapel. First Volume: Harmonization with Chords within the Limits of One Key) in October of 1884.[38]

Its second volume, which included sections on modulation, nonharmonic tones, mixed chords, enharmonicism, and deceptive progressions, appeared in August of 1885, also printed lithographically.[39] Soon after that, Rimsky-Korsakov compressed the two volumes into one, with a slight reduction in the text volume, and published it under the title *Prakticheskii uchebnik garmonii* (Practical Manual of Harmony) in 1886 with the publisher Büttner.[40] There are no substantial differences between the two versions regarding theoretical issues. The second version, however, has a different organization of material. Rimsky-Korsakov eliminated, for instance, the division of the text into rules and explanatory sections as found in the first version. He also clarified definitions and simplified

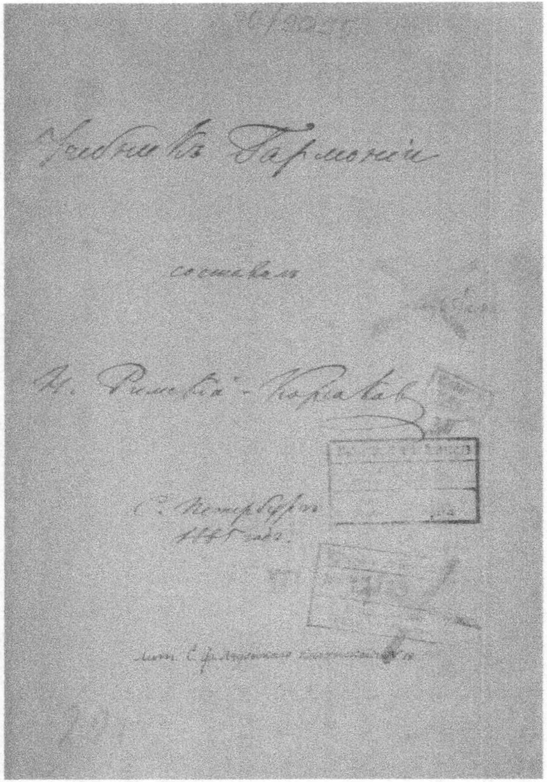


N. A. Rimsky-Korsakov, *Uchebnik garmonii*, 1884–1885 lithograph edition, title page. *Courtesy of Rossiiskii Gosudarstvennyi Muzykal'nyi Teleradiotsentr, Moscow, Russia.*

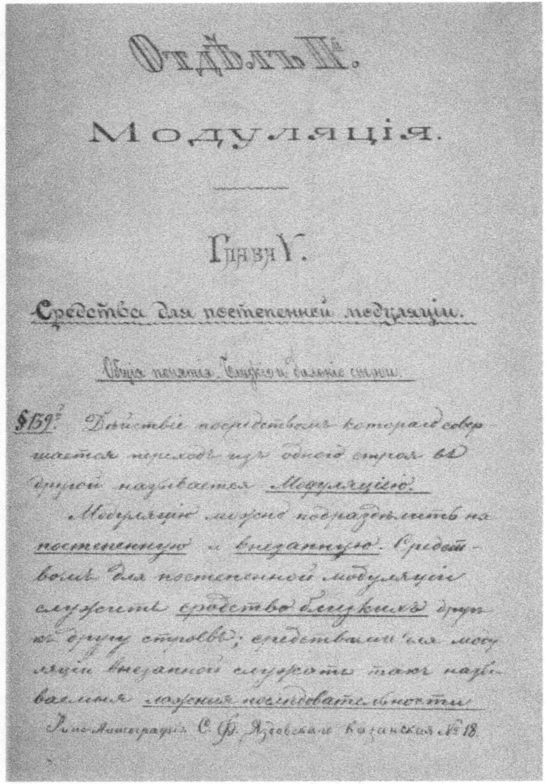


N. A. Rimsky-Korsakov, *Uchebnik garmonii*, 1884–1885 lithograph edition, modulation chapter opening page. *Courtesy of Rossiiskii Gosudarstvennyi Muzykal'nyi Teleradiotsentr, Moscow, Russia.*

some of the modulation exercises. All these changes had the purpose of making the manual more efficient for students' use.

There were seven subsequent editions of the *Practical Manual of Harmony* during Rimsky-Korsakov's life.[41] Some slight changes were introduced by the author in the third edition of 1893, which included "items that proved necessary in practice: concealed fifths and octaves, semi-plagal cadences ..., ascending sequences; also some remarks relative to modulating plans."[42] All later changes to the manual were made by Rimsky-Korsakov's pupils, Maximilian Steinberg and Jazeps Vitol [Vitols], who were in charge of all posthumous editions, in particular the ninth and the twelfth editions.

This analysis of Rimsky-Korsakov's harmonic theory primarily refers to the 1886 edition as reprinted in the collected works, occasionally in comparison with the 1884/1885 lithographic edition.

# Chapter 3

# Introduction to the Theory

Before considering Rimsky-Korsakov's theory in historical context and tracing the lineage of his work, let us establish the basic principles of Rimsky-Korsakov's theory of key relationships and modulations, considering it as a system.

After Rimsky-Korsakov's full immersion in theoretical studies with the commencement of his conservatory duties, which included a very full teaching load for several years, his creative development reached a stage wherein he formed the clear position on harmony that prompted him to write his own treatise in 1884.

Two major factors affected this transformation. One was that Rimsky was tasked with teaching the theoretical disciplines at the St. Petersburg Conservatory, yet he was dissatisfied with the harmony manuals in circulation.[43] He realized that it was time to create a harmony treatise, one that would accurately reflect what he practiced and believed in. In the foreword to the first Russian edition of the *Practical Manual of Harmony*, Rimsky-Korsakov explains the motivation for writing this treatise:

> In most of the existing manuals of harmony we find a detailed analysis of various chords and their resolutions, rules for the reading of

> the now-obsolete figured bass, attempts to explain the causes of such phenomena as the objectionable quality of parallel fifths, etc., but little or no practical advice or pedagogical systems for harmonization of melodies and the proper selection of chords. The same may be said in regard to the study of modulation. Manuals, laying stress on various dissonant chords as means for modulation, omit the very basis of modulation—the relationship of keys and common chords.[44]

In Rimsky-Korsakov's view, the manuals to which he had access gave inadequate treatment to two important aspects of harmonic theory. First, they lacked practical advice for composers on how to harmonize melodies and select proper chords. Second, he was entirely dissatisfied with their approaches to the issue of modulation. The most central deficiencies in these manuals' treatment of modulation were the poor discussion of the issue of "tonal relationships and common chords" and the absence of the large-scale tonal design that Rimsky considered essential for the study of harmony.

In his own manual, by contrast, Rimsky systematically develops the topic of melody harmonization. In unit II, "Harmonization by chords within a single key," he introduces various chords available for harmonization of melodies, as well as rules for connecting these chords and details of voice leading.[45] In unit 4, "Elaboration of melody,"[46] he concentrates on melodic ornamentation in harmonic context, including the use of passing tones, neighbor tones, and suspensions.

The topic of modulation is treated primarily in unit 3, "Modulation,"[47] and additionally in unit 5, "Enharmonicism and sudden modulation".[48] We start, however, with unit 1, "Preliminary notions,"[49] where scales and chords are clearly laid out as a basis for Rimsky-Korsakov's further discussion of modulation.

# Chapter 4

# Scales and Chords

Rimsky-Korsakov defines four types of scale as the basis for his harmonic system:[50]

**EXAMPLE 1.** Four basic scales

a) *Natural'nyi mazhornyi lad* (natural major)

b) *Iskusstvennyi garmonicheskii mazhornyi lad* (artificial harmonic major)

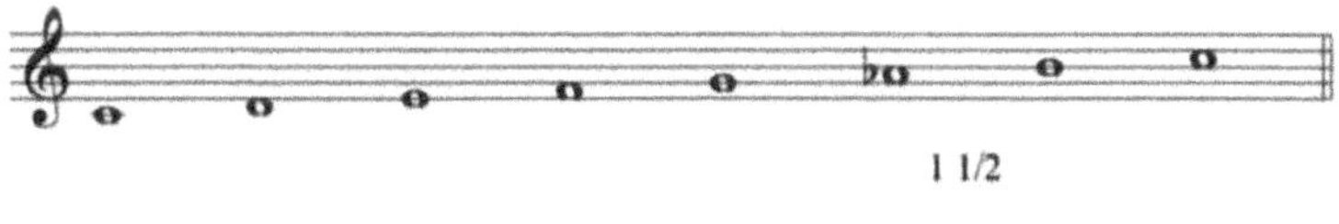


*(Continued)*

**(Continued)**

c) ***Natural'nyi minornyi lad*** **(natural minor)**

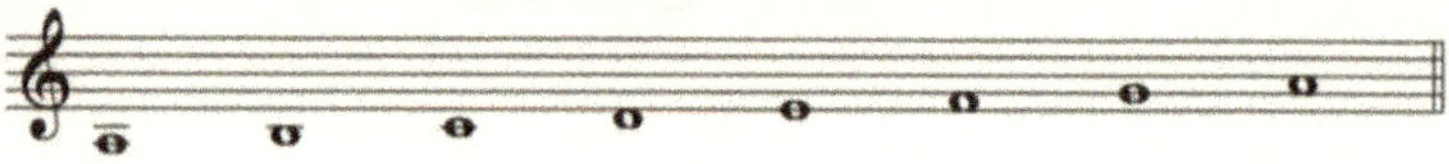

d) ***Iskusstvennyi garmonischeskii minornyi lad*** **(artificial harmonic minor)**

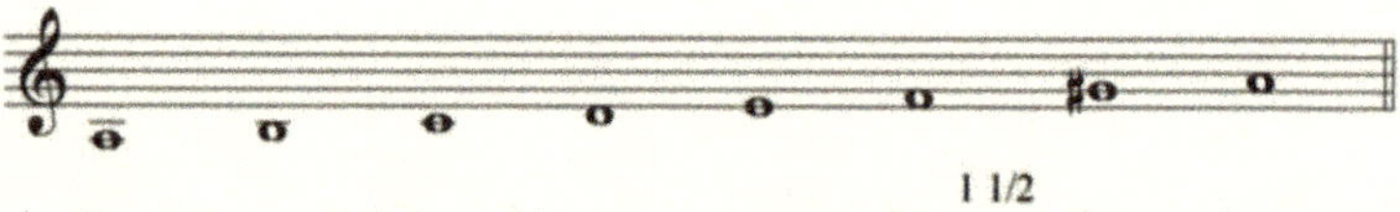


From these basic scales Rimsky-Korsakov derives a set of fundamental chords:[51]

EXAMPLE **2.** Fundamental chords

a) *Natural'nyi mazhornyi lad* (natural major)

b) *Iskusstvennyi garmonicheskii mazhornyi lad* (artificial harmonic major)

c) *Natural'nyi minornyi lad* (natural minor)

d) *Iskusstvennyi garmonischeskii minornyi lad* (artificial harmonic minor)

Next, Rimsky-Korsakov excludes the augmented triad on the flatted VI scale degree in harmonic major.[52] He does not provide an explanation for this exclusion, but the fact that the augmented triad cannot be used as a tonic triad was likely assumed as an obvious reason. Considering both types of C major scale, natural and artificial (harmonic), there is a total of nine triads for major:

EXAMPLE 3a

Similarly, there is a total of nine triads in minor, when both types of A minor scale are considered and the augmented triad on III in harmonic minor is similarly excluded:

EXAMPLE 3b

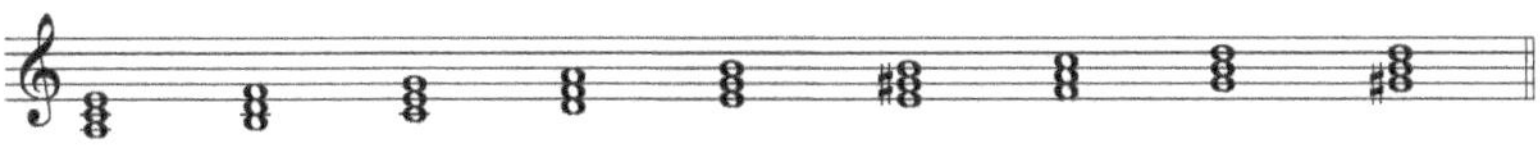

Thus, the four types of scales introduced by Rimsky-Korsakov at the beginning of his treatise represent the first layer of fundamental elements of his harmonic system. The two sets of triads built on the scale degrees of these four scales, one set for major and the other for minor, represent the next layer of the system, or "source keys," which in turn will form a group of closely related keys.

# Chapter 5

# Modulation and First-Degree Key Relationships

Rimsky-Korsakov's chapter on modulation, also the topic to which the whole of unit 3 is devoted, begins with a Preliminary Notions section. There, he offers a concept of modulation and immediately divides it into two distinct types: "The action by which a transition from one key to another is executed is called *modulation*. Modulation can be *gradual or sudden, diatonic or chromatic*."[53] It is important to note from the outset that Rimsky clearly distinguishes between these two categories of modulation.

Next, Rimsky provides corresponding grounds for each type of modulation: "*The kinship of keys* serves as the means for gradual modulation, while *deceptive and enharmonic progressions* serve as the means for sudden modulation."[54] Rimsky-Korsakov thus indicates that in this chapter one of the main motives for writing the treatise, as stated in the Foreword, will be explicated: his conception of modulation based on "kinship of keys" rather than on "deceptive and enharmonic progressions." Indeed, the remainder of unit 3 revolves around this issue of gradual or diatonic modulation, which Rimsky further develops into a unique and elaborate modulatory system. In contrast, sudden or chromatic modulation takes up only a small part of unit 5.[55]

The way Rimsky-Korsakov structures this chapter on modulation reveals his preoccupation with relationships between tonalities. It starts with a section on closely related keys, followed by a section on second-degree keys and concluding with a section on remote keys. Rimsky also places material about the various techniques of gradual modulation immediately after the discussion of closely related keys rather than at the center of his discussion about modulation in general.

Rimsky starts out by identifying the keys most closely related to the source keys: those associated with the first scale degrees corresponding to all triads other than the tonic. Out of these nine fundamental chords (see examples 3a and 3b), Rimsky-Korsakov separates a new set of six chords, which he calls the "full triads" because they are capable of functioning as the tonic triads of the keys in first-degree relationship to the source key.[56] He derives the full triads by excluding the tonic triad of the source key, which can be major, minor, or diminished (as are the triads on II in harmonic major, the VII in natural major, the II in natural minor, and the raised VII in harmonic minor): "*The six keys whose triads are contained in the given key* are considered to be the close keys, or keys *in the first degree of relationship* to a given key."[57]

**EXAMPLE 4.** Six keys in first-degree relationship

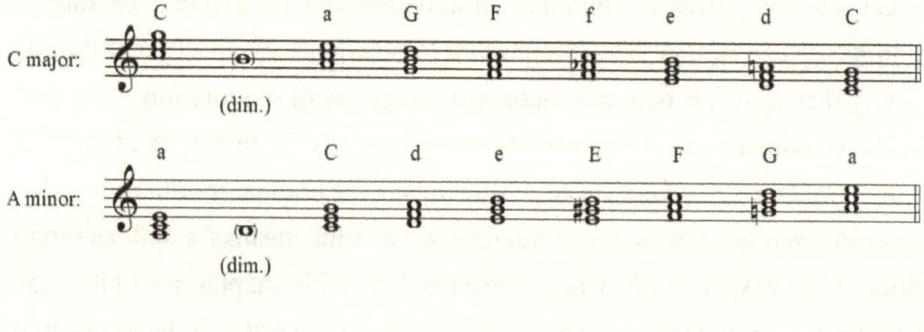

# Chapter 6

# Aspects of Modulation between First-Degree Keys

Rimsky-Korsakov defines the pivotal triad as the main principle to be used for executing a modulation between first-degree keys: "The passage from one key into another is based on those chords that are common to both given keys."[58] The source key is named the "antecedent key" and the key of destination the "subsequent key":[59]

> 1) Modulation begins in the antecedent key. One of the triads common to both the antecedent and subsequent keys should be selected, but the tonic triad of the subsequent key should be avoided. 2) This [common] triad must be reinterpreted as [the triad of] the corresponding [scale] degree of the subsequent key and modulation is finally accomplished by adjoining a cadence or a cadence-like progression in the subsequent key.[60]

Since the tonic triads of keys related in the first degree are chords common to both keys, modulation between these keys is simple and direct. The following examples illustrate such modulations into all six first-degree keys. Rimsky-Korsakov uses parentheses to indicate the change in function of each common triad as it undergoes modulation:[61]

EXAMPLE 5

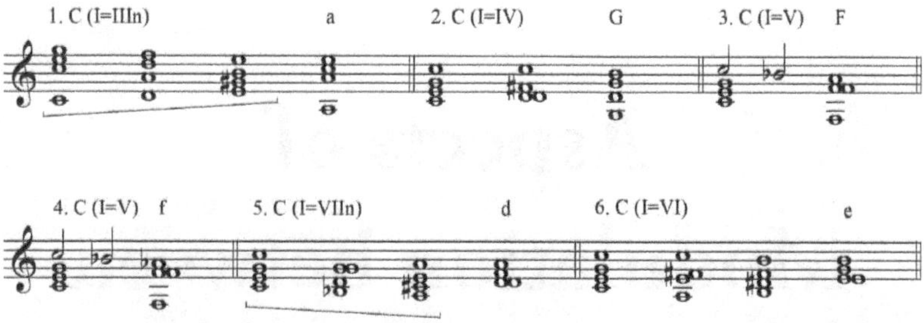


Note that Rimsky singles out each case in which a chord in the antecedent key is altered to serve as the dominant of the subsequent key: for example, in the modulation from a major key to its subdominant, either major or minor (C to F; C to f).

In contrast to the simple modulations between such keys, as shown in example 5, Rimsky further instructs that the new key be approached by first using the deceptive cadence and then following it with the subdominant: "In modulating from a major key into the keys of the major and minor subdominant (C to F; C to f), a more complicated method is most often used, going first to a deceptive cadence, so that one has a chance to obtain after it the subdominant harmony of the subsequent key."[62]

EXAMPLE 6

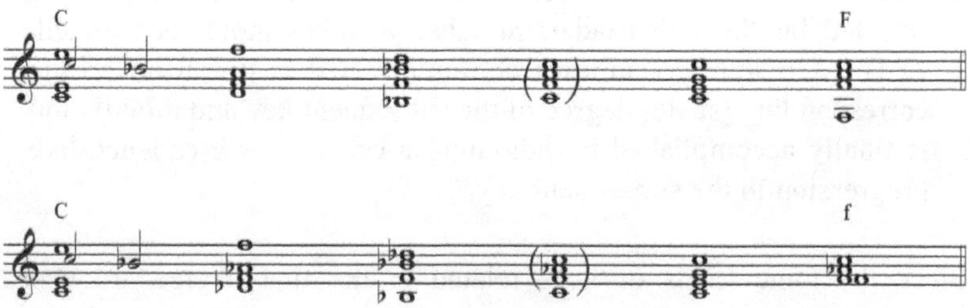


Rimsky-Korsakov's guidance on deceptive cadences reveals his general inclination to neutralize the effect of harmonic progressions of keys along the circle of fifths. The deceptive cadence interrupts such modulations, and the subdominant of the subsequent key also marks a certain barrier to further modulation.

Rimsky-Korsakov also offers another alternative as a means of avoiding harmonic successions of keys on the circle of fifths: intermediate modulation through the relative of the subsequent key:

> In order to accomplish a satisfactory modulation from a given minor to its subdominant (a – d), one resorts to a more complex method, leading first to the major key relative to the subsequent key: a – F – d: [example].
>
> Sometimes in order to pass from a given major key into the key of its major subdominant one resorts to a more complex modulation: C – d – F [example].[63]

It is remarkable that, under such circumstances, where no intermediate key would seem to be necessary to modulate smoothly from A minor to D minor, or from C major to F major, Rimsky-Korsakov prefers a three-key modulation, using the relative keys of the subsequent keys (the relative F major of the subsequent D minor, and the relative D minor of the subsequent F major) instead of going directly to the new keys. Rimsky shows a similar tendency in his discussions of other harmonic progressions along the circle of fifths, particularly in his explication of modulatory plans for second-degree keys.

# Chapter 7

# Second- and Third-Degree Key Relationships

In the 1884/1885 version of the treatise, Rimsky-Korsakov divides all keys into only two types: those that are closely related to the main key and those that are remotely related to the main key. In the treatise's shorter and later version of 1886, he further refines the area of the remote keys, dividing them into two degrees of proximity.

Several principles in the commentary on modulation between keys related in the first degree (by common chords) also apply to the whole system of keys within the overall context of gradual modulation. At the end of the section on first-degree keys in unit 3 of the *Practical Manual*, Rimsky-Korsakov defines the remote keys and explains how they may be reached. He considers all keys outside the first-degree keys (that is, second- and third-degree keys) as remote keys. He further states, however, that modulation from one key to another is still based on chords common to both keys (understood here as triads representing keys in an abstract sense). This notion of the pivotal triad is an extension of the original principle applied in modulations between first-degree keys.

Rimsky-Korsakov relates a set of twelve keys in the second degree to a source key as follows: "As belonging to the 2nd-degree relationship to a given key, we consider *those keys whose tonic triads are not contained in that key, but which nevertheless have at least one triad in common.*"[64] To summarize, Rimsky-Korsakov defines the second-degree relationship as the sharing of a triad (which, again, stands in for a key) other than the tonic. In every possible case, this compounds the first-degree relationship, because every triad is shared as the tonic of a first-degree key. Consequently, every second-degree modulation can be executed as a succession of two first-degree modulations. In other words, one definition implies the other.

The derivation of the second-degree keys is demonstrated in examples 7a and 7b below. For F major, indicated in the third row of the column listing first-degree keys in relation to C major, the other first-degree keys will be G minor, A minor, B-flat minor, B-flat major, C major, and D minor. Of these, after the elimination (shown by parentheses) of C major as a duplicate of the source key and D minor and A minor as first-degree keys of C major, the remaining three (G minor, B-flat minor, and B-flat major) are related to C major in the second degree. Similarly, there are six keys closely related to each of the remaining five keys of C major (A minor, G major, F minor, E minor and D minor). After eliminating duplicates, source keys, and keys related in the first degree, there will be a total of only twelve unique keys in second-degree relationship. These are highlighted in bold type throughout the following example and are placed separately in the left column (the asterisks designate keys that may also be reached by way of other closely related keys). Thus, for C major and A minor these comprise:

EXAMPLE 7. Twelve keys in second-degree relationship to C major

| C: | Second-degree keys | | | | | (First-degree keys to a given key) | | | | | |
|---|---|---|---|---|---|---|---|---|---|---|---|
| [a] | **E** | | | | | (C) | (d) | (e) | **E** | (F) | (G) |
| [G] | **b*** | **c*** | **D*** | | | (a) | **b*** | **c*** | (C) | **D*** | (e) |
| [F] | **g*** | **b♭*** | **B♭*** | | | **g*** | (a) | **b♭*** | **B♭*** | (C) | (d) |
| [f] | **A♭** | **b♭*** | **c*** | **D♭** | **E♭** | **A♭** | **b♭*** | (C) | **c*** | **D♭** | **E♭** |
| [e] | **b*** | **B** | **D** | | | (G) | (a) | **b*** | **B** | (C) | **D** |
| [d] | **g*** | **A** | **B♭*** | | | (F) | **g*** | (a) | **A** | **B♭*** | (C) |

*(Continued)*

**(Continued)**

| a: | Second-degree keys | | | | | (First-degree keys to a given key) | | | | | |
|---|---|---|---|---|---|---|---|---|---|---|---|
| [C] | f | | | | | (d) | (e) | f | (F) | (G) | (a) |
| [d] | g* | A* | B♭* | | | (F) | g* | (a) | A* | B♭* | (C) |
| [e] | b* | B* | D* | | | (G) | (a) | b* | B* | (C) | D* |
| [E] | f# | g# | A* | B* | c# | f# | g# | (a) | A* | B* | c# |
| [F] | g* | b♭ | B♭* | | | g* | (a) | b♭ | B♭* | (C) | (d) |
| [G] | b* | c | D* | | | (a) | b* | c | (C) | D* | |

*Keys that may also be reached by way of other closely related keys

The following musical example illustrates second-degree keys in C major by their tonic triads on the staff, accompanied by the keys' letter-symbols above. Roman numerals underneath the letters indicate the scale degrees of the source key. Letter-symbols underneath the staff designate those first-degree keys through which each second-degree key at the top of the column may be reached. Example 8 also shows this same information for A minor.

**EXAMPLE 8**

Twelve keys related in second degree to C major

*(Continued)*

**(Continued)**

Twelve keys related in second degree to A minor

Second-degree keys

| b♭ | B♭ | b | B | c | c♯ | D | f | f♯ | g | g♯ | A |
|---|---|---|---|---|---|---|---|---|---|---|---|
| ii♭ | II♭ | ii | II | iii | iii♯ | IV | vi | vi♯ | vii | vii♯ | I |

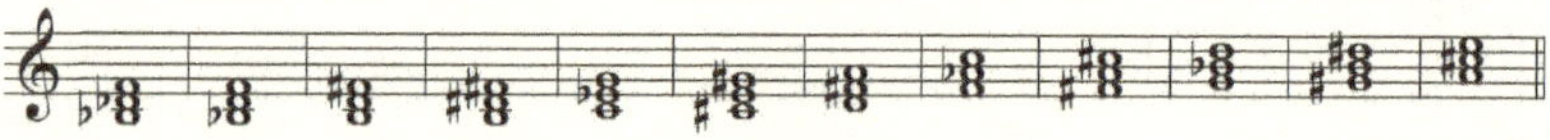

First-degree keys

| F | d | e | e | G | E | e | C | E | d | E | d |
|---|---|---|---|---|---|---|---|---|---|---|---|
|  | F | G | E |  |  | G |  |  | F |  | E |
| VI | iv | v | v | VII | V | v | III | V | iv | V | iv |
|  | VI | VII | V |  |  | VII |  |  | VI |  | V |

The last degree of relationship encompasses the remaining five keys, which are identified by Rimsky-Korsakov as third-degree keys, or "remote keys": "With the exception of 1st- and 2nd-degree keys, all other keys that do not have common triads with the source key are considered *remote keys*."[65] Keys related in the third degree to the source key are derived from the second-degree-relationship keys by tracing the set of nearest keys (i.e., first-degree keys) to each of the twelve second-degree keys. After eliminating duplicates, source keys, and keys related in the second degree, there will be a total of only five unique keys in the third-degree relationship. The same principle of derivation (i.e., tracing a new set of nearly related keys to reach new keys) is applied to obtain keys in the third degree of relationship, just as it was done for the second-degree keys.

The following musical example illustrates five third-degree keys by their tonic triads on the staff, accompanied by the keys' letter-symbols above the staff. Roman numerals underneath the letters indicate the scale degrees of the source key. Letter-symbols underneath the staff designate those second-degree keys through which each third-degree key at the top of the column may be reached (the second-degree keys are common to both first-degree keys and third-degree keys). Example 9 also shows this same information for A minor.

**EXAMPLE 9.** Five keys in third-degree relationship

Five keys related in third degree to C major

Third-degree keys to C major

| c♯ | (d♭) | d♯ | (e♭) | f♯ | (g♭) | F♯ | (G♭) | g♯ | (a♭) |
|---|---|---|---|---|---|---|---|---|---|
| i♯ | (ii♭) | ii♯ | (iii♭) | iv♯ | (v♭) | IV♯ | (V♭) | v♯ | (vi♭) |

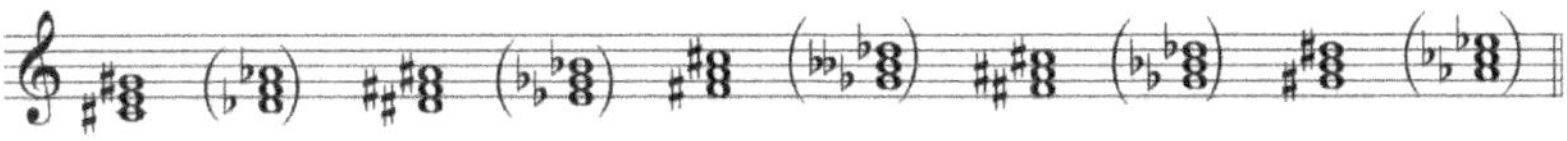

Second-degree keys to C major

| A | A♭ | B | b♭ | E | D♭ | B | b♭ | E | E♭ |
|---|---|---|---|---|---|---|---|---|---|
| E | | | B♭ | A | | b | D♭ | B | |
| B | | | D♭ | D | | | | | |
| | | | | b | | | | | |
| VI | VI♭ | VII | vii♭ | III | II♭ | VII | vii♭ | III | III♭ |
| III | | | VII♭ | VI | | vii | II♭ | VII | |
| VII | | | II♭ | II | | | | | |
| | | | | ii | | | | | |

Third-degree keys to A minor

| D♭ | (C♯) | e♭ | (d♯) | E♭ | (D♯) | G♭ | (F♯) | A♭ | (G♯) |
|---|---|---|---|---|---|---|---|---|---|
| IV♭ | (III♯) | v♭ | (iv♯) | V♭ | (IV♯) | VII♭ | (VI♯) | I♭ | (VII♯) |

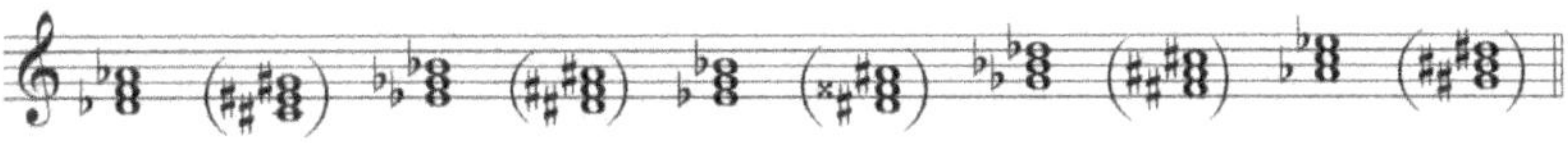

Second-degree keys to A minor

| b♭ | | b♭ | B | B♭ | | b♭ | b | b♭ | |
|---|---|---|---|---|---|---|---|---|---|
| f | f# | B♭ | | f | | | B | f | |
| | | | | c | | | | c | c# |
| | | | g# | g | g# | | g# | | |
| ii♭ | | ii♭ | II | II♭ | | ii♭ | ii | ii♭ | |
| vi | vi# | II♭ | | vi | | | II | vi | |
| | | | | iii | | | | iii | iii# |
| | | | vii# | vii | vii# | | vii# | | |

# Chapter 8

# Deceptive Progressions and Enharmonicism

In unit 5 of the treatise, "Enharmonic and sudden modulation," Rimsky-Korsakov deals with the second category of modulation or "sudden" modulation, to which he referred briefly in unit 3.[66] Since sudden modulation may travel at high speed across a wide span of the tonal space instead of operating on the slower, gradual basis of key relationships, it is introduced in a separate section of the treatise devoted to the discussion of chromatically altered chords.

In Rimsky-Korsakov's scheme, chromatically altered chords are divided by Rimsky-Korsakov into two types:

1) altered chords that do not contain any new combinations of tones. These chords only appear on scale degrees where they cannot be formed without chromatic passing notes:[67]
   a. the "false" dominant seventh on scale degree II in both major and minor
   b. the diminished seventh chord on the raised II scale degree in major and on the raised IV scale degree in minor
   c. major triad on the flatted II scale degree in both major and minor

2) altered chords that contain new combinations of tones: chords with the augmented fifth and augmented sixth[68]
   a. The chords with the augmented fifth include:
      1. the dominant seventh with the flatted fifth in both major and minor
      2. the augmented triad
      3. the dominant seventh with the augmented fifth in major
   b. Chords with the augmented sixth are built on scale degrees II and IV in harmonic major and minor and result from the alteration of these scale degrees:
      1. the augmented sixth chord in both major and minor
      2. the twice-augmented dominant seventh chord in first inversion in major
      3. the augmented dominant seventh chord in first inversion in minor
      4. the augmented dominant seventh chord in second inversion in both major and minor
      5. the twice-augmented dominant seventh chord in second inversion in major

Rimsky-Korsakov later also adds that sudden modulation can be effected by means of the enharmonic capability of numerous "deceptive progressions."[69] Deceptive progressions are defined by him as "any combination of two chords where each chord belongs to a different key or mode"[70] and include deceptive cadences, deceptive progressions of triads, and deceptive progressions of the dominant seventh, as shown below in examples 10a through 10c:[71]

**EXAMPLE 10(a)** Deceptive cadences

**EXAMPLE 10(b)** Deceptive progressions of triads

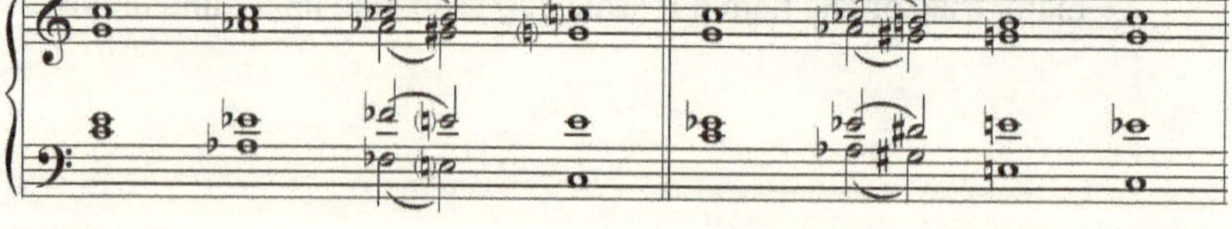

EXAMPLE **10(c)** Deceptive progressions of dominant seventh chords and first inversions

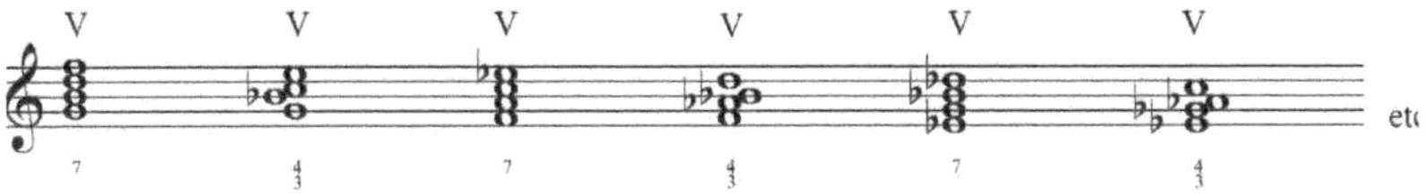


Rimsky-Korsakov identifies the deceptive cadence and deceptive progressions of the dominant seventh as the most notable and widely used deceptive progressions.

Rimsky takes care to note what he considers techniques fundamental to good harmonic development. Also, in a way, he extends his concept of gradual modulation when he instructs that smooth voice leading must be observed and that a greater incidence of common tones between the two chords makes a deceptive progression sound softer and more appealing.[72] Commenting on the use of deceptive progressions for sudden modulation, Rimsky-Korsakov states that they may be employed for modulation to close keys or remote keys. He notes, however, that a good musical taste requires that the new key should not be farther than a second-degree relationship from the source key, since only gradual modulation can satisfactorily connect more remote keys.[73]

# Chapter 9

# The Modulatory Plan

One of the most exceptional sections offered in Rimsky-Korsakov's harmony treatise is the one in which he explains the modulatory plan. Here, with respect to approaching more remote keys by means of gradual modulation, Rimsky-Korsakov further refines his understanding of tonal navigation and offers a set of guidelines. He describes keys in terms of a hierarchical system, which he demonstrates in a large-scale tonal plan for a composition—its modulatory plan. In doing so, Rimsky positions the idea of the modulatory plan as in fact a primary goal and essential element of his theory of key relationships. The concept of a modulatory plan is undertaken mainly in unit 3 of the *Practical Manual of Harmony* and introduced in the section on second-degree keys.

In the 1884/1885 edition, Rimsky-Korsakov had offered a complete table of modulatory plans for moving from A major and A minor to remote keys (see example 11).[74] The second and third degrees of relationship were not yet differentiated in this earlier version of the treatise. Consequently, all the remote keys appear there in one section, divided only by their major and minor orientation. The degrees of relationship marked in

**EXAMPLE 11**

**A. From major to major**

| Modulation | key degree | modulatory plan |
|---|---|---|
| 1) C – D | II | C – e – D |
| 2) C – B♭ | [II] | C – d – B♭ |
| 3) C – A | [II] | C – d – A |
| 4) C – E♭ | [II] | C – f – E♭ |
| 5) C – E | [II] | C – a – E |
| 6) C – A♭ | [II] | C – f – A♭ |
| 7) C – B | [II] | C – e – B |
| 8) C – D♭ | [II] | C – f – D♭ |
| 9) C – G♭ | III | C – f – D♭ – G♭ |
| 10) C – F# | [III] | C – G – b – F# |
| 11) C – C# | IV | C – d – A – f# – C# |
| 12) C – C♭ | [IV] | C – d – B♭ – e♭– C♭ |

**B. From major to minor**

| Modulation | key degree | modulatory plan |
|---|---|---|
| 1) C – b | II | C – G – b<br>C – e – b |
| 2) C – g | [II] | C – F – g<br>C – d – g |
| 3) C – f# | III | C – d – A – f# |
| 4) C – c | II | C – f – E♭ – c |
| 5) C – c# | III | C – a – E – c#<br>C – d – A – c#<br>C – e – B – c# |
| 6) C – f | close key | |
| 7) C – g# | III | C – e – B – g#<br>C – a – E – g# |
| 8) C – b♭ | II | C – f – A♭/D♭ – b♭<br>C – a/d – F – b♭ |
| 9) C – d# | III | C – e – B – d# |
| 10) C – e♭ | [III] | C – d – B♭ – e♭ |
| 11) C – a# | IV | C – G – b – F# – a# |
| 12) C – a♭ | III | C – f – E♭ – a♭ |

**C. From minor to major**

| Modulation | key degree | modulatory plan |
|---|---|---|
| 1) a – D | II | a – G – D<br>a – e – D |
| 2) a – B♭ | [II] | a – F – B♭<br>a – d – B♭ |
| 3) a – A | [II] | a – E – f# – A |
| 4) a – E♭ | III | a – C – f – E♭ |
| 5) a – E | close key | |
| 6) a – A♭ | III | a – C – f – A♭<br>a – F – b♭ – A♭<br>a – G – c – A♭ |
| 7) a – B | II | a – C/G – e – B<br>a – E – g#/c# – B |
| 8) a – D♭ | III | a – C – f – D♭<br>a – F – b♭ – D♭ |
| 9) a – F# | III | a – G – b – F# |
| 10) a – G♭ | [III] | a – F – b♭– G♭ |
| 11) a – C# | III | a – E – f# – C# |
| 12) a – C♭ | IV | a – F – b♭ – G♭ – C♭ |

**D. From minor to minor**

| Modulation | key degree | modulatory plan |
|---|---|---|
| 1) a – b | II | a – G – b |
| 2) a – g | [II] | a – F – g |
| 3) a – f# | [II] | a – E – f# |
| 4) a – c | [II] | a – G – c |
| 5) a – c# | [II] | a – E – c# |
| 6) a – f | [II] | a – C – f |
| 7) a – g# | [II] | a – E – g# |
| 8) a – b♭ | [II] | a – F – b♭ |
| 9) a – d# | IV | a – G – b – F# – d#<br>a – E – g# – d# |
| 10) a – e♭ | [IV] | a – C – f – D♭ – e♭<br>a – d – B♭ – e♭ |
| 11) a – a# | [IV] | a – E – f# – C# – a# |
| 12) a – a♭ | [IV] | a – C – f – E♭ – a♭ |

square brackets in the second columns of sections A and B were penciled in by Rimsky-Korsakov. This had to have been done at some point before 1886, given that the 1886 version of the treatise contains the remote keys classified into second and third degrees of relationship. The fourth degree of relationship was eliminated in the 1886 edition.

Also, in the 1886 version of the manual, Rimsky-Korsakov withdrew entirely the detailed table of modulatory plans shown in example 11. Instead, he provided a set of more general guidelines for creating modulatory plans from major to major, minor to minor, major to minor, and minor to major. In this later version, however, as mentioned, Rimsky-Korsakov further refined his classification of the remote keys, dividing them into second and third degrees of relationship.

The 1886 edition's chapter on second-degree keys offers some samples of modulatory plans. To modulate from C major to D major, for example, one should locate those keys that are in first-degree relation to both C major and D major. These common keys are G major and E minor.[75] Two modulatory plans are then possible:

EXAMPLE **12**

| 1) | C | — | G | — | D |
|---|---|---|---|---|---|
| | | 5 | | 5 | |
| 2) | C | — | e | — | D |
| | | 3 | | 2 | |

Rimsky-Korsakov adds an explanation:

> In the *first plan* we have three major keys in succession, going each time a perfect fifth up, which tends toward monotony of the modulatory plan; therefore, preference should be given to the *second plan*, where we have a minor key, represented by its tonic triad, interpolated between two major keys; in it the first modulating step will be a third up, the next—a second down.[76]

From this commentary we learn that alternating between major and minor keys is recommended in creating modulatory plans. Moreover, the following statement from the same paragraph clearly prohibits the use of three keys of the same mode in a row: "The succession of three major or three minor keys must be avoided."[77] The choice of keys found in the Table of Modulatory Plans of 1884/1885 is consistent with the guidelines offered in the later 1886 edition. Uniformity of mode is thus perceived by Rimsky-Korsakov as an undesirable feature of a modulatory plan.

A second issue raised in Rimsky-Korsakov's commentary concerns the intervals in the first plan, which modulates from C to G to D. Rimsky specifically dislikes modulation around the circle of fifths. In the next statement, he advises against the repetition of intervals of a fourth or fifth in modulatory plans, a notion also explicated earlier in the context of modulation between the first-degree keys:[78]

> Modulation from a major key into minor, situated a major second lower (C major—B-flat minor) and from a minor key into major, situated two steps higher by a fifth or a fourth in succession:
>
> 1) C — F — b♭
>
> 4 4
>
> 2) a — E — B
>
> 5 5
>
> It is therefore preferable to modulate through the keys relative to the subsequent keys:
>
> 1) C — (f — D♭) — b♭
>
> [5 3 3]
>
> 2) a — (E — g#) — B
>
> [3 3 5]

or through the keys relative to the antecedent key:[79]

1) C — (a — F) — b♭

[3 3 5]

2) a — (C — e) — B

[3 3 5]

Thus, Rimsky-Korsakov's alternative for avoiding the undesirable succession of fourths or fifths in modulations is the use of relative keys.

In the 1884/1885 version of the treatise, Rimsky-Korsakov describes the sequence of keys on the circle of fifths as "unpleasant monotony which is even more intensified by the fact that all three keys are major keys."[80] His more extensive commentary in the same source on these two modulatory plans, corresponding to plans B8 and C7 in example 11, clarifies the author's dislike of such progressions, as well as pointing to the use of relative keys to avoid this problem:

> The passage from C into B-flat [minor] could be executed using a shorter plan: C – f – b-flat; but then we have two fifths in sequence (C – f, f – b-flat), to avoid which it is best to include one of the intermediate [relative] keys D-flat or A-flat. A similar remark may be made in regard to modulation from A [minor] to B; here the shortest plan will be: a – e – B, to avoid the two fifths in a row (a – e, e – B) it is best to include the intermediate [relative] keys C or G. The same is true for the two other plans mentioned above regarding modulation from C to b-flat, and a to B.[81]

Clearly, the principle of ruling out repetitive modulatory plans was already at work in the formulation of the Table of Modulatory Plans in example 11.

Toward the end of the chapter on modulation in the 1886 edition, Rimsky-Korsakov offers an exercise to create modulatory plans for moving into all keys related in the second degree. In the instructions to this exercise, he again states directly that sequences of keys that are a fifth or fourth apart must be avoided: "Write out modulatory plans for all modulations from the keys of C major and A minor into all second-degree keys, avoiding any two successive modulatory steps by fourth or fifth."[82] Another example further illustrates his aversion to plans in which each key is reinterpreted as a dominant of the subsequent key:[83]

| | | | | | | | | |
|---|---|---|---|---|---|---|---|---|
| Good | | | | | | | | |
| 1) | C | — | (f | — | D♭) | — | e♭ |
| | | [4 | | 3 | | 2] | |
| 2) | C | — | (d | — | B♭) | — | e♭ |
| | | [2 | | 3 | | 4] | |
| Poor (steps by fourth) | | | | | | | | |
| 3) | C | — | (f | — | B♭) | — | e♭ |
| | | [4 | | 4 | | 4] | |
| 4) | C | — | (f | — | b♭) | — | e♭ |
| | | [4 | | 4 | | 4] | |

Finally, Rimsky-Korsakov acknowledges the exceptional role of the minor subdominant in the context of modulatory plans to the remote keys. It provides an essential link to keys that differ by four scale degrees from the source key:

> Going from a minor key, one must start with a modulation to a key different in four scale degrees (the minor subdominant); going from a major key, the same should be done, but after first going to the relative or other close minor:[84]

1) b♭ — F — a — e

2) A♭ — f — C — a — E or A♭ — c — G — a — E

# Chapter 10

# Analysis of Rimsky-Korsakov's Harmonic System

In summary, the principal concepts of Rimsky-Korsakov's harmonic system are as follows:

1) A choice between natural and harmonic forms of both major and minor scales
2) A clearly articulated concept of hierarchical tonal space, in which the spectrum of keys is coordinated in terms of their degree of proximity to (or distance from) the source key. The hierarchy of tonal space is expressed through the idea of key relationships. This leads to the next essential element:
3) The modulatory plan: a guide to movement within the tonal space
   a. An aversion to successive steps on the circle of fifths in modulatory plans, which are instead reached by way of substituting relative major and minor keys
   b. A preference for alternating between major and minor keys in modulatory plans

Rimsky-Korsakov's preoccupation with relationships of keys and modulation, defined from the outset as a goal of his treatise and presented systematically in his *Practical Manual of Harmony*, took root in his compositional practice. After all, it is a very rare occasion for such a treatise to be written by a composer. The composer's concern for the large-scale tonal design of his work was an important part of his compositional process, from the early works to the very last ones. Recalling the composition of his early symphony *Antar* in 1868, Rimsky-Korsakov wrote in his autobiography:

> A certain incoherence is felt in the choice of the key of C-sharp minor for the second movement in connection with the key of F-sharp [major] in the first movement and B minor in the third movement. But, speaking generally, the play of tonalities in the individual movements of the composition is interesting, beautiful, and legitimate. The distribution of the keys shows that there was awakening in me at the time a sense of the interplay of tonalities and their interrelation—an understanding that served me well throughout my subsequent musical activity.[85]

Thirty-four years later, Rimsky-Korsakov briefly reflected on his pervasive and conscious approach to tonal design and modulations in one of his last compositions, the opera *Kashchei the Immortal* of 1902: "the play of tonalities and the modulatory scheme, as always with me, were not due to chance."[86]

Rimsky-Korsakov's selfless and laborious process of completing Musorgsky's works displays the same persistent search for coherence in large-scale tonal designs of compositions and for logic in harmonic progressions. While working on the opera *Khovanshchina* in 1883, Rimsky-Korsakov recorded his aversion to Musorgsky's abrupt shifts of keys, as well as his own desire to improve such harmonic progressions: "[I] had to make modulations in certain places. This was a man [Musorgsky] who seemed not to recognize any ... modulations. He would finish in A-flat major and immediately continue in D major. All such roughness I managed to smooth out."[87]

By writing his harmony treatise, Rimsky-Korsakov brought out his theoretical conception of tonal relationships and demonstrated various ways to link in logical progression a great number of what were traditionally considered to be remote keys. In the 1884/1885 version of the treatise, we find his statement about the crucial role of the minor subdominant triad for obtaining the lowered sixth degree of the scale that he includes in the system of the major key. Its inclusion eventually leads to the new system of the relationships of keys presented later in the treatise: "Thus, we see that … the minor subdominant, which brings closer those keys that are four accidentals apart, is in fact a most powerful means for gradual modulation into considerably remote keys."[88]

As a consequence of including the minor subdominant among the closely related keys in the system of a major key,[89] along with the five other traditionally acceptable keys (the relative minor or submediant, the dominant, the major subdominant, the mediant, and the minor supertonic), Rimsky-Korsakov comes to regard the system of a major key as encompassing five possible accidentals: for C major, these would be F-sharp, coming from G major and E minor; B-flat from F major and D minor; and an additional three, E-flat, A-flat, and D-flat, coming from F minor. The minor key also encompasses five possible accidentals: for A minor, these would be F-sharp, coming from G major and E minor; B-flat, coming from F major and D minor; and an additional three, C-sharp, G-sharp, and D-sharp, coming from E major:

EXAMPLE 13

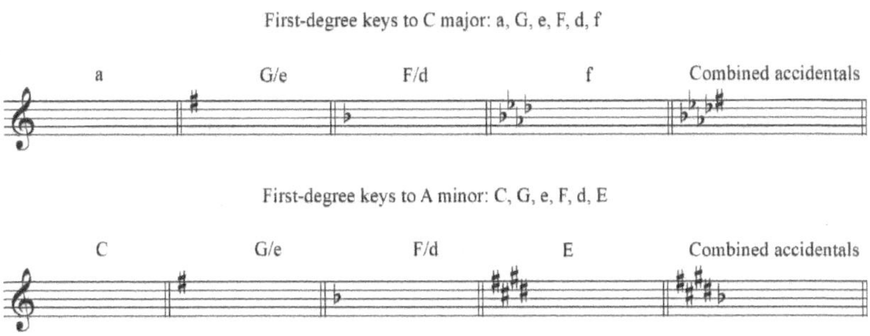


It is only in the 1884/1885 edition of the treatise that Rimsky-Korsakov provides his argument for integrating the minor subdominant into the major key system. Drawing a parallel with the system of the relative minor key, where the major dominant figures so prominently, Rimsky-Korsakov asserts that the minor subdominant in the major key may be—by comparison to, and also mirroring, the minor system—as natural an element to the major key system as the major dominant is to the minor:[90]

> If we turn our attention to the relationship of the V and I scale degrees of a minor key, where the major triad on V is located a fourth below the minor triad on I:
>
> 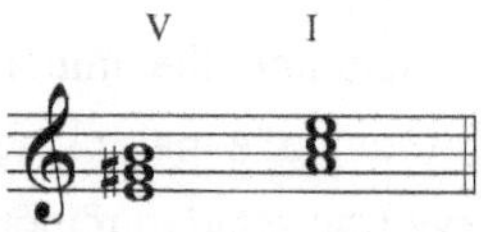
> 
>
> then we come to the conclusion that this kind of relationship is not to be found in a major key; nevertheless, this perfectly natural-sounding progression makes one wish to apply it also in the major key. Indeed, if we resort to altering the natural minor scale by means of an accidental, raising its VII scale degree, then it is possible to resort to a similar artificial alteration of the major scale. If we introduce an accidental, lowering the VI scale degree, into the major scale, then the following artificial kind of major scale results [called the harmonic major scale, in contrast to the natural one[91]] ...
>
> 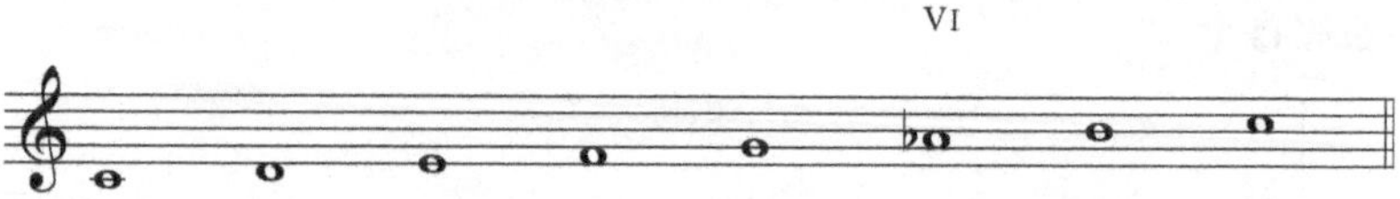
> 
>
> The main triads, built on its [harmonic major] scale degrees, will be the following ...:
>
> 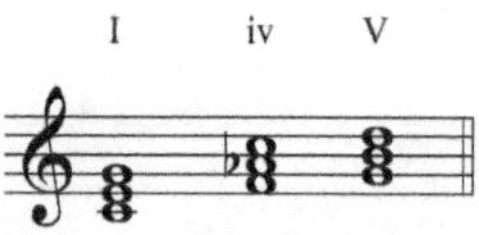
> 
>
> Thus, by including the above-mentioned accidental in the major scale, we obtain a similar relationship between the triads on I and IV, as found in the harmonic minor scale between triads on V and I scale degrees. ...

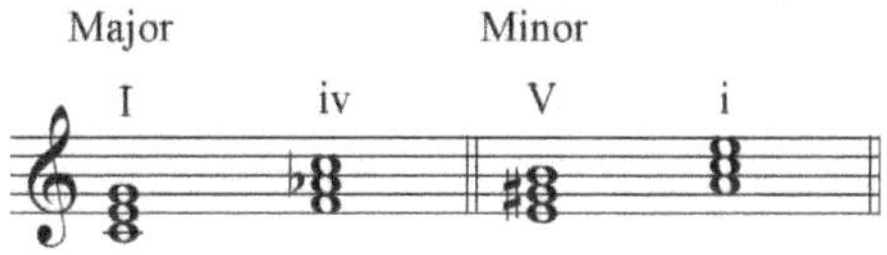


Rimsky-Korsakov perceives the key of the minor subdominant in major as resulting from a special relationship between the source major key and its relative minor. While already sharing the same collection of pitches in their natural forms, the harmonic ("artificial") source-major scale acquires its flatted sixth scale degree by association with the raised seventh scale degree of its harmonic relative minor. This relationship of mutual reference between the major key and its relative minor key may be extended further to the relationship of keys in Rimsky-Korsakov's harmonic system.

Let us first consider Rimsky-Korsakov's layout of the six first-degree keys to C major and to A minor (see example 4 above). In the 1886 edition, Rimsky-Korsakov arranged the chords representing the tonic triads of these keys in the downward direction for C major and in the upward direction for A minor, aligned.[92] The triads of each key presented in this manner appear in a mirror pattern: any major triad of the major key is mirrored by a minor triad in the minor key, and vice versa. This results in two major triads per major key and two minor triads per minor key (G major and F major in C major, and D minor and E minor in A minor), and four minor triads per major key as well as four major triads per minor key (A minor, F minor, E minor, and D minor in C major, and C major, E major, F major, and G major in A minor). Similarly, the major dominant triad of the minor key is mirrored by the minor subdominant triad of the major key. Although a similar formal symmetry may be traced between any major and minor keys, it is significant that, in the case of relative keys, it applies to a single pitch collection. As shown in example 14 below, graphically arranging the first-degree keys for both a major key and its relative minor helps to illuminate the symmetry between the keys:[93]

EXAMPLE 14. First-degree keys

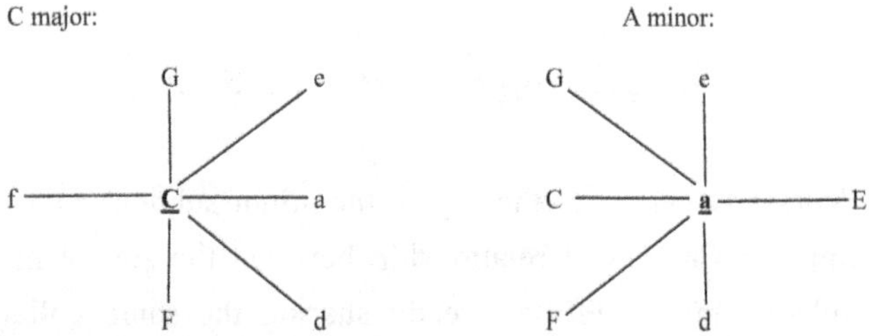


The two charts of the relative keys above exhibit perfect replication of form, but in reverse order. The mirror symmetry between the major key and its relative minor key, so evident in this example, is manifested throughout Rimsky's various explanations of the system, but it is only acknowledged in the earlier 1884 version of the treatise, and in an indirect manner. Nevertheless, this relationship permeates not only the pattern of the first-degree keys but the remainder of the system as well.

Let us now extend the chart to second-degree keys. Here the degree of relationship to the tonic is illustrated by the number of steps taken to reach a certain key. For example, in the map for C major, the first-degree key of G major is shown as one step away from the tonic C. D major, a second-degree key, is represented as two steps away from tonic C and is shown as reachable through G major:

EXAMPLE 15. Second-degree keys

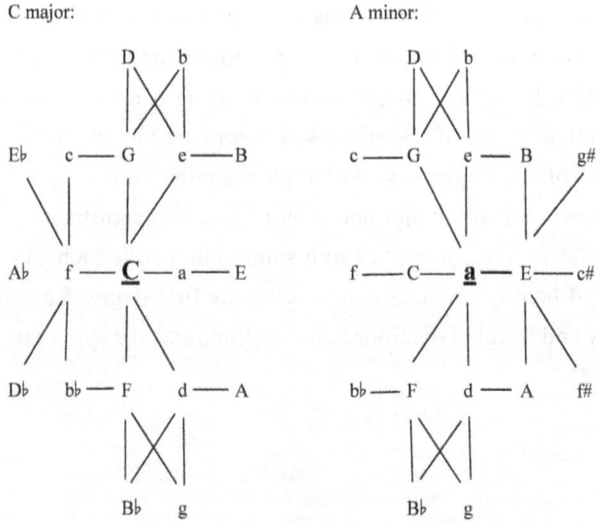

Extending the chart to second-degree keys reveals that the symmetry is also evident at this level. The mirror symmetry observed on the level of the first-degree relationship between the source key (C major or A minor) and its relative key (A minor or C major) is replicated on the level of the second-order relationships between the source major key (C major) and its minor subdominant (F minor) and the source minor key (A minor) and its major dominant (E major).

When one compares the detailed modulatory plans for major and minor keys found in the 1884/1885 edition, the correspondence between the plans for C major and those for A minor is striking: they mirror each other perfectly. One may also explore the existence of symmetry between modulations "from major to major" and "from minor to minor" by comparing sections A and D from Rimsky's Table of Modulations (example 11), as given in the table below (the distance between tonics is measured in half-steps and marked in parentheses underneath each plan).

If we compare, for example, the first four plans in each section, the interval spaces between any two keys in one plan will be preserved in the other, but the order will be reversed. Also, the order of modes in the corresponding keys will be the opposite. For example, plan A1 moves from major to minor to major, while plan B1 moves from minor to major to minor, and so forth:

| A: from major to major | | | | | | D: from minor to minor | | | | | |
|---|---|---|---|---|---|---|---|---|---|---|---|
| 1) | C | — | e | — | D | 1) | a | — | G | — | b |
| | | (4) | | (2) | | | | (2) | | (4) | |
| 2) | C | — | d | — | B♭ | 2) | a | — | F | — | g |
| | | (2) | | (4) | | | | (4) | | (2) | |
| 3) | C | — | d | — | A | 3) | a | — | E | — | f# |
| | | (2) | | (5/7) | | | | (5/7) | | (2) | |
| 4) | C | — | f | — | E♭ | 4) | a | — | G | — | c |
| | | (5/7) | | (2) | | | | (2) | | (5/7) | |

Such mirroring relationships may be traced throughout the remainder of the table of modulatory plans.[94]

The two guidelines specified by Rimsky-Korsakov for the construction of both major and minor modulatory plans shed light on the composer's overall conception of the relationship between keys and, thus, of tonal space. Rimsky-Korsakov instructs to avoid any two consecutive steps on the circle of fifths in modulatory plans. Instead, he recommends alternating between major and minor keys. Also, in four modulatory plans, he elects to insert additional keys, eschewing the simpler progressions available on the circle of fifths.[95] This choice of additional keys consistently falls on the relative keys of either the antecedent or subsequent key of the initial plan:

| | | | | | | | | | | | | | | | |
|---|---|---|---|---|---|---|---|---|---|---|---|---|---|---|---|
| not | C | — | f | — | b♭ | but | C | — | f | — | A♭/D♭ | — | b♭ |
| | C | — | F | — | b♭ | | C | — | a/d | — | F | — | b♭ |
| | a | — | e | — | B | | a | — | C/G | — | e | — | B |
| | a | — | E | — | B | | a | — | E | — | c#/g# | — | B |

Rimsky also advises to avoid another type of progression: direct modulation to parallel keys. We find such statements in both editions of the treatise. In the 1884/1885 edition, this concept appears in his table of modulatory plans (see plans B4 and C3 from example 11). In the 1886 edition, Rimsky is more articulate about resorting to the use of the relative key (of the antecedent or consequent key) as an intermediate key for smooth modulation to parallel keys:

> In modulations to a parallel key in both major and minor, because of the equality of tonics, one must use an additional key in between, namely: the relative of the subsequent key:
>
> 1) C — f — E♭ — c
>
> 2) a — E — f# — A
>
> One should use these means exclusively [in such modulations].[96]

Combining the tables of keys for C major and A minor, and adding the third-degree keys, we obtain the following diagram:

EXAMPLE 16

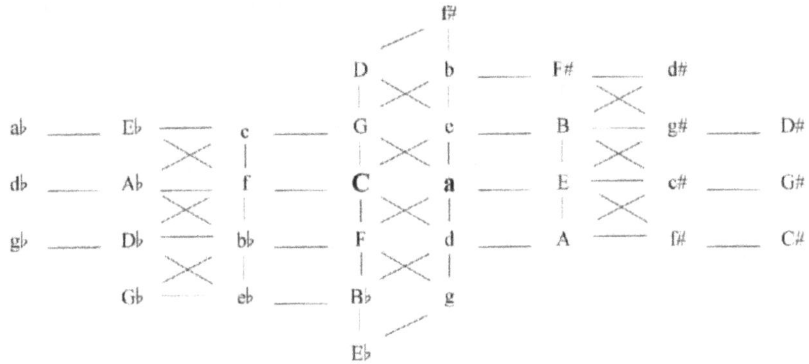


As illustrated here, three aspects of Rimsky-Korsakov's tonal map emerge as its structural concepts:

1) the source major key and its relative minor are fused into one area because of their complementary nature, forming a dual center or extended tonic (C major/A minor)
2) the extended tonic engages the two source keys' neighboring key areas by encompassing one key from each, along with their relative minors (for major, the harmonic minor triad of F minor; and for the minor key, the harmonic dominant, E major)[97]
3) the source keys of the extended tonic (C major/A minor) and their neighboring key areas (e.g., A-flat major/F minor and E major/C-sharp minor) are removed from one another by an interval of a major third

Rimsky-Korsakov's tonal map exhibits an integration of both hierarchical and symmetrical principles. The structure's hierarchy stems from extending the principle used to define closely related keys by using it for the purpose of reaching distant keys as well. Another source of hierarchy is the tripartite definition of levels of relationship (first-, second-, and third-degree). Thus, the spectrum of keys evolves around the tonic in three degrees of proximity: out of twenty-three keys remaining after the source tonic key, six belong to the immediate tonic area or first-degree keys, twelve belong to the adjacent area or second-degree keys, and five to the remote tonic area, or third-degree keys.

In addition, the system exhibits pervasive symmetrical patterns, much like those associated with twentieth-century music's nonhierarchical, symmetrical structures based on the octatonic and the whole-tone scales. These scales, which Rimsky-Korsakov recognized,[98] were not introduced as such in the *Practical Manual of Harmony*, except indirectly in a couple of short examples of sequences.[99] Rimsky-Korsakov's employment of the octatonic scale (better known in Russia as the "Rimsky-Korsakov scale"[100]) and the whole-tone scale has been widely acknowledged and examined.[101] The connection between these scales and his harmonic system, however, may be explored further.

The model in example 19 of Rimsky-Korsakov's tonal map displays symmetry along the horizontal tonic axis (F minor to **C major** to A minor/ C major to **A minor** to E major). The symmetry is present inside one key in its immediate and adjacent areas:

C major (f — C — a) A minor (C — a — E)

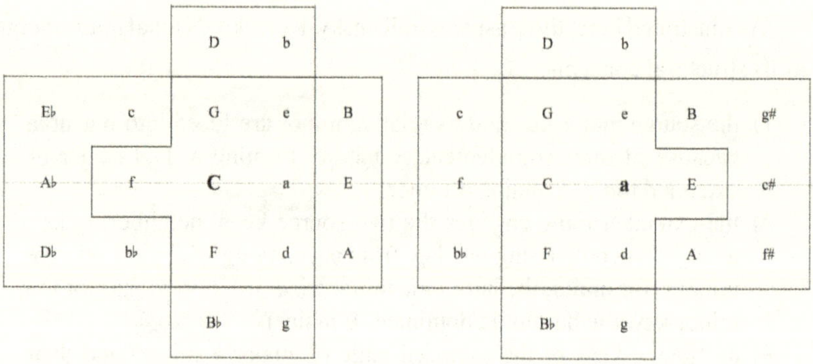


We can also observe a mirror symmetry between the relative keys (C major to A minor) found in the immediate area (first-degree keys):

The symmetry is replicated in the adjacent area of the keys in second-degree relationship to both C major and A minor. The source major key's relationship with its minor subdominant (F minor to C major) is mirrored in the source minor key's relationship to its major dominant (A minor to E major):

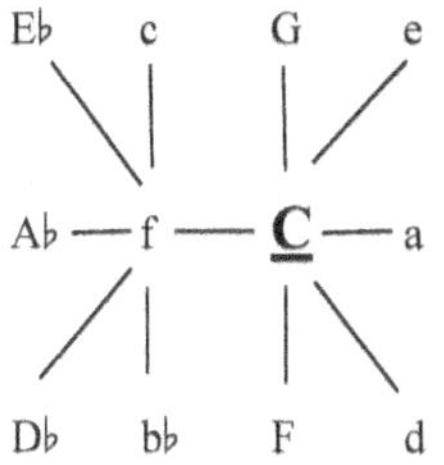


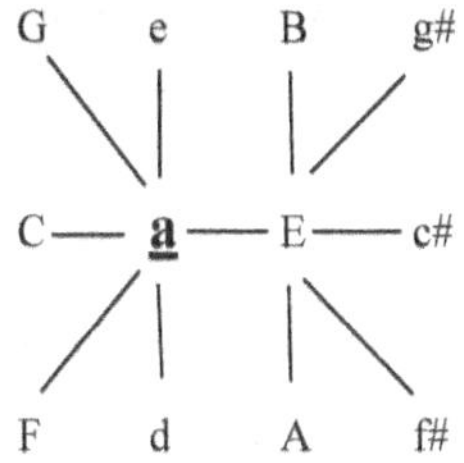


Finally, the same mirror symmetry may also be observed between the complete major source key area (i.e., including immediate, adjacent, and remote areas) and that of its relative minor key (and vice versa).

In addition to a circle of fifths found in the tonic column (G major to C major to F major) of the immediate area, the model also contains a circle of major thirds (A-flat to C major to E major) that spreads into the adjacent area, a feature associated with the structure of the whole-tone scale. While the use of the circle of fifths is explicitly discouraged by Rimsky-Korsakov, the author frequently emphasizes two advantages of the circle of thirds relationship.

First, following Rimsky-Korsakov's prescription for alternating keys of opposite mode, the modulations from C major to A*b* major and to E major, which are both 2nd-degree keys to C, may be performed only by way of F minor and A minor respectively, and provide the shortest routes in tonal context:

<u>C – f – Ab</u> <u>C – a – E</u>

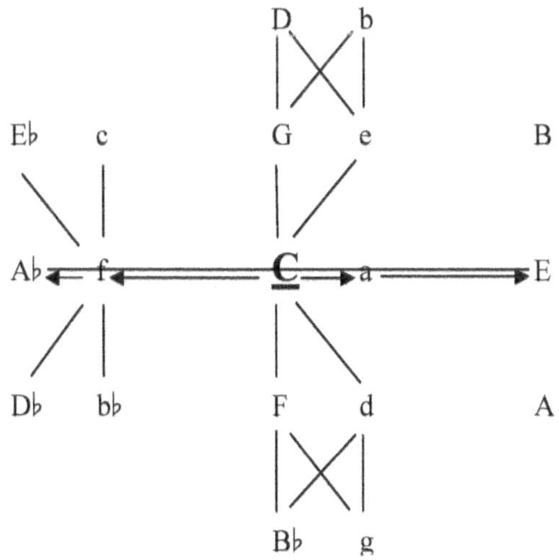

Second, the economy of these two modulatory paths is possible only because they exploit two essential elements of the system: (1) the relationship between the relative keys (F minor to A-flat and C major to A minor), and (2) the relationship between a source minor key and its major dominant (A minor to E major), or its counterpart, the relationship between a source major key and its minor subdominant (C major to F minor). The latter is characteristically described by Rimsky-Korsakov as a "most powerful means for gradual modulation into considerably remote keys."[102]

In addition to facilitating modulation by a major third, the relationship between a source minor key and its major dominant or the source major key and its minor dominant also allows for smooth and gradual modulations into keys situated a minor third apart, a feature characteristic of a single octatonic structure, possible in the context of Rimsky-Korsakov's tonal map. The keys of E-flat major and A major are similarly related to C major in the second degree, and the shortest modulatory paths to reach them again employ minor keys: D minor and F minor, respectively:

C – f – E♭ C – d – A

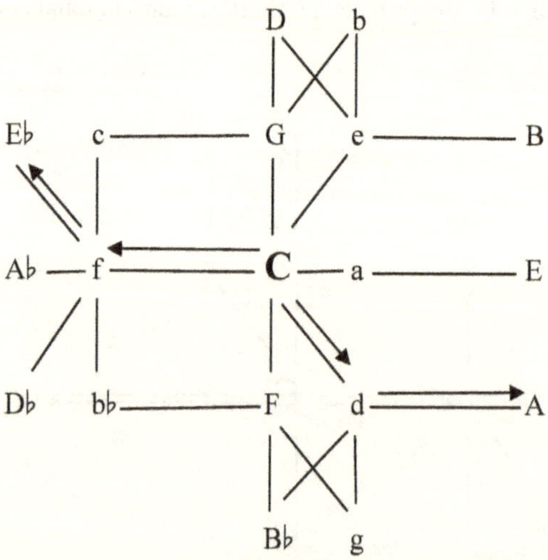

It is the relationship between the source major and its minor subdominant (C major to F minor) and the source minor and its major dominant key (D minor to A major) which accounts for the brevity of the modulatory path of these passages.

By offering a detailed, comprehensive discussion of keys and their relationships as well as providing specific instructions for their practical implementation, Rimsky-Korsakov achieved one of the main goals that he set for creating his own distinctive harmony treatise: to write a treatise that instead of "laying stress on various dissonant chords as means for modulation" offers discussion of "the very basis of modulation—the relationship of keys and common chords."[103]

# Part Two

# Rimsky-Korsakov's Harmonic Theory and the Nineteenth-Century German Theoretical Tradition

# Chapter 11

# Channels of German Influence

Designed for practical instruction rather than as a scholarly work, Rimsky-Korsakov's harmony treatise contains no references to other authors or treatises. In the absence of direct evidence regarding specific theoretical works to which Rimsky-Korsakov was exposed, it is necessary to establish which sources are most likely to be relevant in the context in which Rimsky-Korsakov worked. With this as a basis, we will then go on to a detailed comparative analysis of these sources.

The *Practical Manual of Harmony* was written by Rimsky-Korsakov after he had been on the faculty of the St. Petersburg Conservatory nearly a decade. During this first decade, Rimsky-Korsakov had to become closely familiar with the methods and traditions of the conservatory. His perception of a need for a new textbook on harmony must therefore be considered in the context of these traditions.

The St. Petersburg Conservatory was established in 1862, nearly nineteen years after the Leipzig Conservatory and a dozen years after the Berliner Musikschule, to meet a need for a school to train professional musicians for the Imperial Court. The Russian Musical Society (RMS), nicknamed

"Rubinstein's *Musikverein*" by a critic,[104] provided the foundation for the conservatory, which perpetuated its aesthetics and philosophy. The sole patron of both the RMS and the conservatory was the brilliant and willful Grand Duchess Elena Pavlovna, a former Württemberg princess. Most of the cosmopolitan faculty that had been employed for the RMS courses now taught at the new conservatory.[105]

As the first institution of its kind in Russia, the conservatory was fashioned primarily after conservatories recently established by Russia's southern neighbor, Germany. When Rimsky-Korsakov entered the St. Petersburg Conservatory in 1871 as professor, despite its nearly ten years of existence, its theoretical and pedagogical approaches were little more than a compilation of programs copied from various German schools—a fact recognized and recorded in the St. Petersburg Conservatory's Faculty Council Journal on September 4, 1873: "Freshmen would choose the piano or one of the orchestral instruments as their specialty. ... The elementary theory course. ... was copied from the programs of German teachers' seminaries."[106] A determining factor underlying the German orientation in the teaching of theoretical disciplines at St. Petersburg Conservatory was that its first five directors received their education in Germany as demonstrated in the following table. Two of them, Nikolai Zaremba and Iuly Johansen, taught theory at the conservatory. Connections between the first five conservatory directors and the specific theorists from Germany with whom they studied are listed below.

| *Directors of the St. Petersburg Conservatory (19th Century)* | *Period* | *Teacher and Period in Germany* |
|---|---|---|
| Anton Rubinstein (1829–94) | 1862–67 | Dehn (Berlin), 1844–46 (following in Glinka's footsteps) |
| *Tchaikovsky: 1861 RMS classes with Zaremba, graduated in 1866* | | |
| *Nadezhda Purgold, Rimsky's wife, studied with Zaremba in mid–1860s.* | | |
| Nikolai Zaremba (1821–79)<br>1859 RMS,<br>1862 St. Petersburg Conservatory<br>(Theory professor) | 1867–71 | A. B. Marx (Berlin) until 1854 |

*(Continued)*

**(Continued)**

| *Directors of the St. Petersburg Conservatory (19th Century)* | *Period* | *Teacher and Period in Germany* |
|---|---|---|
| Mikhail Azanchevsky (1839–81), 1870 St. Petersburg Conservatory, 1876 donated his library to the St. Petersburg Conservatory | 1871–76 | Hauptmann (Leipzig), 1858/1861–64 Richter (Leipzig), 1862 |
| *Rimsky-Korsakov becomes conservatory professor in 1871.* | | |
| Karl Davydov (1838–89) | 1876–87 | Hauptmann (Leipzig), 1858, 1859 Gewandhaus success, taught at the Leipzig Conservatory, from 1865 active in St. Petersburg |
| Anton Rubinstein | 1887–91 | (see above) |
| Iuly Johansen (1826–1904), taught theory at St. Petersburg Conservatory 1867–98 | 1891–98 | Hauptmann, Richter (Leipzig), to 1848 |

Anton Rubinstein (1829–1894) was the head of the RMS (1859–1867) and director of the conservatory from its opening in 1862 until 1867, and again from 1887 to 1891. He studied counterpoint and harmony with Siegfried Dehn in Berlin from 1844 to 1846.[107] These lessons were likely private, since Dehn did not begin to teach at the Königlische Akademie der Künste until 1849. Dehn's treatise, *Theoretisch-praktische Harmonielehre mit angefügten Generalbassbeispielen*, was among the popular harmony manuals in late nineteenth-century Germany and could also have been known in the St. Petersburg musical establishment through Mikhail Glinka, who had studied with Dehn in Berlin a decade earlier than Rubinstein did.

The second director of the conservatory, from 1867 to 1871, was Nikolai Zaremba (1821–1879), who taught music theory and composition at the conservatory during its first decade and had taught composition previously at the RMS courses as well. Zaremba had studied in Berlin with Adolf Bernhard Marx before returning to St. Petersburg in 1854.[108] It is not known whether he took private lessons with A. B. Marx or attended his lectures at the University of Berlin, since Marx had been teaching at the University since 1828 and the Stern'sches Konservatorium (Stern Conservatory) since 1850. It is also noteworthy that Nadezhda Purgold, Rimsky's future wife, studied at the conservatory in the mid-1860s, during Zaremba's tenure.

Mikhail Azanchevsky (1839–1881), honorary librarian of the conservatory library and later the conservatory's director from 1871 to 1876, had studied music theory in Leipzig with Ernst Friedrich Richter and Moritz Hauptmann between 1861 and 1864.[109] In both cases, the instruction might have been private, or it may have been a part of the Leipzig Conservatory courses, since both Richter and Hauptmann had been teaching at the conservatory since its founding in 1843. Azanchevsky's extensive and valuable book collection later became the foundation of the St. Petersburg Conservatory Library. Azanchevsky gained a reputation as a progressive director who brought new people to the faculty, revitalized the curriculum, and changed the entire atmosphere of the institution.[110] Rimsky-Korsakov was among the new people who joined the conservatory's faculty under the directorship of Azanchevsky.

Karl Davydov (1838–1889), the fourth director (1876–1887), had studied at the Leipzig Conservatory with Moritz Hauptmann in 1865.[111] A famous cellist, he toured extensively in Europe and also taught (presumably cello) at the Leipzig Conservatory.

Iuly (Julius) Johansen (1826–1904), director from 1891 to 1898, was the author of a popular counterpoint manual.[112] From 1867 to 1898, Johansen taught a course at the conservatory on "theory of composition," which included harmony instruction.[113] Born in Copenhagen, Johansen moved to Russia in 1848 at age twenty-two and lived in St. Petersburg beginning in 1852. He had studied with Ernst Friedrich Richter and Moritz Hauptmann in Leipzig, presumably in the mid-1840's.[114] Although there is no known harmony treatise by Johansen, Rimsky-Korsakov indicates a direct connection between Johansen, Liadov (a student of Johansen and Rimsky-Korsakov's friend and colleague), and his own harmonic system:

"Essentially, Liadov's system was an outgrowth of his professor Iu[ly] Johansen's system, and mine of Liadov's."[115]

To summarize, four German theorists directly influenced the leaders of the St. Petersburg Conservatory leaders: Siegfried Dehn, Adolf Bernhard Marx, Ernst Friedrich Richter, and Moritz Hauptmann. Unfortunately, it is not known whether any books by these authors were in Rimsky-Korsakov's personal library, since a large part of it was destroyed during the Leningrad siege of 1942. A harmony manual by another German author, however, was found in the surviving part of Rimsky-Korsakov's personal library: the Russian translation of the *Praktische Harmonielehre mit vier und fünfzig Aufgaben* of Ludwig Bussler.[116]

Another important source of influence cannot be ignored in examining the context in which Rimsky-Korsakov formulated his harmonic theory: the St. Petersburg Conservatory Library, to which he had full access. Harmony manuals and theoretical treatises that contain sections on harmony by the above-mentioned German authors were available in the conservatory library along with several Russian translations. The complete library of the RMS was transferred to the conservatory in 1862. Since all volumes of this collection bear the Society's stamp, it is very likely that any book in the library carrying this stamp was acquired before 1862. Later acquisitions bear the St. Petersburg Conservatory Library stamp. It is impossible to establish the date of the conservatory's other acquisitions more specifically, because no dates were marked on the books. By 1871, when Rimsky-Korsakov entered the St. Petersburg Conservatory, Russian translations of the following four German treatises were a part of its library's collection: A. B. Marx's *Allgemeine Musiklehre* (1839), E. F. Richter's *Lehrbuch der Harmonie* (1853), J. C. Lobe's *Katechismus der Musik* (1851), and Ludwig Bussler's *Praktische Harmonielehre in vier und fünfzig Aufgaben* (1875).[117]

In addition, although a direct link to Gottfried Weber can neither be established through Russian translations nor personal contact with first-generation St. Petersburg Conservatory professors, his theoretical treatise was a part of the conservatory library collection and bears an RMS stamp. Thus, it may well have attracted Rimsky-Korsakov's attention through its reputation.

Based on these considerations, the treatises of seven German theorists, Gottfried Weber, A. B. Marx, S. Dehn, J. C. Lobe, E. Richter, M. Hauptmann, and L. Bussler appear essential for our further consideration.[118] We now turn to the examination of these authors' approaches to the field of tonal relationships, which allows for a consideration of Rimsky-Korsakov's theory in this context, including the identification of elements in his theory that proceed or diverge from these German antecedents.

# Chapter 12

# Modulation and Key Relationships in Nineteenth-Century German Music Theory

The work of several German music theorists of the 19th century finds reflection in Rimsky-Korsakov's ideas of tonal space and could have helped shape Rimsky's thinking. In particular, some aspects of each author's work on the relationship of keys can be related in varying degrees to parts of Rimsky-Korsakov's distinctive harmonic theory. Moritz Hauptmann's significant concept of *Moll-Durtonart*, for example, was countered by Rimsky-Korsakov's inclusion of the harmonic major concept in his harmonic theory. This important correlation prompts a discussion of Hauptmann's treatment of harmony and modulation as our starting point.[119]

## Moritz Hauptmann

Hauptmann, who studied with Louis Spohr, was a professor at Leipzig Conservatory, director of Thomasschule, and the founder of Bach-Gesellschaft. His pupils included Joseph Joachim, Hans von Bülow, and Arthur Sullivan. Hauptmann's profoundly influential work, *Die Natur der Harmonik und der Metrik* of 1853, stands out among the many nineteenth-century harmony treatises because of its unique blend of abstract theoretical and

Moritz Hauptmann (1792–1868). *Wikipedia.*

philosophical thinking. His work is also distinctive because it bears a clear stamp of Hegelian philosophy.[120] Just as Hegel's philosophical system is based on the interaction of the two basic poles of thesis and antithesis, so is Hauptmann's harmonic theory based on the interaction of positive and negative elements.

Hauptmann's idea of modulation is an integral part of his wider perception of a musical system as an organic whole. Defining a set of fundamental principles from the start, Hauptmann then applies them on all levels, from elementary units, such as intervals, to the complex system of tonality itself.

Thus, the triad is understood by Hauptmann as a "unity" (*Einheit*) comprised of intervals and the key as a unity made up of triads. In Hauptmann's system, each note of the triad is assigned its special meaning: the root (I) represents unity; the fifth (II), separation (*Trennung*); and the third (III), union (*Verbindung*):[121]

| I | | II | | III |
|---|---|---|---|---|
| C | — | e | — | G |

Hauptmann's discussion of the harmonic properties of key and modulation is based on the important notion that "a key can take shape harmonically only in a succession of chords."[122] In this context, Hauptmann emphasizes a crucial distinction between major and minor keys in modulation. In a chain of major keys positioned on the circle of fifths, with an additional key built on each original key's major third, there is no limitation on the direction of modulation, for it is equally possible to modulate in the direction of either flat keys or sharp keys (see illustration below).[123]

In contrast, minor keys possess a particular quality, described by Hauptmann as "isolated, without the power of passage into others,"[124] which precludes such freedom of direction for modulation. On a circle of fifths with each key's minor third interposed, the result is a strictly one-way movement in the triadic manner Hauptmann describes: "the chord series belonging to the notion of the minor key starts from a moment of contradiction and forms a chain of major triads in one direction, and a chain of minor triads in the other" (see illustration below).[125]

Thus, Hauptmann defines the relationship between keys on the basis of their proximity in a chain of triads based on the circle of fifths. The proximity among major keys (which form a circle of fifths in each chart) coincides with the number of steps they are removed from the source key, so that, for example, A major and E-flat major are both related in the third degree to C major:[126]

Hauptmann – series for the major keys

| II | | I | III | II | | I | III | II | | I | III | II | | I | III | II | | I | |
|---|---|---|---|---|---|---|---|---|---|---|---|---|---|---|---|---|---|---|---|
| I | III | II | | I | III | II | | I | III | II | | I | III | II | | I | III | II | |
| A♭ - | C - | E♭ - | g - | B♭ - | d - | F - | a - | C - | e - | G - | b - | D - | f# - | A - | c# - | E - | g# - | B | … |

Hauptmann – series for the minor keys

| | | | | | | | | | | | | I | III | II | | I | III | II | |
|---|---|---|---|---|---|---|---|---|---|---|---|---|---|---|---|---|---|---|---|
| | | | | | | | | | | I | III | II | | I | III | II | | I | |
| A♭ - | c♭ - | E♭ - | g♭ - | B♭ - | d♭ - | F - | a♭ - | C - | e♭ - | G - | b - | D - | f# - | A - | c# - | E - | g# - | B | … |
| II | III | I | | II | III | I | | II | III | I | | | | | | | | | |
| I | | II | III | I | | II | III | I | | | | | | | | | | | |

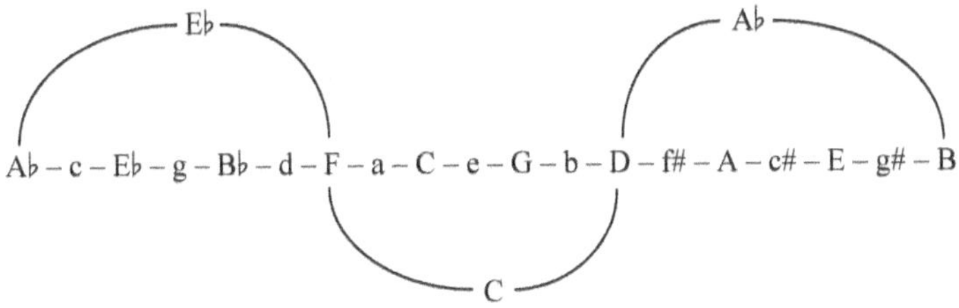


Hauptmann further states, however, that the main criterion for the relationship of keys isn't "merely … the greater quantity of like material," but the presence of a common dominant or subdominant: "The keys of subdominant and dominant … are much more intrinsically [related] in that the tonic triad of the tonic key comprises the dominant triad in the subdominant key and the subdominant in the dominant; and similarly, the tonic triads of the dominant and subdominant keys comprise respectively the dominant and the subdominant triads in the tonic key."[127] This criterion allows Hauptmann to relate the more remote keys of the third and fourth degrees of relationship quite persuasively. By taking the fifth of C major. G. and interpreting it as the third of E-flat major, it becomes possible to modulate more quickly from C major to E-flat major, a key related in the third degree, than by going first through F major and then through B-flat major:[128]

C major – E-flat major

II

F — a — C — e — G — b — D

III

A♭ — c — E♭ — g — B♭ — d — F

Hauptmann offers a similar example for modulation from C major to A major, another key related in the third degree. By taking the fifth of C major in the third-meaning, or by interpreting G as the third of E-flat major, it becomes possible to modulate more quickly from C major to E-flat major, a key related in the third degree, than by going first through F major and then B-flat major:

C major – A-flat major

I

F — a — C — e — G — b — D

III

D♭ — f — A♭ — c — E♭ — g — B♭

Hauptmann also provides an example of direct modulation from C major into another key related in the fourth degree, E major.

It is remarkable that Hauptmann finds a way to trace a closer relationship between keys related in the third and fourth degree than between keys related in the second degree.[129] Hauptmann postpones his explanation of how one can actually connect the keys of the third and fourth degree through modulation until after the introduction of a new concept: the minor-major key system.

One of the most innovative features of Hauptmann's harmonic theory is the idea of harmonic dualism, which greatly affects his view of key relationships.[130] Hauptmann develops a new notion of a minor-major key resulting from the interaction of the major and minor systems. Hauptmann conceives the minor key as a negation of the major key, as well as of its principal element, the tonic triad: "In the minor key there is a negative impulse, the negation of the positive or major triad, mainly, the [tonal] center or **tonic**."[131] The minor-major key is then presented as a fusion (or, speaking in Hegelian terms, a synthesis) of the two principal elements of Hauptmann's theory, the negative (minor) and the positive (major), into one key. Here, the major triad is placed in the center or tonic position, and the minor triad in the subdominant of this key system: "we may also conceive the notion of the key system, so that it shall contain this negation, the minor triad, as an essential determination, yet not give it prominence as a principal element, i.e. not place it in the middle of the system. Then the positive, or major, triad represents the middle, and its negation, the minor triad, takes its place as **subdominant** chord."[132] Hauptmann illustrates the minor-major key system in the key of G:[133]

Hauptmann – minor-major key-system

| II | | III | | I | | | | I | | II | | III |
|---|---|---|---|---|---|---|---|---|---|---|---|---|
| C | — | e♭ | — | G | — | b | — | D | — | f# | — | A |
| | | | | I | | III | | II | | | | |

In the context of Hauptmann's aforementioned discussion of modulation from C major to A-flat major, he summarizes the greater advantage of the minor-major key system for reaching remote keys compared to the major key system: "we immediately gain a region lying towards the subdominant side that in successive modulation would be reached only by progression through three keys. Therefore, the more distant keys that lie on this side are in general more easily accessible along this path."[134]

Hauptmann proposes two kinds of key relationships in the context of the minor-major key system. First, he declares as related two keys that are quite remote on the circle of fifths, the minor-major key (e.g., G minor-major, which is G major with a lowered sixth scale degree) and the key of its minor subdominant (C minor): "To the key of C minor, the key of G major with minor sixth, which we term minor-major, alone can appear related; while related to the latter [G minor-major], which is its principal key, the key of C minor is quite unrelated to the key of G major."[135]

Second, based on the commonality of functions (tonic and dominant) shared by the parallel major and minor keys, as well as their capability for changes of meaning from positive to negative and vice versa, Hauptmann classifies the parallel major and minor as nearly related: "To every key the opposite key with like name will always stand in close relationship; the minor key to the major with like name, the minor-major to the minor or major key with like name, and so too inversely. The change here acts upon the tonic interval of the fifth, which passes from positive to negative or from negative to positive meaning."[136] Hauptmann's acceptance of the minor subdominant key and the parallel minor key into the realm of keys closely related to a source major key is highly significant because it explains how to accomplish the shortcut passage into keys related in the third and fourth degrees: from C major into E-flat major, A major, E major, or A-flat major. A comparison of the following two modulatory plans from C major to A-flat major clearly illustrates this:[137]

C – F – B♭ – E♭ – A♭

C – f – A♭

The key of the minor subdominant is used for modulation from C major to A-flat major. F minor also helps to make a shorter connection between C major and E-flat major:[138]

C – F – B♭ – E♭

C – f – E♭

The parallel minor key performs the same minor subdominant role, as shown in modulations from C major to E major and A major:[139]

C – e – E (instead of C – G – D – A – E)

C – a – A (instead of C – G – D – A)

While he does briefly discuss some aspects of the relationship of keys in the context of the minor-major key, Hauptmann does not approach these issues as a separate topic in his treatise. As a result, details of key relationships are neither treated thoroughly nor presented systematically, with statements about this subject scattered throughout the treatise. It is possible, however, to trace the implications of several specific ideas proposed by the author regarding the relationship of keys.

First, Hauptmann relates all major keys in a circle of fifths, determining their degrees of relationship by the number of steps along the circle by which they are removed from the source key. Thus, we conclude that he treats F and G as keys in the first degree of relationship to C major; B-flat and D, in the second degree; E-flat and A, in the third degree; and A-flat and E, in the fourth.

However, since Hauptmann finds that the possibility of modulation in the minor keys is limited to only one direction along a circle of fifths,[140] in his system the minors keys related by first, second, third, and fourth degree cannot be clearly established. Consequently, based on their separation by fifths, it remains possible to identify the key of F minor as related to C minor in the first degree; B-flat minor, in the second; E-flat minor; in the third; and A-flat minor, in the fourth:

| | C major: | C minor: |
|---|---|---|
| first degree | F, G | f |
| second degree | B♭, D | b♭ |
| third degree | E♭, A | e♭ |
| fourth degree | A♭, E | a♭ |

Second, by integrating a minor-major key into the harmonic system, Hauptmann effectively expands the region of keys related to a major key by including the minor subdominant and parallel minor key. As a result, Hauptmann provides very effective means for reaching more distant keys with short modulatory plans. Two other minor keys are also treated as closely related, because their triads are contained in the tonic triad: the relative minor key and the mediant minor key.[141] Therefore, we may summarize that the following six keys are considered by Hauptmann as closely related to a major key as represented by C major: F major, G major, F minor, C minor, A minor, and E minor.

C major: F, G, f, c, a, e

In a minor key, there are also six keys considered by Hauptmann as closely related to a minor key. As represented in the key of C minor, these include the keys of the minor dominant (G minor), the minor subdominant (F minor), the minor-major dominant (G), the parallel major key (C major), the relative major key (E-flat major), and the submediant major (A-flat major), are closely related.[142]

C minor: F, g, G (minor-major), C, E-flat, A-flat

Gottfried Weber (1779–1839). *Magnoliabox.*

## Gottfried Weber

Weber's *Versuch einer geordneten Theorie der Tonsetzkunst (*1817–1821) is considered one of the most significant composition theory treatises of the nineteenth century, for it had a great influence on the European scholarly community.[143] Its popularity is reflected by its three editions and their translation into French, English, Danish, and Dutch.[144] This work was among the first treatises of the century to offer a comprehensive discussion of the relationships between keys.

In this treatise, Weber conceptualizes the closeness between any two keys as resulting from the closeness of their scales: "The major or minor keys most nearly related to any major key are thus those whose scales are most like the latter."[145] He recognizes two main scales: natural major and harmonic minor. Weber lists four keys as the "most nearly related keys"[146] or keys in the first degree of relationship.[147] Based on similarity of scale, for C major, the four most closely related keys are G major, F major, A minor, and C minor,[148] and for A minor, they are E minor, D minor, C major, and A major.[149]

| Weber: keys related in first degree | |
|---|---|
| C major: | G, F, a, c |
| A minor | e, d, C, A |

To determine the next set of keys, those related in the second degree to a source key, Weber uses a method derived from the one just described: "The more remote relationship depends upon the following simple principle: the nearest relatives of my nearest relatives are my relatives in the second degree: i.e., those keys standing in the second degree of relationship to a key are the ones most nearly related to its nearest relatives."[150] Under keys of second-degree relationship to a major key (again represented by C major), Weber lists eight: D major, E minor, A major, D minor, B-flat major, F minor, E-flat major, and G minor.[151] Similarly, in the case of A minor, the keys related in second-degree are: B minor, E major, F-sharp minor, D major, G minor, F major, C minor, and G major.[152]

| Weber: keys related in second degree | |
|---|---|
| C major: | D, e, A, d, B-flat, f, E-flat, g |
| A minor | b, E, f-sharp, D, g, F, c, G |

Finally, Weber places six remote keys in third-degree relationship to C major, similarly derived. In the key of C major, the third-degree keys are: B minor, E major, F-sharp minor, E-flat minor, A-flat major, and B-flat minor.[153] For A minor, they are: B minor, C-sharp minor, F-sharp minor, E-flat major, F major, and B-flat major.[154]

| Weber: keys related in third degree | |
|---|---|
| C major: | b, E, f-sharp, e-flat, A-flat, b-flat |
| A minor | b, c-sharp, f-sharp, E-flat, F, B-flat |

It is clear that, overall, common-tone relationships are central to Weber's view. The first three keys in first-degree relationship to C major (G major, F major, and A minor) each have six tones in common with the C major scale, while the fourth, C minor, shares five common tones (C, D, F, G, and B).[155]

Significantly, as in the case of C major just mentioned, but more so, the proximity of first-degree keys in minor is unequal. As Weber explains, the two fifth-related first-degree relationship keys in minor have fewer common tones—only four: in A minor, these first-degree keys are E minor and D minor. However, the relative major shares six common tones, as between A minor and C major. The parallel major contains five common tones, as in A major and A minor. In some of the second- and third-degree related keys, there are even fewer common tones. Although E and D minor have fewer common tones with A minor than G and F major have with C major, Weber treats the former (E and D minor) similarly as nearly related keys to A minor based on the fact that they exhibit greater similarity of scales than other minor keys.

Among the first-degree related keys in major, Weber includes the parallel minor key (illustrated using C minor), a point that deserves special attention. This key has five scale degrees in common with the source key, one less than G major, F major, and A minor. The parallel minor shares this property with four scales that Weber places in the category of second-degree related keys (D minor, D major, E minor, and B-flat major). Since the proximity of the C major and C minor scales does not match that of the other three first-degree related keys (G major, F major, and A major), the close relationship between the parallel keys cannot be explained by common scale degrees. Weber, however, asserts that, unlike other closely related scales with different tonics, the parallel keys, C major and C minor, share the same tonic and the same second, fourth, fifth, and seventh scale degrees, which makes this relationship indeed a very close one:

> the tonic note of C major is also the tonic note of C minor; and thus, both keys revolve around one and the same center, around the principal

> tone C, like being the children of one parent, like twin sisters, though of different character (mode), but one and the same person, only of two different dispositions. Just as the tonic of C major is also the tonic [of] C minor, the second degree of C major is the second degree of C minor also; the fifth (the dominant) of C major is also the dominant of C minor; the leading tone of C major is likewise the leading tone of C minor; we find on the fifth degree of both keys precisely the same harmonies, namely in C major and minor the harmonies [of the G major triad] and [G dominant seventh]. The similarity of these twin sisters is, accordingly, so great, that it almost ceases to be a mere similarity and passes into an absolute identity; it is certainly far too great to admit of not regarding two keys which are as similar to each other as these are in so many points and indeed positively alike, as being at least most nearly related to each other.[156]

From this we may conclude that Weber proposes a second criterion for the relationship of keys: commonality of functions. If the relationships of C major to F major, G major, and A minor stem from common tones, that of C major and C minor stems from identity as a whole.[157] The two scales, C major and C minor, differ only in the chromatic inflection of the third and the sixth scale degrees and are described by Weber as variants of one another rather than as separate, but similar, entities.

After introducing the fundamental principles of relationships between keys and sorting the keys by their degree of closeness to a source key, Weber proceeds to arrange all keys in one table:[158]

It is important to note that, when all the keys are combined in this table, two other kinds of key relationships appear: vertical and horizontal. Weber places each major and minor key on its own circle of fifths and arranges these in alternating vertical lines. Relationships between major and minor keys are interpolated into the horizontal axis, with each horizontal line alternating between relative major and minor keys (e.g., C major and A minor) and tonic and parallel major and minor keys (e.g., C major and C minor): "this species of relationship, here shown in the form of a horizontal line, may be called a *horizontal relationship*, in contradistinction to the ascending and descending species of relationships exhibited under numbers 1.) and 2.) [the dominant and subdominant]:"[159]

TABLE OF THE RELATIONSHIPS OF KEYS.

| C | a | A | f♯ | F♯ | d♯ | D♯ | b♯ | B♯ | g× |
|---|---|---|---|---|---|---|---|---|---|
| F | d | D | b | B | g♯ | G♯ | e♯ | E♯ | c× |
| B♭ | g | G | e | E | c♯ | C♯ | a♯ | A♯ | f× |
| E♭ | c | C | a | A | f♯ | F♯ | d♯ | D♯ | b♯ |
| A♭ | f | F | d | D | b | B | g♯ | G♯ | e♯ |
| D♭ | b♭ | B♭ | g | G | e | E | c♯ | C♯ | a♯ |
| G♭ | e♭ | E♭ | c | C | a | A | f♯ | F♯ | d♯ |
| C♭ | a♭ | A♭ | f | F | d | D | b | B | g♯ |
| F♭ | d♭ | D♭ | b♭ | B♭ | g | G | e | E | c♯ |
| B♭♭ | g♭ | G♭ | e♭ | E♭ | c | C | a | A | f♯ |
| E♭♭ | c♭ | C♭ | a♭ | A♭ | f | F | d | D | b |
| A♭♭ | f♭ | F♭ | d♭ | D♭ | b♭ | B♭ | g | G | e |
| D♭♭ | b♭♭ | B♭♭ | g♭ | G♭ | e♭ | E♭ | c | C | a |

e♭ – E♭ – c – **C** – a – A – f♯

Thus, the tables incorporates the two criteria for closely related keys that constitute the heart of Weber's conception of tonal space: commonality of tones and commonality of functions, with the former exhibited between relative keys and the second between parallel keys.

## Adolf Bernhard Marx

A discussion of key relationships may be found in Marx's first volume of the popular and highly acclaimed *Die Lehre von der musikalischen Komposition, praktisch-theoretisch* of 1837–1847. Similarly to Weber, Marx considers

Adolf Bernhard Marx (1795–1866). *Muzykal'naia entsiklopediia*, vol. 3. (Moscow: Sovetskaia entsiklopediia. Sovetskii kompozitor, 1976), 449–450.

resemblance between scales to be the main guide for determining the degree of relationship between keys. Like Weber, two kinds of scale are used by Marx in the harmonic context: (1) natural major,[160] and (2) harmonic minor.[161] The relationships between major keys may be found in the first section, "Finding the First Harmonies," of part 3, "Harmony of the Major Scale."

Marx treats neighboring major keys on the circle of fifths as the most closely related,[162] and therefore can be considered as keys in the first degree of relationship: "Two major keys are called closely related when they deviate from one another in only one tone. For example, C major and G major differ only in the tone F, C major and F major only in the tone B, etc. Each key has its closely related key on both sides of the circle of fifths."[163]

According to Marx, then, the degree of relationship between major keys depends on the number of tones that differ between them. In the same way, D major and B-flat major are both related in the second degree to C major because their respective scales differ by two tones, and they are related to each other in the fourth degree, since their scales differ by four tones.[164] From this statement we may conclude that, according to Marx, there is also a fourth-degree relationship between major keys that differ by four tones and that, consequently, there must be a third-degree relationship between major keys, although the latter is not stated. Marx, however, does not discuss the fourth degree further nor does he offer additional details. A similar chapter devoted to the minor key, part 6, "The Harmony of the Minor Scale," contains no examination of relationships between keys.[165] Only the relationship between major keys is described in Marx's treatise.

Several additional ideas about the relationship of keys may be found in part 8 of the treatise, "Modulation into Remote Keys," where Marx first discusses various chords used for modulation (the dominant seventh and ninth chords, the diminished seventh chord, and the diminished, major, and minor triads). In section 6 of part 8, "Order of Modulation for More Extended Compositions," Marx introduces his ideas on the large-scale logic of modulations within a composition. He divides a longer passage of music into three "main [tonal] seats [*Sitze*]."[166] In a major key, these are:

1) the tonic key
2) the dominant key (which can be followed by its nearest relation, the relative minor key)
3) the subdominant key (which can be preceded by its relative key and best prepares the final arrival into the tonic key)[167]

The relative key may be placed adjacent to the source key, either initially, before the subdominant, or towards the closure.

Marx – order of modulations in major

| Major | | | Minor | | | Major | | |
|---|---|---|---|---|---|---|---|---|
| C — | D — | G — | e — | a — | d — | F — | G — | C |

To summarize this section of the treatise: Marx refers to relative keys as close keys, first by exactly describing the relative minor key as the nearest related key to the dominant key,[168] and then by including E minor immediately following G major, as well as placing D minor, as a relative minor, before the subdominant key of F major. If the main tonal seats demonstrate the large-scale progression and are guided by close key relationships, the other keys, which were not underlined in Marx's treatise, may be regarded as representing the small-scale or local-level progression, which is similarly guided by the close relationships of keys.

Marx also states his preference for combining the major and minor keys within a modulatory plan into clusters: in the above example, a group of major keys—C, D, G—is followed by a group of minor keys—E, A, D—which is then followed by another major group–F, G, C. It should be noted that, due to the perspective produced by this grouping, a dominant-tonic relationship emerges between some keys in the plan, such as D major and G major, E minor and A minor, A minor and D minor, and G major and C major.

The order of modulations in minor keys seems more problematic for Marx, because of the key's aforementioned "gloomy and unstable character."[169] To demonstrate modulation in a composition in a minor key, Marx chooses the following keys as the main close areas:[170]

1) the tonic key
2) the relative major key
3) the subdominant key

The source key is placed in the first area, just as it was in the major-key chart. The second area of minor, which is supposed to be occupied by a key of opposite mode (major), is considered problematic by Marx since the keys of the dominant and subdominant are both minor.[171] For this second area, Marx therefore chooses the relative major key. To the relative major key is attached its dominant, which in turn is followed by the (minor) dominant of the source key. The third region is occupied by the subdominant, similarly to the major modulation plan's third tonal seat. The minor subdominant key may be preceded, according to Marx, by its relative major, although it is not considered by Marx to be as natural and easy to use in this context as are the other keys in the chain.[172] In Marx's chart demonstrating the order of modulation in minor, the principal areas are underlined:

Marx – order of modulations in minor

| Minor | Major | | | | | Minor |
|---|---|---|---|---|---|---|
| a | — C | — G | — e | — F | — d | — a |

In Marx's discussions of the order of modulation in major and minor compositions, the relationship between A minor and its relative key, C major, is treated as a close one, and in his use of the clusters of keys Marx adheres to his idea of alternating between contrasting modes.

However, Marx finds these techniques insufficient in the minor key. For example, in the modulation plan in A minor presented above, Marx considers it a logical but awkward alternative to F major, and he therefore places it before the key of the subdominant in the chain. However, in discussing the alternative minor modulation plan shown below, Marx also demonstrates that, if A minor replaces F major, two dominant-tonic relationships arise (E minor to A minor and A minor to D minor), and a clustering of major and minor keys then becomes possible:

Marx – alternative order of modulations in minor

| Minor | Major | | Minor | | | |
|---|---|---|---|---|---|---|
| a // | C — | G // | e — | a — | d — | a |
| | | | | [5] | [5] | |

Marx's statements on the relationship of keys may be summarized in the following three principles:

1) The relationship between major keys is judged on the closeness of their scales and according to their distance from one another on the circle of fifths. As a result, the dominant and subdominant keys are the most nearly related to a source major key: in C major, the keys of F major and G major.
2) Although not explicitly stated, in a minor key the keys of the dominant and subdominant (whose scales differ by three tones in the context of harmonic minor) are also closely related: in A minor, the keys of D minor and E minor.
3) The relative major and minor keys, whose scales differ by only one tone in the case of harmonic minor, are also considered closely

related. In the large-scale modulatory plans for major and minor, relative keys are systematically attached to their respective source major or minor key: in C major, the key of A minor, and in A minor, the key of C major.

An examination of Marx's later and shorter treatise, *Allgemeine Musiklehre* of 1839, supports the preceding summary on the relationship of keys and also provides additional details. A short chapter, "Relationships of the Scales," offers a brief exposition in which two degrees of relationship are specified:[173]

Marx's first- and second-degree keys to C Major

| | | | | | |
|---|---|---|---|---|---|
| 1st | | F | a | G | and C minor |
| 2nd | B♭ | d | | e | D |

Marx's first- and second-degree keys to A Minor

| | | | | |
|---|---|---|---|---|
| 1st | d | C | e | and A major |
| 2nd | F | | G | |

In addition to those already introduced in *Die Lehre*, this includes one new key among the first-degree-related keys in major and minor: the parallel key (i.e., the tonic key of opposite mode). This new key differs in two scale degrees, since Marx uses the harmonic minor scale as the principal type of minor scale in both treatises. Marx justifies the inclusion of this key in the first degree of relationship by the parallel keys' shared tonic, dominant, and subdominant scale steps.[174] The dominant and subdominant relationships, described as "inner affinities," also play a decisive role for Marx.[175] Marx considers the minor dominant and minor subdominant as related in the first degree to the source minor key, in spite of the differences in three scale degrees that, in another context, would render them less closely related.

Marx's and Weber's tonal systems display many similarities. The following table illustrates and compares their perspectives on first- and second-degree-key relationships based on common tones. For the minor source key, common tones are calculated in the context of the harmonic minor scale used by Weber and Marx in their treatises.

| | **C** | | | | **a** | | | |
|---|---|---|---|---|---|---|---|---|
| First degree | | | | | | | | |
| Weber | G | F | a | c | e | d | C | A |
| Common tones | [6] | [6] | [6] | [5] | [4] | [4] | [6] | [5] |
| Marx | G | F | a | c | e | d | C | A |

| Second degree | | | | | | | | | | | | | | | | |
|---|---|---|---|---|---|---|---|---|---|---|---|---|---|---|---|---|
| Weber | D | e | A | d | B♭ | f | E♭ | g | b | E | f# | D | g | F | c | G |
| Common tones | [5] | [5] | [4] | [5] | [5] | [4] | [4] | [4] | [3] | [4] | [4] | [4] | [3] | [5] | [5] | [5] |
| Marx | D | e | | d | B♭ | | | | | | | | | F | | G |

For Marx, relationships in the major key work exactly as they do in Weber's theory: scales with six common tones are included in the first degree and those with five, in the second degree, with the exception of giving the parallel minor first-degree status. The only difference between Weber and Marx is that, in the second-degree category, Weber includes four scales with only four common tones (A major, F minor, E-flat major, and G minor).

Relationships in the minor key work in almost the same way for Marx as they do for Weber. The same keys constitute those related by one degree; however, the number of common tones is less consistent than in major, ranging from four to six. Keys with five common tones comprise the those related by two degrees, with the exception of the parallel major, which is given first-degree status.

Clearly, the two systems are remarkably similar: the groupings of first-degree relationships in major and minor keys are identical in Weber and Marx's theories. The differences arise only in the second-degree group, where Marx introduces only four keys in major and two in minor, as opposed to Weber's eight each in major and minor. This difference may stem from Marx's less systematic approach to the relationship of keys, while the equivalence of the first-degree group in Weber and Marx may be explained by their similar approaches to establishing the most nearly related keys. In both cases, relationships are based on the principles of common-tone relationships, relationships on the circle of fifths (i.e., those of the subdominant and dominant), and commonality of functions (i.e., parallel majors and minors).

## Siegfried Dehn

Dehn devotes an entire chapter of his *Theoretisch-praktische Harmonielehre mit angefügten Generalbassbeispielen* of 1840 to a discussion of the relationship between keys. The two scales considered are the natural major and harmonic minor, just as in Weber and Marx.[176] He lists five keys as keys closely related to C major: D minor, E minor, F major, G major, and A minor.[177] Dehn notes, however, that three of the five keys—F major, G major, and A minor (in the harmonic form of the minor scale)—are comparatively closer to the source key, because they differ from it by only one scale degree, while the other two keys—E minor and D minor—differ by two (again, in harmonic minor).[178] Thus, while Dehn's measurement of key relationships in terms of common scale degrees is similar to the theories of Weber and Marx, Dehn demonstrates a more precise awareness of the varying degrees of closeness characterizing the five keys in the closely related category.

Dehn further develops his idea of affinity between keys by introducing the concept of common triads: "those tonalities are most nearly related whose tonic triads (or triads on the tonic note of the key) occur as full triads in both keys."[179] Dehn illustrates this statement by showing how the triads G major, E minor, A minor, F major, and D minor are derived (the C major triad is distinguished by its open noteheads):[180]

Having introduced the concept of common triads early in the discussion of the relationship of keys, Dehn later demonstrates its application and, in the process, reveals his conceptualization of this relationship in greater detail. Giving priority to the relationship between the relative major and minor keys (C major and A minor),[181] Dehn establishes a structural pattern

Siegfried Dehn (1799–1858). Wikimedia.

in which the relative minor key is linked to each of its nearest major keys (initially, to G major and F major), and he then reiterates this pattern to build a fluid system of keys. Eventually, the following chart of key relationships is offered:[182]

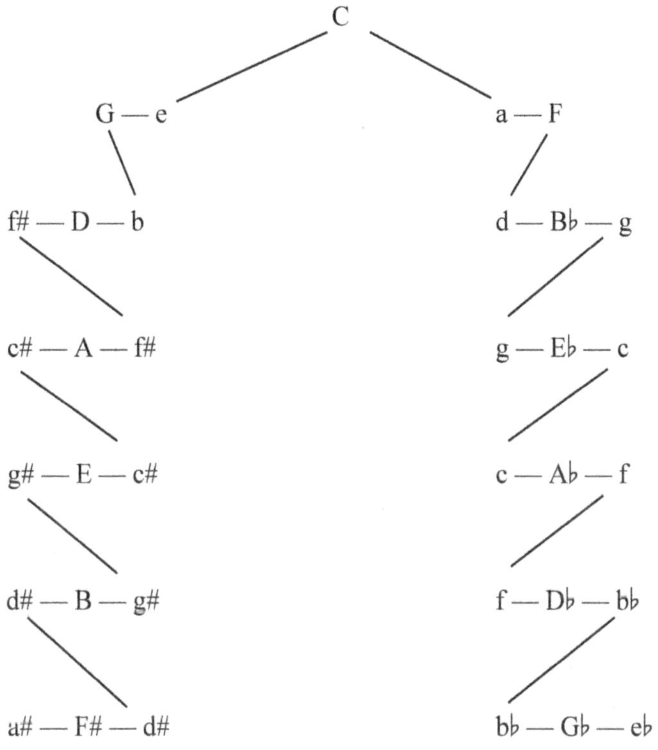


The concept of common triads operates by means of the interlocking triad principle (e.g., the tonic triad of C major, C – E – G, interlocks with that of its mediant E minor, E – G – B, by sharing notes E and G, as well as with that of its submediant A minor, A – C – E, by sharing notes C and E). Each level is a chain of interlocking triads, alternating between minor and major (except for the uppermost level, which is occupied by the source key). Excepting B minor and D minor, each minor key (F-sharp minor, C-sharp minor, G-sharp minor, and D-sharp minor on the sharps side of the chart, and G minor, C minor, F minor, and B-flat minor on the flats side) is placed on a level's outer edge and duplicated on the inner edge of the next level below.

Dehn also notes a secondary feature resulting from this structure: the appearance of a circle of fifths for both major and minor keys. The keys on the circle-of-fifths are reached, according to Dehn's chart, via relative or median/submediant keys. Dehn points out that the center and edges of the two columns form vertical circle-of-fifths patterns.[183] Several musical examples are offered that illustrate possible modulations within these circles, and it is mentioned that such modulations are often used in musical practice.[184]

Overall, then, the chart demonstrates that Dehn's approach to the relationship of keys is based on two principles, both of which stem from the concept of common triads: (1) relative majors and minors, also understood as mediant and submediant chords, and (2) interlocking triads. This approach allows him to extend the chain of keys in both directions on a circle of fifths, either toward the dominant or (in this case) sharp side or toward the subdominant or flat side.

The chart's seven levels reflect gradually increasing distance from the source key. If only major keys are considered, the keys on the first level after the tonic (occupied by G major and F major) belongs among Dehn's five closely related keys,[185] while the second level is more distant (D major and B-flat major), the third level even more so (A major and E-flat major), and so on. Among the minor keys, the same principle is at work: the first level (E minor and A minor) denotes the nearest keys. With the exception of D minor, treated by Dehn as a close key, the three minor keys of the second level (F-sharp minor, B minor, and G minor) are more distant, while the third level (C-sharp minor, F-sharp minor, G minor, and C minor) is even more distant, and so forth.

Comparing Dehn's concept of key relationships with those of Weber and Marx brings to light some important differences. Where Weber and Marx rely on commonalities of scale degree and function to determine the closeness of keys, Dehn builds his system of key relationships on the basis of relative minor and major keys and of interlocking triads. In Dehn's system, the prominence of the dominant and subdominant functions is secondary; instead of serving as the prime determinant of the group of close keys, as it did in Weber and Marx, it merely follows as a consequence of the structure of his chart.

Another significant difference involves the parallel minor key. For Weber and Marx, the closeness of the parallel minor results from the commonality of functions between keys of the same tonic. However, Dehn does not include the parallel minor in his list of close keys.[186] Neither does it appear among the close keys in his chart, where it is shown only on the third level, a level that contains remote keys (the other minor keys on this level are G minor, C-sharp minor, and F-sharp minor).

Another difference between Dehn's tonal map and those of Weber and Marx is that Dehn does not create a separate chart for the minor key. However, given that the principles of relative minor and major keys and of interlocking triads lie at the foundation of Dehn's system, it is possible to build an A minor chart based on his C major chart (see above):

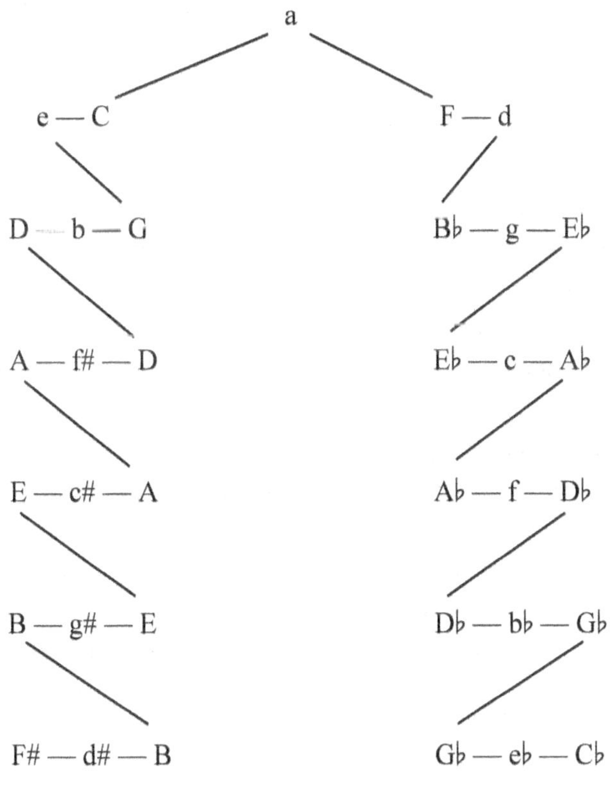

Applying Dehn's definition of closely related keys results in a set of keys closely related to A minor. Among them, the tonic triads of the following five keys are of greatest significance because according to Dehn they "occur as full triads":[187] C major, E minor, G major, F major, and D minor. Dehn's chart is distinctive and demonstrates his focus on triads rather than common tones as the basis for modulation between keys.

## Johann Christian Lobe

Discussion of the relationship of keys may be found in all three of Lobe's widely used treatises, *Lehrbuch der musikalischen Composition* (vol. 1, 1850), *Katechismus der Musik* (1851) and *Katechismus der Compositionslehre* (1872). Lobe's ideas about key relationships remain consistent throughout all three works, differing only in length. These ideas prominently exhibit the influence of Weber's early-century treatise—so much so that Lobe's work should be understood as belonging within the same tradition. The differences between the two theorists' ideas, such as Lobe's recognition of not just the harmonic minor scale (as in Weber) but also the melodic minor scale,[188] are of little consequence.

Lobe, taking C natural major and A harmonic minor as his two basic scales,[189] uses the principle of scale similarity to determine relationships between keys.[190] In his discussion of the relationship between the major keys, Lobe defines close scales or first-degree keys as differing from the source scale or key by only one tone.[191] As a means of comparing the degrees of relationship exhibited by two keys of the same mode, Lobe considers their location on the circle of fifths. For example, two major keys that neighbor C major on the circle of fifths, G major and F major, differ from the source key in only one tone and are described by Lobe as being within one degree of relationship to it. By extension, the greater the distance between two major keys on the circle of fifths, the more remote their degrees of relationship from the source key: D major and B-flat major each have two tones different from C major and are thus related to it in the second degree.[192] Lobe's approach here is similar to that adopted by Marx.

In his discussion of the relationship between the minor keys, defining levels of relationship is more complicated. Lobe argues that the keys of the dominant and subdominant are closely related to a source minor key, even though the similarity of their scales is not as close as in major, since they differ by two tones from the source minor (rather than by one tone). By way of example, in the key of A minor, the dominant E minor and the subdominant D minor are in the first degree of relationship to the source key, and it therefore follows that B minor and G minor are in the second degree of relationship to A minor.[193]

Finally, Lobe discusses the relationship between keys of opposite mode (major and minor). Again, the closeness of scales is said to determine the relationship, as it did between keys of the same mode. Lobe identifies two new keys related in the first degree to a major key, the relative minor and the parallel minor, as well as two new keys in first-degree relationship to a minor key, the relative major and the parallel major. Weber and Marx also categorized the relative and parallel major and minor keys as closely related to their source keys. Unlike Weber or Marx, however, Lobe simply lists them among the first-degree keys without providing any details to support this inclusion. Thus, a total of four keys are treated by Lobe as being related in the first degree to a source key, major or minor, and they match the four first-degree keys in Weber and Marx as well as in Weber's graphic representation of these keys:[194]

1) the key of the dominant
2) the key of the subdominant
3) the relative key
4) the parallel key

Put differently, in Lobe's theory, there are four keys related to the source key in the first degree.[195] Having traced the four first-degree keys in C major, as listed above, Lobe uses the same principle to expound a set of eight keys related to a source key in the second degree, applying a method of derivation similar to the one used by Weber. After eliminating duplicates, there are eight keys related in the second degree:

| | | | | | | | | |
|---|---|---|---|---|---|---|---|---|
| C major: | g | d | e | f | D | B♭ | A | E♭ |
| A minor: | b | E | g | D | F | G | c | f# |

Lobe's eight second-degree-related keys match those of Weber, but not those of Marx. It may therefore be presumed that Lobe's concept of the relationship of keys, despite having features in common with Marx's, reflects its lineage from Weber's *Versuch* more faithfully. In addition to offering the same eight keys related in the second degree, Lobe's graphical charts of both the first-degree keys and the second-degree keys' derivation are nearly identical to those of Weber, as shown below:[196]

First-degree keys

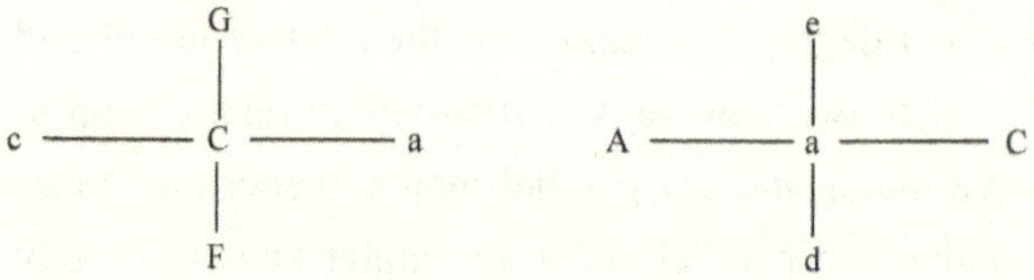


Second-degree keys

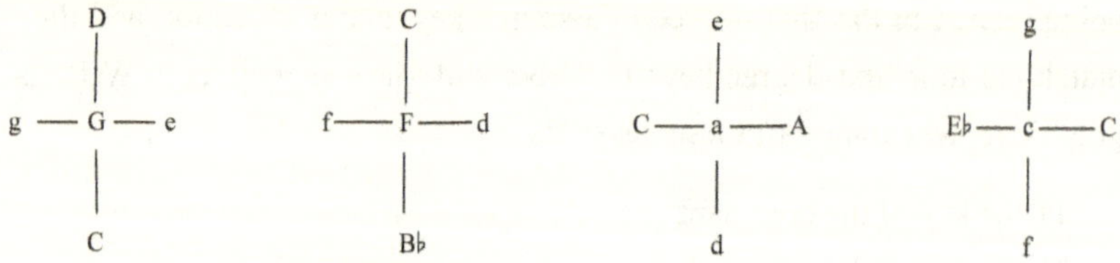


## Ernst Friedrich Richter

In chapter 11 of his *Lehrbuch der Harmonie* of 1853, "On the Modulation of a Passage of Music," Richter defines modulation as a "digression from one key into another."[197] As his choice of words suggests, Richter is not particularly interested in the large-scale tonal design or the relationship between keys. Rather, his focus is on techniques for performing modulations, which he explicates in chapter 16, "On the Means for Modulation." In Richter's words, "the art of modulation consists in finding those harmonies which are related to two or more keys, so as to use them to get from one key to the other."[198] Richter distinguishes between two kinds of modulation, sudden and gradual: "First: occurring suddenly, passing briefly by and through, or, second: prepared more slowly, seeking the new key as a target and taking it as a foundation for a prolonged period of time."[199] It is only here that Richter hints at the division of keys into close and remote categories: "This kind of modulation [sudden] is suited only to the most nearly related keys, and although more distant ones can be reached by special and decisive means, nevertheless in their development very natural and organic combinations must prevail, if they are not to appear unintelligible and clumsy."[200] At the end of the chapter on modulation, a series of figured bass exercises is given, which might have been a source of Rimsky-Korsakov's criticism of the available harmony treatises in the foreword to his treatise.[201] Unsurprisingly, in the chapter titled "On the Means for Modulation," the technical discussion of different uses for various chords is considerably more extensive than the discussion of modulatory concepts.[202]

An examination of several examples discussing the technical side of modulation reveals a few scattered indications of Richter's idea of key relationships and the criteria used to determine them. For example, modulations from C major to D minor, G major, and A minor are demonstrated in Richter's example 192, though they are not expressly identified as closely related keys.[203] However, in the text between two examples given much later, Richter speaks of "the more distant key of E[-flat]" in relation to modulation from C major to F major, G minor, and A minor.[204] The key of E-flat major in the earlier of these two examples is approached via B-flat major and F major, which are clearly less distant—though, again, this is not explicitly stated.

Towards the end of the chapter titled "On the Means for Modulation," an implicit theory of key relationships begins to emerge based on common tones in pivot chords. Richter puts special emphasis on common tones in performing a modulation: "The harmonic connection produced by tones that are identical or held over will be most readily comprehensible."[205] He then further explains that all keys can be reached using this principle of common tones, with the exception of three keys: in the key of C major, the exceptions are E-flat major, E major, and F-sharp major. Richter shows in an example that modulation into these three keys demands a four-chord progression, whereas other modulations can be accomplished in three chords.[206] In the key of A minor, the destination keys requiring a four-chord progression are C major, E-flat major, F-sharp major, and A-flat major.[207] To summarize Dehn's reasoning, the principle of modulation in both major and minor relies on tones shared in common between the source tonic and the destination key's dominant seventh.

Richter offers no further discussion in *Lehrbuch der Harmonie* on the technical side of gradual modulation, nor does he give advice on the choice of keys or elaborates regarding their distances, for a clear reason: to Richter, these questions pertain to the theory of form.[208] Accordingly, in his other treatise, *Die Grundzüge der musikalischen Formen und ihre Analyse* of 1852, a small chapter is devoted entirely to modulation. However, Richter's approach to modulation is from a structural perspective, and thus his purpose is to review the various locations appropriate for modulation rather than the relationships of keys in the modulatory processes.[209] Dividing modulation into transient and complete types and then further into melodic and harmonic types, Richter concentrates on the use of modulation at cadential points and on the location of modulation within a phrasal period. In other words, the author offers little specific guidance regarding tonal relationships. It is casually revealed, however, that the key of the dominant is considered to be the closest key in major. In contrast, Richter considers the major dominant in a minor key to be remote. Instead, Richter treats the relative key and the minor dominant as close keys in minor: "The key of the dominant is chosen because first, it is closest to the main key, and second, it is considered the peak of the climax. Likewise, it is difficult to choose the major key of the dominant in a minor-key piece, since it stands in a distant relation to the minor key. Therefore, the relative key or the minor key of the dominant are usually used."[210] In summary, Richter's impact on the field of tonal relationships is comparatively minimal. The author is primarily concerned with the localized technical execution of modulations, rather than the overall tonal design within a movement or composition.

## Ludwig Bussler

Ludwig Bussler (1838–1901) was a German theorist from Berlin and a student of Siegfried Dehn.[211] Bussler's name appears only in the Foreword to the first edition of Rimsky-Korsakov's *Practical Manual of Harmony*, but he is the only theorist mentioned by Rimsky anywhere in his writings in the context of harmonic treatises. Criticizing most harmony manuals for their lack of practical devices for harmonizing melodies and choosing chords, Rimsky-Korsakov notes that "Bussler's harmony manual is an exception in this regard."[212] The manual Rimsky-Korsakov refers to was likely the Russian translation of the *Praktische Harmonielehre in vier und fünfzig Aufgaben*,[213] which the composer had a translated copy of in his library.[214] Significantly, the numerous notes Rimsky-Korsakov wrote in the margins contain remarks regarding his disagreement with Bussler on harmonic techniques rather than conceptual issues and are concerned with aspects of voice leading, resolutions, and doublings.

Below, the two manuals' tables of contents are presented side by side for comparison. Rimsky-Korsakov's text of 1885 is organized very similarly to Bussler's harmony manual in terms of both structure and content, except that Rimsky-Korsakov discusses modulation in unit 2, while Bussler does so in part 3:

| **Bussler** | **Rimsky-Korsakov** |
|---|---|
| *Praktische Harmonielehre* (1875) | *Uchebnik garmonii* (1884/1885) |
| I. On the chords of the key | Unit I. Harmonization within one key |
| The principal chords | Ch. 1 Main triads in major and minor |
| A. The consonant principal chords | Ch. 2. Dissonant chords of the dominant |
| B. The dissonant principal chords | Ch. 3. Secondary degrees in major |
| The subordinate chords | Ch. 4. Secondary triads and 7th chords in minor |
| Thorough-bass notation | |
| II. The tones foreign to a harmony | Unit II. Modulation |
| Passing notes | Ch. 5. Means for gradual modulation |
| The suspensions | Ch. 6. Modulation and deviation to close keys |
| | Ch. 7. Modulation to remote keys |
| | Ch. 8. Pedal points |

*(Continued)*

**(Continued)**

| **Bussler** | **Rimsky-Korsakov** |
|---|---|
| *Praktische Harmonielehre* (1875) | *Uchebnik garmonii* (1884/1885) |
| III. Harmonic modulation | Unit III. Nonharmonic tones |
| A. Dissonant principal chords | Ch. 9. Passing and embellishing notes |
| B. Deceptive progressions | Ch. 10. The Suspensions |
| C Progressions of triads | Ch. 11. Melodic Figuration |
| IV. The altered or mixed chords | Unit IV. Mixed chords, enharmonic and false progressions |

One major difference between Bussler and Rimsky-Korsakov is that Bussler's harmonic theory recognizes only the natural major and harmonic minor scales.[215] Indeed, this is logical, because, although the manual discusses modulation, its primary goal, as stated in the Introduction, concerns the harmonization of melody: "The chief object of the lessons in harmony will be the adding of harmonies to—harmonization of—given melodies."[216] Most of the exercises offered in Bussler's volume require the student to supply harmonies to support melodies rather than build harmonies upon a figured bass (which is only required in one part of the section on thorough-bass notation). It is also noteworthy that the presentation of harmonic techniques and devices begins with simple notions and advances to the more complex. Both features of Bussler's text undoubtedly attracted Rimsky-Korsakov's approval, given that Rimsky addresses the same issues, organized similarly, in the Foreword to the *Practical Manual of Harmony*.

There is, however, very little common ground between Bussler's concepts in the discussion of modulation and those in Rimsky-Korsakov's treatise. Bussler concentrates on the various techniques for connecting chords in modulation. The issue of the relationship of keys is mentioned only in passing in his manual and without much detail. It is possible to deduce that there are three keys that Bussler treats as closely related to a source key, since all of the examples from the short section called "Modulation to Adjacent Keys" contain modulations into these keys, but these examples are not presented as comprehensive:[217]

| | | | |
|---|---|---|---|
| C major: | G | F | c |
| A minor: | e | d | A |

It is only at the end of this section that Bussler states that "the distance on the circle of fourths and fifths determines the degree of relationship."[218] It may thus be concluded that, in addition to the two keys in the same mode as a source key, its parallel key is considered a close relative. Bussler, however, proclaims that "the transition from C minor and reversely, is not *properly* a modulation; because the relation to a particular tone as fundamental or *key-note* is not abandoned, but merely the *mode* is changed."[219] Moreover, at the beginning of his discussion of modulation, Bussler defines it as a "means to pass over to another key. We say of a piece, that it modulates, when different keys occur in it."[220] Due to these two contradictory treatments of the parallel key, it is impossible to reconstruct Bussler's precise definition of the set of closely related keys. On the one hand, the examples of modulation to the parallel key given in the section titled "Modulation to the Adjacent Keys" suggest that the parallel key is regarded as closely related to a source key. On the other hand, the author states that the modulation equals a change of key, not mode.

Therefore, the only two keys that are clearly regarded as belonging among close keys are those located next to a source key on the circle of fifths: in the key of C major, these are G major and F major; in the key of A minor, G minor and F minor. Bussler does not offer any suggestions about approaching indirectly related keys, nor does he indicate which keys he considers to be remote.

# Chapter 13

# Analysis of German Tonal Models

Ideas concerning tonal space and the various concepts of the relationship of keys expressed by the German theorists and outlined above may also be described in the form of models. Among the seven German theorists discussed earlier only Richter and Bussler do not provide sufficient material for construction of a model and thus cannot be included in the following analysis.

It seems appropriate to begin by considering how different authors determine the first and often definitive group—the most nearly related keys to a source major key (i.e., the first-degree keys, or the first-degree group). Most of the models contain characteristics common to those used by Weber, and therefore a layout similar to the one used by him in his key-relationship charts is adopted for the purpose of easier comparison. Three concepts common to the majority of the authors are highlighted by this particular layout of major and minor keys. First, relative keys possess nearly identical scales (with due allowance for the harmonic form of the minor scale adopted by all the authors) and are treated by all the authors as the most nearly related to a source key. In the charts below all relative minor keys are placed immediately to the right of their respective major keys on the same horizontal line.

Second, the parallel major/minor is included by nearly all the authors in the first-degree group and is placed here on the left of the source key. Third, the difference in scale degrees gradually increases with movement around the circle of fifths. Thus, the dominant and subdominant, being the nearest distinctive keys of the same mode, are placed vertically above and below the source key in one column.

While Weber, Marx, and Lobe consider only four keys as first-degree keys, Dehn includes five in this category and Hauptmann includes six:[221]

Model 1

Weber, Marx, and Lobe
(V, IV, vi, i)

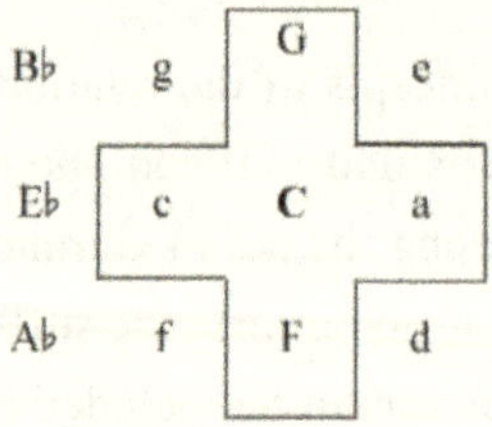


Model 2

Dehn
(V, IV, vi, iii, ii)

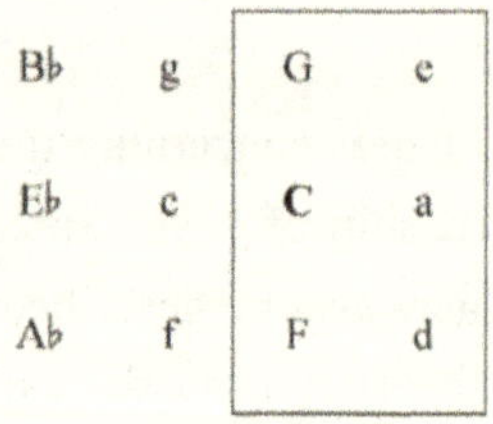


Model 3

Hauptmann
(V, IV, vi, i, iii, iv)

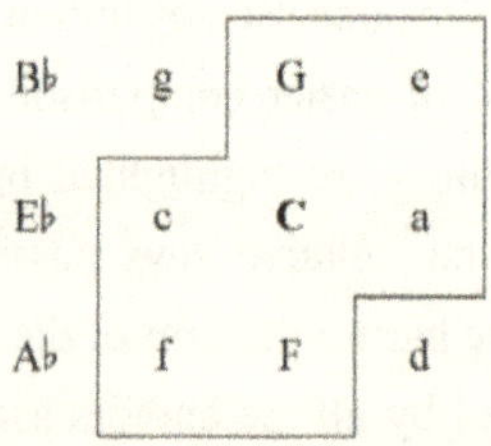

From these three models we observe that Dehn's concept of first-degree keys is distinguished from the others in that only two columns are engaged in his model, whereas the other two models engage three. While agreeing on the inclusion of the dominant, the subdominant and the relative minor in the first-degree keys to C major with the other two models, Dehn's model coincides only with that of Hauptmann in including the mediant minor and is unique in treating the supertonic as a first-degree key. Taking the principle of interlocking triads as a natural means of proximity to remote keys, Dehn establishes the priority of mediant and submediant in determining the relationship of keys. As a result of this principle, we observe the emergence of circle-of-fifths of both major keys and minor keys, which thus performs the function of a secondary element of the system.

If a model describing Weber's, Marx's, and Lobe's concepts of tonal relationships, one which includes four keys in the first-degree relationship, is compared with Dehn's model, a new element is revealed. While the former includes the three keys common to both models, the dominant, the subdominant, and the relative minor, it also engages the parallel minor key as a fourth first-degree key. The argument for the close relationship of this last key to the source major is developed on the grounds of commonality of functions, or the exceptional importance of shared tonics, dominants and subdominants between the major key and its parallel minor key. Because of the inclusion of the parallel minor key in the first-degree group, this model is extended to the new column that contains this key. If the keys in the initial two columns, i.e. two columns that include relative major/minor keys, in our case

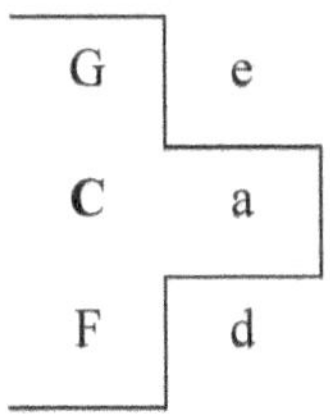

offer a modest range of only one scale-degree difference (B and B-flat or F and F-sharp), then by including the C minor in the first-degree keys, the range of differences jumps from one to three (B and B-flat, E and E-flat, A and A-flat, etc.):

| | | | |
|---|---|---|---|
| B♭ | g | G | e |
| E♭ | c | **C** | a |
| A♭ | f | F | d |

By not including the supertonic and mediant keys, that is, the relative minors of subdominant and dominant, as in Dehn's model, the model of Weber/Marx/Lobe exhibits an elegant balance of two major keys, the dominant and subdominant, and two minor keys, the relative minor and parallel minor.

Hauptmann's model is the most complex of the three encompassing the Weber/Marx/Lobe model, but it is further expanded in two directions by inclusion of the minor subdominant and mediant keys in the first-degree relationship. Two central ideas of his theory are reflected in the range of closely related keys which he offers. First is the concept of interlocking triads, somewhat similar to that of Dehn but greatly elaborated, which is used for the construction of his chains of keys. Hauptmann's second fundamental notion is that the minor triad represents the negation, or reversal of the major triad, an idea based on his theory of the supremacy of the tonic-dominant relationship. It is this principle that leads to his inclusion of both the parallel minor and the minor subdominant keys in the first-degree group. Thus, the minor subdominant key acquires the status of close relation to the source major since it is formed by way of negation of the tonic triad (C – e – G : C – a-flat – F). The parallel minor key is included in the first-degree keys, according to Hauptmann, because it shares the tonic and dominant with the source major, that is, because of the commonality of functions. The resulting first-degree group in Hauptmann is the most extended of the three models.

The first-degree keys to a source minor may be represented by the three following models. Weber, Marx, and Lobe use A minor in their discussion of the minor key, and the first model reflects this in its construction around A minor. Hauptmann's and Dehn's discussions of the minor key, on the other hand, are centered around C minor. Dehn's and Hauptmann's maps are transposed to A minor for easier comparison:

<u>First-degree keys in minor:</u>

Model 1a: Weber, Marx, Lobe

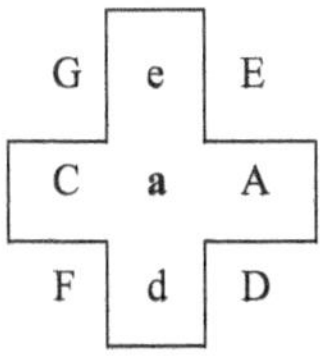


Model 2a: Dehn

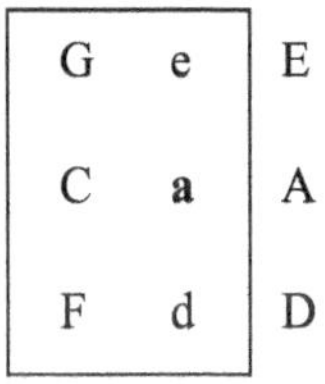


Model 3a: Hauptmann

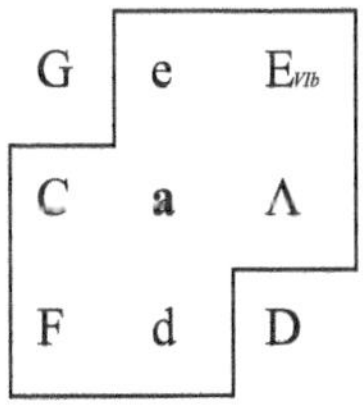


The minor key models exhibit the same structure as the three models for major keys, but two of out of three models occupy different areas of this space. The Weber/Marx/ Lobe model is primarily contained within the source key column (a) and is extended to the neighboring two columns by the inclusion of the relative major (C) and the parallel major (A). Dehn's model occupies the same space and contains the same keys as its major counterpart. Hauptmann's model is concentrated in the source column (a). It is extended to its neighboring two columns by the inclusion of the relative major (C) and the submediant (F) on the one hand, and of the two new keys in comparison with its major counterpart, the parallel major (A) and minor-major (E major with flatted sixth) dominant keys on the other.

Only three authors, namely Weber, Marx, and Lobe, go beyond discussion of first-degree related keys into the domain of indirectly related keys or second-degree keys. Whereas Marx's notion of second-degree keys is limited to four for a major key and only two for a minor key, Weber and Lobe offer a full set of eight 2nd-degree keys to the major key and another eight to the minor key:

Model 1b

Marx:

(II, VII♭, ii, iii)

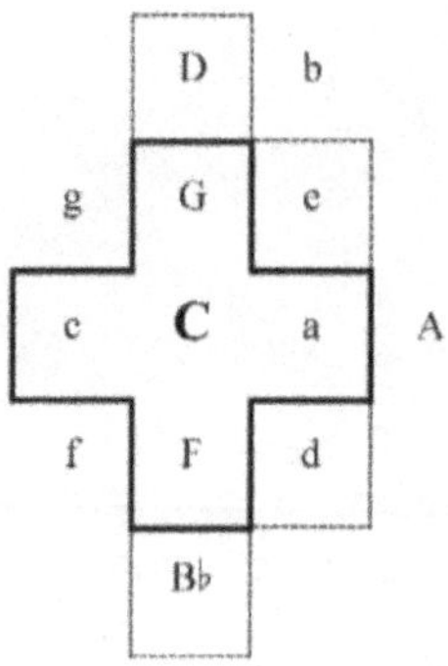


Weber and Lobe:

(II, VII♭, VI, III♭, ii, iii, iv, v)

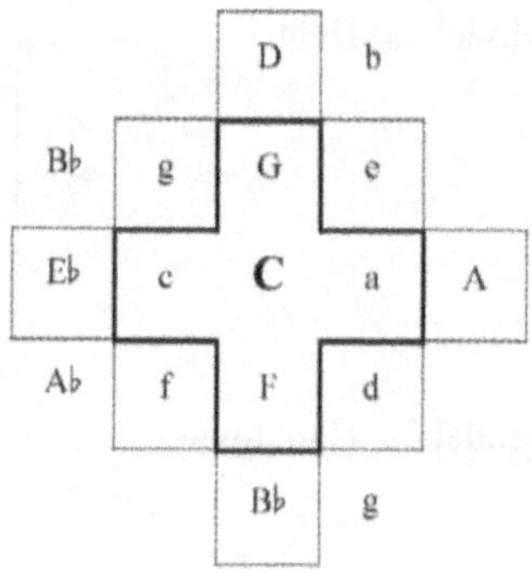


Model 1c

Marx:

(VI, VII)

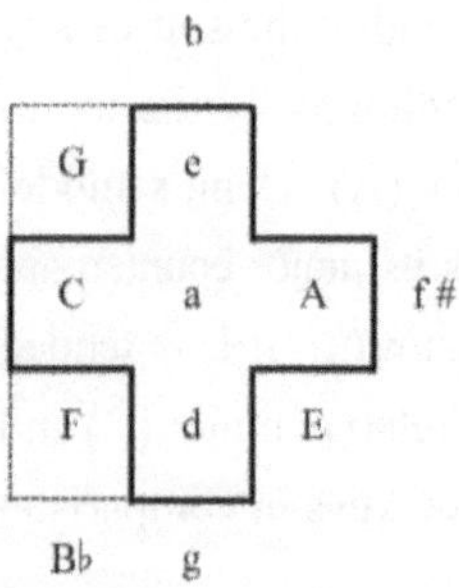


Weber and Lobe:

(VI, VII, IV, V, ii, iii, vi#, vii)

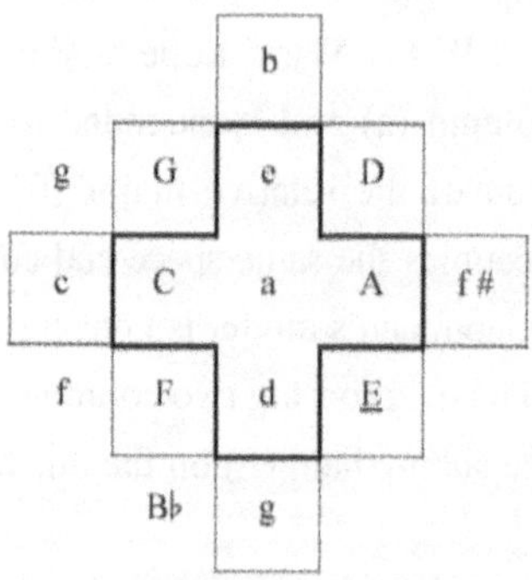

Marx's models display symmetric expansion of the tonal area by including two major keys on the circle-of-fifths (new keys: B-flat and D) and two minor keys (new keys: E and D) in the model for major, and by including only two major keys (new keys: F and G) in the model for minor.

The Weber/Lobe models encompass those of Marx but exhibit systematic expansion in all directions. By the acquisition of four major keys (D, B-flat, A, E-flat, in major and F, G, D, E in minor) and four minor keys (E, D, G, and F in major and C, F-sharp, G, B in minor), both models lb and 1c unfold consistently in two opposite directions. Each model acquires four total additional keys.

# Chapter 14

# Rimsky-Korsakov's System in the Context of Nineteenth-Century German Theory

Rimsky-Korsakov's acute interest in developing his own system of key relationships reflects both his active participation in a wider nineteenth-century discussion on tonal relations and his dissatisfaction with the systems proposed by other authors. The issue of modulation based on the relationship of keys was a very important part of Rimsky-Korsakov's motivation in writing a new treatise. In its consistent treatment of modulation in a larger tonal context, Rimsky-Korsakov's approach is highly advanced in comparison with those of the German theorists discussed in chapters 12 and 13. In most cases, it was necessary to deduce each theorist's conception of tonal relationships by gathering scattered ideas and statements. Rimsky-Korsakov, however, delivers a clearly articulated, systematic map for navigating tonality, not just by placing his discourse of modulations in the context of key relationships but also by presenting an elaborate discussion of degrees of relationship and of gradual modulation.

In the present section we shall examine both common and distinctive features found in Rimsky-Korsakov's perception of tonal relationships and in the works by German theorists. Considering the fact that we do not have sufficient material regarding Dehn's and Hauptmann's views of second-degree keys, our discussion is necessarily limited to a comparative analysis of the first-degree models. The six keys included by Rimsky-Korsakov in this group are: in C major, A minor, G major, F major, F minor, E minor, and D minor; in A minor, the six first-degree-related keys are C major, D minor, E minor, E major, F major, and G major.[222] In the figure below, the charts compare Hauptmann's and Rimsky-Korsakov's first-degree keys. In addition to the relationships represented by vertical and horizontal lines, both systems also generated relationships represented by diagonal lines. This secondary feature of the two-dimensional representation emerges only when the key on the diagonal line and the keys on both the horizontal and vertical lines are in an identical degree of relationship to the source key.

Hauptmann:

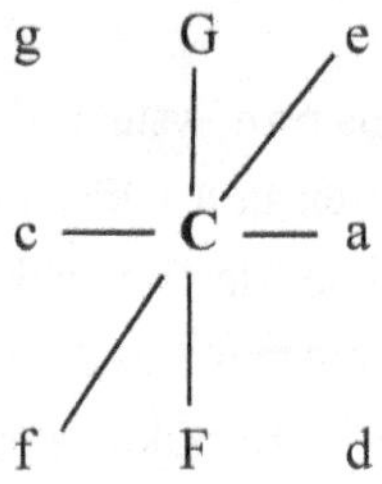


Rimsky-Korsakov:

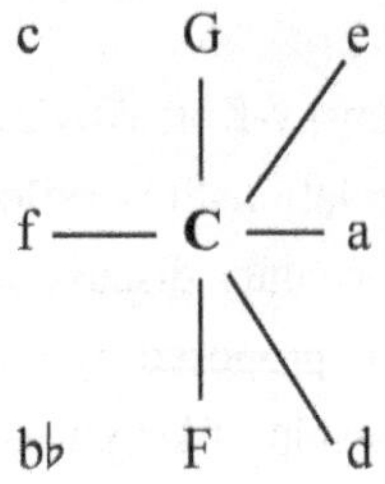


In the Hauptmann chart for the source key of C major, the first-degree key of F minor can be reached horizontally by way of C minor and vertically via F major. F minor is more closely related in the Rimsky-Korsakov chart. However, the column of minor keys to the left of the tonic is shifted one key up, so that F minor shares the horizontal line with C major. This shift is caused by the different relationship Rimsky identifies between C major and its minor subdominant, F minor. In Rimsky-Korsakov's system, modulation to F minor cannot proceed through either C minor or F major, because C minor and F minor are both separated from their relative majors by two degrees of relationship.

Two models of Rimsky-Korsakov's tonal space follow, one for C major and one for A minor, showing visually how many elements his theory shares in common with the German theories.:

Model 4

(V, IV, vi, iii, ii, iv)

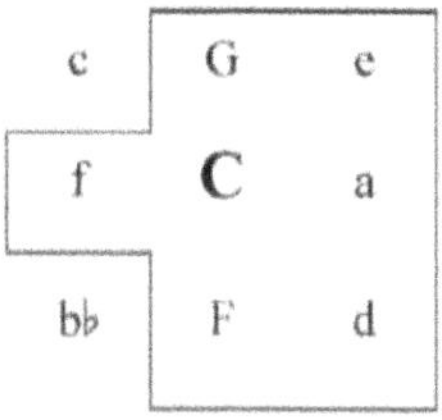


Model 4a

(v, iv, III, V, VI, VII)

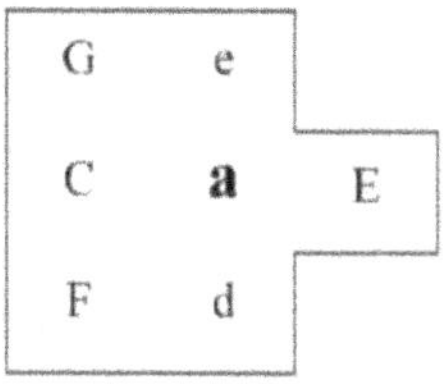


The following model graphically illustrates that there are four first-degree keys common to all four models: the dominant, the subdominant, and the relative major or minor.

Major key

Weber, Marx, Lobe, Dehn,

Hauptmann, and Rimsky-Korsakov

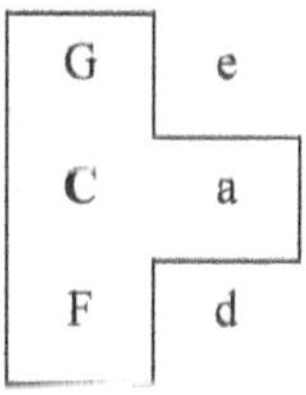


Minor key

Weber, Marx, Lobe, Dehn,

Hauptmann, and Rimsky-Korsakov

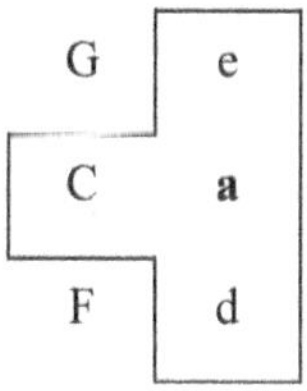


From this point, however, the models begin to diverge.

Rimsky-Korsakov and Dehn, in contrast to the other authors, share the idea that two of the minor keys, the supertonic (ii) and mediant (iii), are closely related to a source major key. Their agreement on this matter may be traced to two sources: the similarity of their approach to closely related keys based on the notion of "full common triads,"[223] and the important role in both of their systems of the relative major and minor keys. Hauptmann, by contrast, includes only the median minor key (iii) among the first-degree keys, and Weber, Marx, and Lobe place the supertonic and mediant in the area of second-degree keys. As a result, only in the Rimsky-Korsakov and Dehn models are the fifth-related major keys (F major – C major – G major) and their relative minor keys (D minor – A minor – E minor) both brought fully into the first-degree area.

One key is common to all of the German theories of close relationship except the Dehn and Rimsky-Korsakov models: the parallel minor or major. It is revealing that Rimsky treats the parallel key as related in the second degree to the source key.[224] The criterion used by the German authors to support the inclusion of the parallel minor or major in the first-degree group was the commonality of chord functions shared by keys despite their opposite modes (rather than scale proximity). Specifically, this commonality was based, beginning with Weber, on the importance of the tonics, dominants, and subdominants shared by the major and minor parallel keys. For Rimsky-Korsakov, however, commonality of functions is not a primary consideration in determining the first-degree group of keys. This difference is visually apparent in German models 1a, 2a, and 3a in chapter 13, where the parallel minor key is always found in the left column of the first-degree area. In Rimsky-Korsakov model 4, this space is occupied by a different key.

Rimsky-Korsakov also differs significantly from prevailing German ideas on first-degree key relationships, and in this case the difference is shared with Hauptmann: the minor subdominant in a major key (e.g., F minor in C major) and the major dominant in minor (E major in A minor).[225] While the inclusion of the major dominant can be explained by the widely accepted reliance on the harmonic minor scale throughout the literature, adding the minor subdominant requires a more complicated rationale. Rimsky-Korsakov and Hauptmann treat the minor subdominant key as a first-degree key to a major, because both admit an unconventional scale among their closely related scales: the major scale with flatted sixth (the minor-major or harmonic major).[226] Having this unusual feature as well as five out of six keys in common (C major: G major, F major, A minor, E minor, and F minor; for A minor: E minor, D minor, C major, E major, F major), it is remarkable that the models of Hauptmann and Rimsky's first-degree keys for major and minor are so different in appearance (model 3 first appeared in chapter 13; models 4 and 4a appeared previously in the present chapter):

**Major key:**

Model 3

Hauptmann

(V, IV, vi, i, iii, iv)

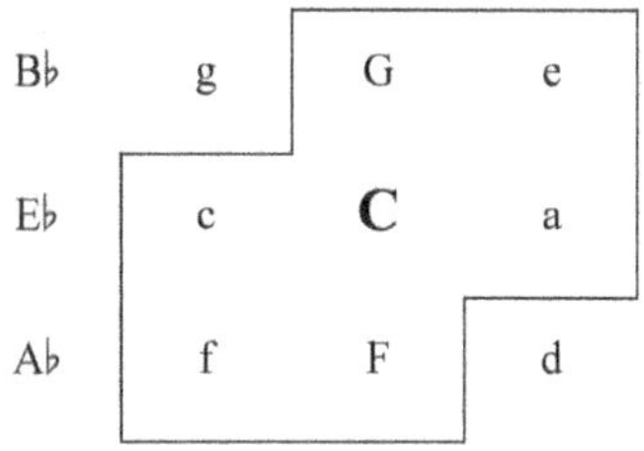


Model 4

Rimsky-Korsakov

(V, IV, vi, i, iii, iv)

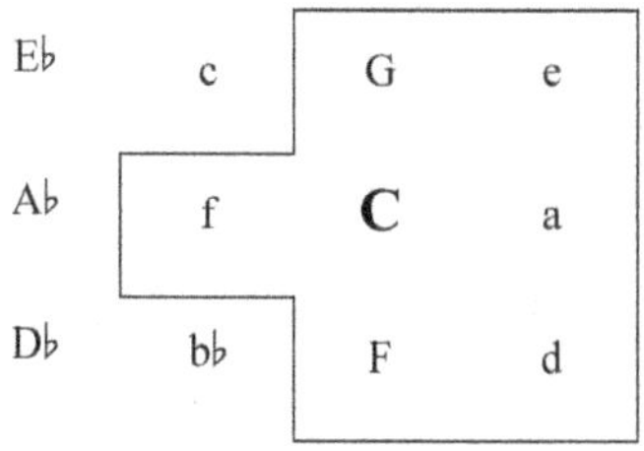


**Minor key:**

Model 3a

Hauptmann

(v, iv, III, I, V, VI)

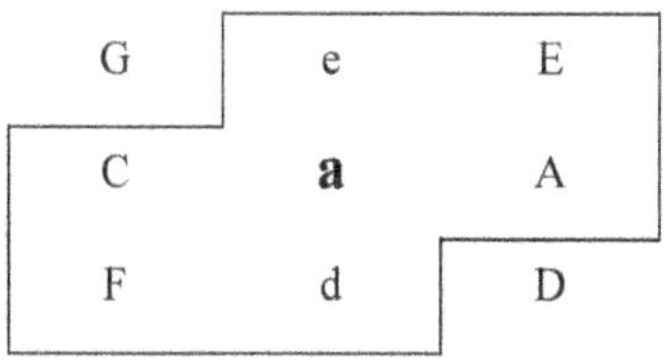


Model 4a

Rimsky-Korsakov

(v, iv, III, V, VI, VII)

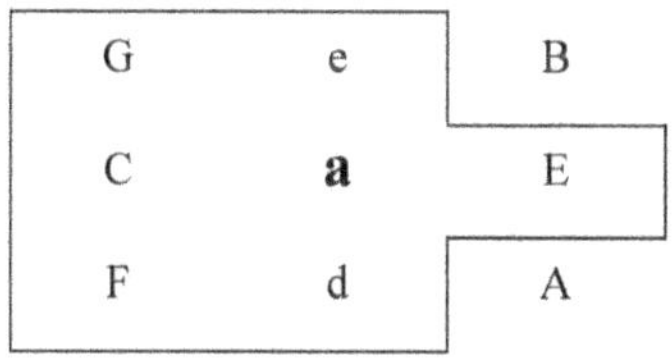


While the Rimsky-Korsakov models fully encompass the source and relative key columns and engage only one key from the next column, the Hauptmann models exhibit a different structure: they too include the entire source column, but they are extended by two keys on each side.

Another important distinction of the Rimsky-Korsakov model is that the key of the minor subdominant is located in the same place occupied by the parallel minor in the Hauptmann model and in the Weber, Marx, and Lobe model. Examining the general structural characteristics of all four models is helpful for understanding this difference, particularly the distinction between horizontal and vertical lines.

The vertical tonic line or tonic column consists of keys of the same mode (major or minor); in other words, the keys are related to one another as entities of the same type. The keys in the vertical tonic line are spaced in equal intervals of a fourth or fifth and, just as these intervals are the inverse of one another, so are the chords built on their scale degrees reciprocally functional (e.g., C major is the subdominant of G major and G major is the dominant of C major). These relationships along vertical lines are maintained in all of the vertical lines throughout all the models.

Horizontal lines are built upon different principles, and it is here that the models most strongly diverge. In contrast to the vertical line content, the models' horizontal lines all contain alternating major and minor keys with varying intervals between them. The horizontal lines of the models thus comprise keys related to one another as entities of opposite type. The principle of the horizontal line can be extended to connect the horizontal lines of the models for both major and minor. For example, in addition to C major and A major, the Rimsky-Korsakov models contain F minor (model 4) and E major (see model 4a) on this extended horizontal tonic line. The Hauptmann models for both major and minor, like the other German models except for the Dehn model, contain C minor (see models 1 and 3) and A major (see models 1a and 3a):

| Rimsky-Korsakov | | | | | | | |
|---|---|---|---|---|---|---|---|
| C major (model 4): | f | — | **C** | — | a | | |
| A Minor (model 4a): | | | **C** | — | a | — | E |
| C major & A minor combined: | f | — | **C** | — | a | | E |

| Weber, Marx, Lobe, Hauptmann | | | | | | | |
|---|---|---|---|---|---|---|---|
| C major (models 1 & 3): | c | — | **C** | — | a | | |
| A Minor (models 1a & 3a): | | — | **C** | — | a | — | A |
| C major & A minor combined: | c | — | **C** | — | a | — | A |

Rather than a mutual interaction of functions as in the vertical lines, the relationship of keys along the extended horizontal tonic line of the German models is grounded either in their commonality of function, as in the case of a parallel key, or in their commonality of scale degrees, as in the case of a relative keys. Moreover, the Hauptmann model (see model 3) can be seen as an elaboration of the earlier work of Weber, Marx, and Lobe (see model 1), because it too develops the principles of commonality of function and scale degree. Thus, the two keys of opposite mode found on the horizontal tonic line in models 1, 1a, 3, and 3a can be interpreted as reiterating the tonic. In other words, in all of the German theories except Dehn's, the tonic is doubly extended along its horizontal line by means of the relative and parallel minors in both the major and minor keys.

In contrast, Rimsky-Korsakov's horizontal tonic line includes the key of the minor subdominant (in the key of C major: F minor). The composer's introduction of this key into the system was motivated by a desire to integrate the relative major and minor keys by establishing common links between them. Thus, in Rimsky's system, there is a practical dimension to the way the minor subdominant in major is balanced by the major dominant in minor, and there is a functional significance to the scalar equivalency of G-sharp minor and A-flat minor. By establishing a progression for a major key that would also be characteristic of a minor key, in this case the movement from dominant to tonic (V to I), the source C major key is reinterpreted as the dominant of F minor, creating an interaction of functions. In the Rimsky-Korsakov model, this principle of interaction of functions, previously found in the vertical tonic line of all models, can also be traced in the horizontal tonic line between the source major and its minor subdominant or, conversely, between the source minor and its major dominant (for example, A minor to E major). The important difference in the horizontal expression of this principle is that keys of opposite mode are involved, which sets Rimsky-Korsakov's approach to tonal space apart as significantly distinct from those of the German theorists. By establishing the interaction of functions between keys of opposite mode, displayed here along a tonal grid's horizontal tonic line, Rimsky-Korsakov introduces a new type of connection between opposite modes.

The second structural characteristic distinguishing the horizontal tonic line of the models from the vertical one is the emergence of varying intervals between keys. All the German models contain an alternation of intervals of unisons and minor thirds between keys of opposite mode on the horizontal axis, while the Rimsky-Korsakov models alternate between intervals of a fourth or fifth (depending on direction traveled) and a minor third. Keys of the same mode form an interval of a minor third in the German models (C minor to A minor, C major to A major) and a major third in the Rimsky-Korsakov model (F minor to A minor, C major to E major). In the area of second-degree keys, which (as discussed above) are found only in the Weber and Lobe models and in the Rimsky-Korsakov model, the same pattern arises between keys of the same mode. In the Weber and Lobe tonic line, a minor third interval emerges (E-flat major to C major, C major to A major; C minor to A minor, A minor to F-sharp minor); in the Rimsky-Korsakov model, a major third (A-flat major to C major, C major to E major; F minor to A minor, A minor to C-sharp minor):

Major: 1st-degree area

min3

unison min3

German model: c C a

Rimsky-Korsakov model: f — C — a

4/5 min3

maj3

2nd-degree area

min 3 min3

min3 unison min3 unison

Weber & Lobe (model 1b): $E^{-}$ — c — C — a — A

Rimsky-Korsakov: $A^{-}$ — f — C — a — E

min3 4/5 min3 4/5

maj3 maj 3

Minor:

1st-degree area

| | | | | | |
|---|---|---|---|---|---|
| | | | min3 | | |
| | | min3 | | unison | |
| German models: | C | — | a | — | A |
| Rimsky-Korsakov: | C | — | a | — | E |
| | | min3 | | 4/5 | |
| | | | maj3 | | |

2nd-degree area

| | | | | | | | | | |
|---|---|---|---|---|---|---|---|---|---|
| | | min3 | | | | | min3 | | |
| | | unison | | min3 | | unison | | min3 | |
| Weber & Lobe (model 1c): | c | — | C | — | **a** | — | A | — | f# |
| Rimsky-Korsakov: | f | — | C | — | a | — | E | — | c# |
| | | 4/5 | | min3 | | 4/5 | | min3 | |
| | | maj3 | | | | | maj3 | | |

Another crucial difference between the models relates to the overall form of their tonal areas. While the Rimsky-Korsakov models do not exhibit the vertical symmetry found in the other models, they are symmetrical along their horizontal tonic lines:

Major: Minor:

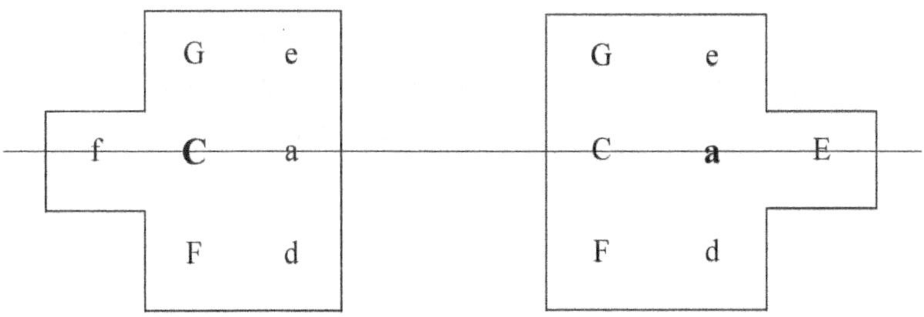


The Weber, Marx, and Lobe models exhibit symmetry around both their horizontal and vertical tonic lines, as shown below. Hauptmann's models, however, exhibit symmetry along neither their vertical nor their horizontal lines, but they can be described as symmetrical only around the tonic center:

Weber, Marx, and Lobe

Major:

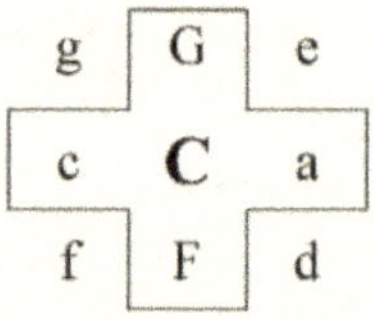


Minor:

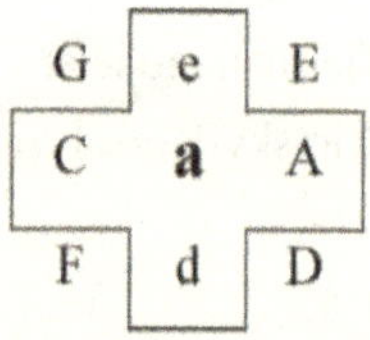


Hauptmann

Major:

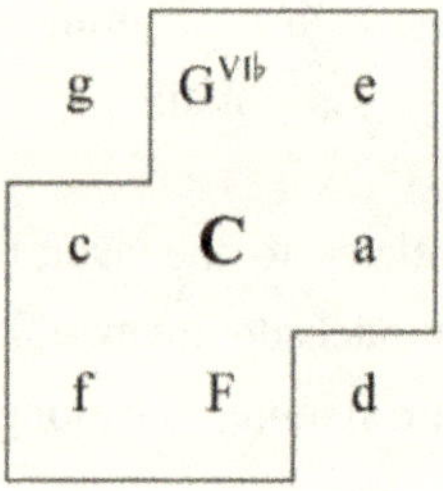


Minor:

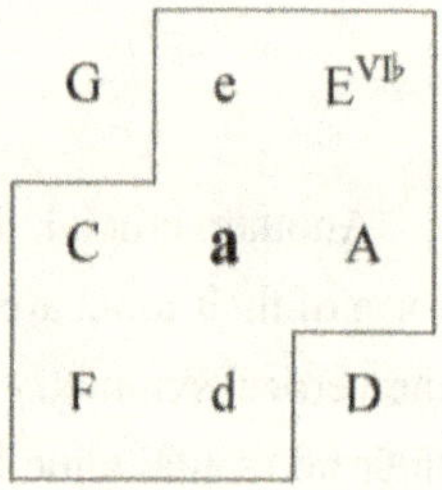


Undeniably, the harmonic system presented in Rimsky-Korsakov's *Practical Manual of Harmony* exhibits an approach to tonal space that is strikingly distinct, although it has some features in common with the major German theories of its time. Indeed, Rimsky's system reflects an independent understanding of tonal space and of the harmonic concepts found in the leading German manuals of the first half of the nineteenth century.

# Part Three

# Rimsky-Korsakov's Harmonic Theory and the Nineteenth-Century Russian Theoretical Tradition

# Chapter 15

# Early Treatises

A variety of theoretical treatises were available in nineteenth-century Russia in before the publication of Tchaikovsky's harmony manual in 1872.[227] Some were written in Russian by Russians or assimilated foreigners, while the remainder consisted of translations of well-received treatises from abroad.[228] The majority of Russian works on music theory in the first half of the nineteenth century consisted of elementary theory and composition manuals. Both types usually incorporated sections on harmony, but manuals devoted exclusively to the subject of harmony were rare.

The Russian music theory literature of the early nineteenth century tended to fall into three main categories. In the first, theoretical works, the most common term found in titles is *Rukovodstvo*, best translated as "manual," "handbook," or "guide." The term implies a basic practical purpose: providing a set of concepts essential to a discipline and establishing rules for their application. The composition books offer introductory descriptions for beginners and often bear titles containing the word *Gramota*, meaning "grammar," or the terms *Nachal'noe osnovanie* ("elementary principles") and *Nachal'noe svedenie* ("elementary information"). The third type comprises titles that use speculative terms such as

*Teoriia* ("theory") and *Nauka* ("science"). Among the Russian treatises of the period, this category is the smallest.[229]

The term *Uchebnik*, best translated as "textbook," which Rimsky-Korsakov used in his title in 1884, only began to appear in the mid-1870s with the publications of Tchaikovsky and Kashkin. Continuing the traditional practical orientation of the *Rukvodstvo*, the *Uchebnik* genre was likewise intended to facilitate technical improvement, but it was addressed primarily to professional rather than amateur readers. Thus, the use of this term in book titles signals a major change: the institutionalization of the field of music, which reflected a new level of status for the discipline. The term *Uchebnik* also corresponds closely to the titles of German treatises of the period. German words such as *Lehre*, as in A. B. Marx's *Allgemeine Musiklehre* of 1848, and *Lehrbuch*, as in Richter's *Lehrbuch der Harmonie* of 1853, may have served as models for the Russian titles published later in the century.

In contrast to the numerous theoretical works written in Russian, the overall number of translations is very small. They fall into two categories: (1) general guides, and (2) practical manuals, which were also prominent in domestic literature. In addition to the German-to-Russian translations of the works by Marx, Richter, Lobe, and Bussler discussed in part 2, there were two other translations of foreign treatises available during the first half of the nineteenth century: Vincenzo Manfredini's *Harmonic and Melodic Rules for the Teaching of All Music*, originally published in Italian in 1797,[230] and François-Joseph Fétis's 1830 French-language book about music for a non-expert readership, *Music Accessible to All, or a Short Description of All the is Needed to Judge and Speak About Art for Those Who Have Not Studied It.*[231]

It is notable that some of the more important and voluminous nineteenth-century German and French theory works containing significant amounts of technical detail or adopting a speculative approach were not translated into Russian. These include Weber's *Versuch einer geordneten Theorie der Tonsetzkunst*, Reicha's *Traité complet de la haute composition musicale*, Fétis's *Traité complet de la theorie et de la pratique de l'harmonie*, Marx's *Die Lehre von der musikalischen Komposition*, Hauptmann's *Die Natur der*

*Harmonik und der Metrik*, Helmholtz's *Lehre von der Tonempfindungen*, and Öttingen's *Harmoniesystem in dualer Entwicklung*. The early-nineteenth-century absence of a wider demand in Russia for advanced theoretical literature offers a plausible explanation for the paucity of translations.

Many theoretical treatises authored in Russian were published throughout Russia before Tchaikovsky's manual. 1801 saw the publication in Moscow of Ivan Komendantov's *Elementary Principles of Harmony, or the Exact Order of the Origin of All Twenty-Two Modes Belonging to Only One Octave*, which contains discussion of chords, intervals, scales, enharmonicism, and cadences.[232] In 1818 in Khar'kov, Gustav Hess de Calvé published *The Theory of Music, or a Discourse About this Art that Includes the History, Purpose, Effects of Music, Thorough Bass, Rules of Composition, a Description of Instruments, Different Sorts of Music, and All that is Related to It, in Detail.* One of the more extensive theoretical works of the period, it contains a large section on the rules of composition, as well as a discussion of instruments, style, form, history, and ethnography. One of its most outstanding features is its presentation of chords in a manner that is at once old-fashioned in its use of figured bass and yet reveals the influence of Kirnberger.[233] Although its progress was slow in the early part of the nineteenth century, Russian theoretical activity had reached a substantial peak by 1820 due to Komendantov's work on elementary harmony and the slightly more substantial and informative treatise by Hess de Calvé.

In the 1830s, traditional private instruction was newly augmented by the introduction of expanded curriculum including musical instruction at the Imperial Court Chapel and the theatrical schools in St. Petersburg and Moscow. These became Russia's first institutional centers of higher musical education, and the surge in pedagogical activity generated a corresponding growth in the production of theoretical works. Accordingly, the tempo of music theory publishing quickened.

In 1830 in St. Petersburg, a Russian translation from the German became available for Johann Leopold Fuchs's *Practical Guide to the Composition of Music, for Independent Study and for the Facilitation of Teachers, with a Supplement of Special Rules for the Composition of Russian Church Music, and Two Music Notebooks, of Which the First Includes Examples and Exercises, and the Second the Answers.*[234] Highly praised by the noted music writer and impresario Alexander Ulybyshev in the press,[235] this systematic and comprehensive survey of harmonic principles includes discussions of intervals, basic chords and inversions, modulation, and cadences. Serving mainly as a compendium of popular Western harmonic ideas, Fuchs's composition manual focuses particularly on Weber's idea of fundamental harmonies. In 1836, Fedor Drobish's *Elementary Information on Practical Music* was published in Russian in St. Petersburg, with a second edition in Moscow in 1854.[236]

New types of manuals began to appear. In St. Petersburg, for example, a short but useful reference book providing reference tables for thorough-bass figuration was published by Ivan Gabretsettel in 1840,[237] and the following year saw the publication of Karl Arnold's Russian-language *Short Guide to the Study of the Rules of Composition.*[238] In Moscow, the first and only volume of Franz Gebel's incomplete multi-volume *Guide to the Composition of Music, or Theoretical-Practical Thorough-Bass Guide* was published in 1842.[239] Also in Moscow, Vikenty Lemokh's *General Guide to the Study of Music* became available in 1846.[240]

Although short manuals of elementary theory and harmony, like those by Drobish, Karl Arnold, Gebel, and Lemokh, remained in demand, there emerged a gradual increase in demand for more specialized treatises. Joseph Hunke's extensive 1852 book, published in Moscow, *A Guide to the Study of Harmony, Adapted for Independent Study*, covered intervals, scales, basic chords and their inversions, modulation, and cadences and was distinctive for its innovative theory of chord connections and progressions.[241] Not long after, in St. Petersburg, Hunke published a three-volume *Guide to the Composition of Music.*[242] These treatises by Fuchs and Hunke are notable for their comparatively extensive volume, comprehensive content, and rigorous technical detail.

1862 was the inaugural year of the St. Petersburg Conservatory, the first professional musical institution in Russia, and the Moscow Conservatory opened in 1866. The example set by these two institutions further stimulated the growth of the musical education system. The results included a rapid elevation of the level of music theory instruction, the emergence of a larger student body with greater professional ambition, and a growing need for new educational materials. During these years, several new manuals on elementary theory were published.

In 1868 in Moscow, Vladimir Odoevsky published a notable volume with the title *Musical Grammar, or the Elements of Music for Amateurs*.[243] Odoevsky's treatise presents the results of his research in acoustics as well as a theory of Russian folk song. These two features distinguish this work from other theoretical manuals of the time. First, the basics of music are explained in an acoustical context.[244] Second, the fundamental differences between Western music and Russian folk music are addressed in great detail. Indeed, this pioneering work was among the first to examine Russian folk music on its own terms, including discussion of its modal qualities (which Odoevsky mistakenly traced to the medieval modes) and rhythmic freedom.

A small number of lesser-known music theory titles were also available in Russia by the time Tchaikovsky's manual was published in 1872.[245] Yuri Arnold's *The Science of Music* of 1875 was a short manual of harmony discussing the basic harmonic elements, including sound, intervals, and chords, explained by means of acoustical phenomena.[246] It shows Hegelian influence,[247] and it is also clearly derivative of Helmholtz's and Öttingen's work. Also in 1875, Nikolai Kashkin published his *Elementary Music Theory Manual*, a short textbook containing discussions of notation, intervals, scales, keys, transposition, and rhythmic notation.[248] In 1878 in Nizhnii Novgorod, Vasily Villoing's *Practical Guide to the Study of Elementary Music Theory* was published.[249] And finally, 1883 saw the publication in St. Petersburg of Andrei Kazbiriuk's *Guide to the Practical Study of Harmony*.[250]

Among the many harmony manuals preceding Rimsky-Korsakov's *Practical Manual of Harmony*, Tchaikovsky's *Guide* stands out for its breadth and its high standard of professionalism. Although it follows the tradition of the Western harmony manuals adopted at the St. Petersburg Conservatory, Tchaikovsky's work does not bear the stamp of any one particular influence and contains an exposition of the composer's own views on harmony.

# Chapter 16

# Liadov and Rimsky-Korsakov

Rimsky-Korsakov acknowledges one important source for his ideas by dedicating the *Practical Manual* to Anatoly Liadov (1855–1914). The son of a notable theater conductor, Liadov graduated from the Conservatory in 1787 having taken two courses with Rimsky: instrumentation in 1873 and practical composition in 1874. Their association, which began during Liadov's conservatory years, continued throughout their lives. In addition to becoming friends, the two composers collaborated on many professional projects together. They were both engaged by Balakirev in the preparation of the new edition of Glinka's compositions,[251] had worked together on the organization of the Russian Symphonic Concerts in 1884, and from 1885 onward were both members of the musical committee on the board of the Beliaeff Leipzig publishing house. They also taught side by side for almost three decades at the Conservatory (1878–1907) and for a decade at the Imperial Court Chapel (1884–1893).

No trace remains of Liadov's theoretical views, except that Rimsky-Korsakov testifies in his autobiography that Liadov's impact upon the *Practical Manual* was important:

> From constant talks with Anatoly [Liadov] regarding this subject [harmony], I came to know his system and methods of instruction and

conceived the idea of writing a new textbook of harmony according to a wholly new system as regards pedagogic methods and sequence of presentation. Essentially, Liadov's system was an outgrowth of his professor Johansen's system, and mine of Liadov's.[252]

Anatolii Liadov (1855–1914). Vasina-Grossman, *V. A. K. Liadov* (Moscow-Leningrad: Muzgiz), 1945.

From this account, it may be concluded that Liadov's methods and system of teaching harmony not only appealed to Rimsky-Korsakov but prompted him to write a new harmony manual "according to a wholly new system." This system, according to Rimsky-Korsakov, consisted in gradually building the student's harmonization technique, starting from the use of tonic, dominant, and subdominant triads and their inversions, and advancing to the use of secondary triads and chords, and then further to modulation, as may be seen in the treatise's table of contents.[253] According to a letter written by Rimsky and dated 17 October 1884, which is when he began to write the section on modulation, Liadov's involvement with the treatise ceased after the initial stage of discussion.[254]

Rimsky-Korsakov further traces this methodological lineage from Liadov to Johansen. Liadov's mentor, Iuly Johansen, was a professor at the St. Petersburg Conservatory who taught theory there from 1867 to 1898 and whose legacy includes a counterpoint treatise but no writings on harmony.[255] That Johansen studied with Hauptmann in Leipzig before moving to Russia suggests that Hauptmann's ideas may have been transmitted to Rimsky-Korsakov via Johansen and Liadov, especially Hauptmann's notions of the minor-major scale and the use of the minor subdominant in a major key.[256] However, no specific evidence supports this connection, since there are no records of Johansen's harmonic ideas or teaching system. Indeed, the prominence of the minor-major scale and its harmonies in Rimsky-Korsakov's pre-conservatory compositions greatly reduces the possibility of an outside theoretical influence on the composer during his years as a professor. Other sources may also have stimulated Rimsky-Korsakov's use of what he terms the "harmonic major" (and Hauptmann calls the "minor-major" scale), such as his training with Balakirev during his youth. The method and the system of presentation adopted in the *Practical Manual of Harmony* can only be partly credited to Liadov and, hence, indirectly to Johansen.

While there is little direct evidence of Liadov's influence on the main ideas presented in the manual, the practical application of at least one of Rimsky-Korsakov's fundamental theoretical concepts, the harmonic major scale, may also be observed in Liadov's music.[257] Moreover, it may also be presumed that Liadov had continued to seek Rimsky-Korsakov's advice throughout the long years of their friendship. In one of Liadov's letters in 1895, he asks for Rimsky-Korsakov's help regarding the choice of keys:

> Suite of Glinka's works … will contain a Mazurka [in] B-flat major, a Nocturne [in] f minor, a Tarantella [in] a minor, and a Polka [in] B-flat major. The two middle numbers are not tonally compatible with B-flat major, – what to do? Transpose? – Where? – If the Nocturne [were] in g minor then what key [should] the Tarantella [be in] (and vice versa). Solve this, Nikolai Andreevich, for God's sake![258]

The tone of Liadov's letter indicates his recognition of Rimsky-Korsakov's authority, at least regarding the issue of tonal plan. Rimsky-Korsakov's letter of reply suggests four alternatives:

> It is harder to answer your [second] question. Two minor keys in the middle … I offer the following four plans:[259]
>
> a) B♭ — e♭ — g — B♭
>
> b) B♭ — g — c — B♭ (best)
>
> c) B♭ — d — g — B♭
>
> d) B♭ — g — d — B♭

Liadov's role, gratefully acknowledged by Rimsky-Korsakov in his dedication, perhaps with some degree of exaggeration, amounted not so much to the development of conceptual issues of the *Practical Manual* as to a gesture of kinship as well as the improvement of the method of presentation, indeed a very important aspect of a practically oriented work.

# Chapter 17

# Tchaikovsky and Rimsky-Korsakov

It must be kept in mind that Tchaikovsky and Rimsky-Korsakov both wrote their manuals specifically for the practical purpose of teaching harmony in an institution of upper-level musical education.[260] Both Tchaikovsky and Rimsky-Korsakov chose to write their own manuals of harmony when confronted with the necessity of teaching; neither aimed to present a theory of harmony, but rather to state the concepts in accessible manner, explain how they work, and acquaint the reader with rules of the discipline as well as their exceptions. They were highly unorthodox authors of treatises for another reason as well: they were not only mature composers but the leading composers of their country. As practitioners who were not especially interested in speculative endeavors, both offered summaries of their compositional approaches in their manuals. Tchaikovsky stated in the foreword to the first edition of his manual:

> From the outset in writing this manual, my intention was least of all the introduction of a new system and new ideas into musical science. Lovers of theoretical pursuits and musical-philosophical intricacies will not find in my book food to satisfy their curiosity. The book does not seek to uncover the reason behind harmonic phenomena, nor does it

P. I. Tchaikovsky (1840–1893). Rimskii-Korsakov, N. A. Polnoe sobranie sochinenii. Literaturnye proizvedeniia i perepiska, vol. 4
(Moskva: Gosudarstvennoe muzykal'noe izdatel'stvo, 1960), 288.

attempt to discover a principle which scientifically unifies the rules that underlie the beauty of harmony, but rather lays out as logically as possible rules that were derived empirically. … Allow me to express doubt that familiarity with current harmonic theories, which are built on sand, can be of any real help to students.[261]

The two treatises should be perceived as valuable documents that express their authors' creative backgrounds and shed new light on details of their craft, including the differences between their approaches to harmony.

Rimsky-Korsakov acknowledges the importance of Tchaikovsky's treatise by mentioning it as the only harmony treatise to which he undoubtedly had access during his intensive study of theoretical literature in the mid-1870s: Tchaikovsky's *Guide to the Practical Study of Harmony* of 1872:

> During the ensuing season [1874–75] I came to be more and more absorbed in studying harmony and counterpoint, both of which I had taken up the season before. Steeped in Cherubini and Bellerman, equipped with a few textbooks of harmony (Tchaikovsky's among them) and every imaginable sort of chorale book, I toiled assiduously, beginning with the most elementary exercises.[262]

Tchaikovsky's *Guide* was recognized as the first definitive Russian theoretical treatise; its authority derived from the prominent composer's reputation and credentials as a Conservatory graduate. It is also known that Rimsky-Korsakov used Tchaikovsky's manual in private harmony instruction.[263] However, that Rimsky-Korsakov was closely familiar with the work and used it in teaching does not necessarily indicate that he inherited his ideas from Tchaikovsky—despite Gerald Abraham's influential claim that "Rimsky-Korsakov taught himself harmony from Tchaikovsky's manual."[264]

The respect and admiration between Rimsky-Korsakov and Tchaikovsky may be described as mutual. It was in 1868, at the beginning of Rimsky-Korsakov's compositional career and before the two men had ever met, that Tchaikovsky, by then an authority figure in the music world, published his first words of support in defense of the young composer, whose recently premiered *Serbian Fantasy* had been heavily criticized by an anonymous writer in a Moscow journal.[265] Tchaikovsky's article ended with the following (which brings to mind Schumann's prophetic words about Chopin and, later, Brahms): "Let us not forget that Mr. Rimsky-Korsakov is still a young man, and that this remarkably gifted man is destined to become one of the best adornments of our art."[266]

From the time Rimsky-Korsakov and Tchaikovsky first met at Balakirev's house, which likely happened on 18 March 1868,[267] until the 1870s, their relationship developed mainly through their host, whom Tchaikovsky trusted and to whom he sent his many new compositions for criticism. It was only after Balakirev temporarily abandoned the musical scene in the early seventies that the relationship between the two composers became more direct and, eventually, quite close.

In 1872, Tchaikovsky dedicated one of his songs, "Pogodi," to Rimsky-Korsakov. Around the same time, he began to visit Rimsky-Korsakov's home when in St. Petersburg, and the composers often played their new compositions for one another. It then that their correspondence began.[268] On several occasions, their works were performed in the same concerts, particularly in the Russian Musical Society series in St. Petersburg. Tchaikovsky considered it an honor to have his music played alongside Rimsky-Korsakov's, as he writes in a letter to his brother Anatoly: "On Saturday I participated in the Russian Symphonic Concert. I am so glad that I had a chance to prove publicly that … I think it very flattering [for myself] to be at a place where the 'main protagonist' is Rimsky-Korsakov."[269]

Their growing friendship was not, however, devoid of a certain amount of mutual criticism, especially on the part of Tchaikovsky. After the Moscow premiere of Rimsky-Korsakov's Third Symphony (in its first version) under the baton of Rubinstein in December of 1874, Tchaikovsky evaluated it in a review as a work in which "technique predominates over the quality of ideas."[270] In 1879, Tchaikovsky expressed his strong dislike of *Paraphrases*, an extended set of variations on a humorous theme written jointly by Rimsky-Korsakov, Cuï, Borodin, and Liadov.[271] Rimsky-Korsakov likewise made critical statements at various times about Tchaikovsky's works, including the incidental music to Ostrovsky's play *Snowmaiden*,[272] the opera *Cherevichki*,[273] another opera titled *Iolanta*,[274] and *The Nutcracker* ballet.[275]

Nevertheless, when Rimsky-Korsakov became intensely absorbed in the study of counterpoint in the late 1870s, he sought Tchaikovsky's opinion and repeatedly sent him sets of fugues for comment. Unlike the members of *The Five*, Tchaikovsky was very enthusiastic about Rimsky-Korsakov's new involvement with this "academic" discipline and was amazed at both the depth of his commitment and his outstanding productiveness (in the summer of 1875 alone, Tchaikovsky received sixty-one fugues from Rimsky). Tchaikovsky shared this astonishment with the influential arts patron Nadezhda von Meck in a letter: "Either he will become a great master, or he will forever get stuck in contrapuntal stuff."[276]

Before he had written his own treatise, Rimsky-Korsakov used Tchaikovsky's *Guide* during the initial lessons when giving private instruction.[277] The *Guide* came out in 1872 and was republished eight times.[278]

As with fugues, Rimsky-Korsakov turned to Tchaikovsky for advice and criticism when working on his harmony treatise, and he sent to him the first part of the 1884 edition once it was published. Tchaikovsky sent Rimsky an extensive commentary with a cover letter dated 6 April 1885.[279] The commentary has not survived, but the Tchaikovsky Archive includes a copy of the 1884 edition containing the marginal notes on which Tchaikovsky presumably based his comments.[280] Rimsky-Korsakov's letter of reply dated 15 April 1885 has also survived.[281] The content of this letter largely matches the issues raised by Tchaikovsky in his page annotations, which suggests that the lost commentary is similar as well. It has not been established whether Tchaikovsky ever read the second part of the treatise, whether in the 1884 version or the condensed 1886 version. No further correspondence between Tchaikovsky and Rimsky-Korsakov regarding the harmony manual has survived, nor is it known whether Tchaikovsky's library contained a copy of the second part.

Tchaikovsky's marginal comments on Rimsky's treatise cover only the Introduction and most of the first chapter, up to unit 2, "Modulation." Most of them are of an editorial nature and concern clarity of presentation and definition. Tchaikovsky voices numerous disagreements regarding matters of counterpoint, such as hidden fifths and octaves, which Rimsky-Korsakov seemed to regard as acceptable in some situations.[282] Very often, Tchaikovsky criticized Rimsky-Korsakov's rules for voice doubling and voice leading and complained about the manual containing too many rules in general.

In terms of concepts, a major difference of opinion becomes apparent with the introduction of the issue of the minor subdominant in major, one of Rimsky-Korsakov's fundamental notions. Tchaikovsky questions the

-8.-

заставляетъ желать примѣнить ее и къ мажорному ладу. Дѣйствительно, если для образованія минорной гармонической гаммы мы прибѣгаемъ къ измѣненію натуральной минорной гаммы посредствомъ случайнаго знака, повышающаго ея VII ступень, то является возможнымъ прибѣгнуть къ подобному же искуственному измѣненію мажорной гаммы. Если мы введемъ въ мажорную гамму случайный знакъ понижающій ея VI ступень, то получится слѣдующій искуственный видъ мажорной гаммы:

VI.

Главныя же трезвучія построенныя на ступеняхъ ея будутъ слѣдующія: I IV V

Такимъ образомъ посредствомъ введенія въ мажорную гамму упомянутаго случайнаго знака мы получаемъ между трезвучіями ея I и IV ступеней тоже искомое отношеніе какое существуетъ въ гармонической минорной гаммѣ между трезвучіями V и I ступеней: Мож. I IV Мин. V I

-9.-

Написавъ искуственную мажорную гамму въ восходящемъ порядкѣ а гармоническую минорную въ нисходящемъ:

Искуствен. маж. I V IV V I

Гармонич. мин. I V IV I

мы увидимъ, что сдѣланное нами измѣненіе VI ступени мажора совершенно аналогично съ общепринятымъ измѣненіемъ VII ступени въ минорѣ, а именно: если терція доминантоваго трезвучія въ минорѣ повышенна случайнымъ знакомъ, то терція субдоминантоваго трезвучія въ мажорѣ понижена.

Вслѣдствіе явнаго благозвучія такого измѣненія субдоминантоваго трезвучія въ мажорѣ, во всемъ нашемъ руководствѣ мы будемъ разсматривать два вида субдоминантоваго трезвучія въ мажорномъ ладѣ: мажорное (натуральное) и минорное (искуственное); итакъ главныя трезвучія мажора будутъ слѣдующія:

I IV IV V

Tchaikovsky's handwritten Notes on Margins of Rimsky-Korsakov's Uchebnik Garmonii. *Courtesy of the Tchaikovsky Museum and Archive, Klin, Russia.*

whole idea of the minor subdominant in major, which is included by Rimsky-Korsakov at the very beginning, in §9 of unit 1, "Harmonization within one key." He also questions Rimsky's grounds for presenting this concept:

> I do not understand this load of rubbish. How is this possible to talk about the pleasant sound of some progression when we do not know anything yet?
>
> One can derive all sorts of things using this kind of reasoning, since "apparently pleasing sonority" means nothing.
>
> Why then is the artificial lowering of the VIIth scale degree in minor not discussed as well?
>
> 
>
> Which is as natural as your lowered sixth.[283]

Rimsky-Korsakov's reply to Tchaikovsky's commentary Tchaikovsky partly explains his reasons for including the minor subdominant in major. Rimsky clarifies its role as a main triad within a key: "The minor subdominant triad is mentioned in the very beginning because it belongs among the main triads, while the major triad on the III scale degree in minor will be mentioned later, when the secondary triads are discussed."[284]

Comparing Tchaikovsky's criticism with the final version of the manual as represented by the 1886 edition, it may be concluded that Rimsky-Korsakov adopted some of the editorial changes suggested by Tchaikovsky but did not agree to any changes in content or methodology, as also illustrated in his letter of reply to Tchaikovsky: "Everything you can convince me of, I shall take into account or change when possible; but I doubt that you will change my mind regarding the essence of things."[285]

Comparing the tables of contents in the two treatises reveals other differences in approach to harmony between Tchaikovsky and Rimsky-Korsakov.[286] The materials are presented in much the same sequence, and both treatises begin with a discussion of consonant combinations followed by dissonant combinations and then proceeding to modulation and melodic figuration, except Rimsky includes a section on enharmonic and sudden modulations at the end:

| Tchaikovsky | Rimsky-Korsakov |
|---|---|
| *Guide* (1872) | *Practical Manual of Harmony* (1886) |
| Introduction | Introduction |
| Intervals | [Chords] |
| Part 1 | |
| Unit 1. Consonant chords, triads. | Unit 1. Preliminary notions |
| | Unit 2. Harmonization by chords within one key: Consonant combinations |
| Unit 2. Dissonant harmonies, 7th and 9th chords | Dissonant combinations of the dominant harmony |
| Unit 3. Modulations | Unit 3. Modulations |
| Part 2. Accidental harmonic forms | |
| Unit 1. (suspensions, anticipations, passing notes, augmented chords, neighboring notes) | Unit 4. Melodic figuration |
| Unit 2. Melodic development of voices | Unit 5. Enharmonicism and sudden modulation |

After defining the intervals in the Introduction, Tchaikovsky begins the first chapter of his treatise with a definition of harmony: "Combinations of musical sounds may be of two kinds: those where the sounds follow each other, and those where they are heard simultaneously. Combinations of the first kind are called melody; combinations of the second kind—harmony."[287] Rimsky-Korsakov does not define harmony in the opening of his treatise, a decision criticized by Tchaikovsky in his remarks written in the margins,[288] but rather postpones it until the end of the introductory section in which he discusses chords: "The study of chord-connections and incidental [sound] combinations and their use in a musical composition is called the study of harmony."[289] Tchaikovsky's definition reinforces the tradition of stressing the vertical or simultaneous aspect of individual harmonies, while Rimsky-Korsakov's definition, identifying harmony above all as a process, emphasizes the connections between chords and their use in composition.

Tchaikovsky's discussion of chords is divided into two sections: consonant chords, which are the triads (unit 1),[290] and dissonant chords, which are the seventh and ninth chords (unit 2).[291] In the 1884 edition, Rimsky-Korsakov's takes a similar approach, discussing consonant chords in unit 1's first chapter and dissonant chords in the second. However, in the 1886 edition, after slightly changing the structure of presentation, he introduces both consonant and dissonant chords in the opening section of unit 1, "Preliminary Notions." Demonstrating a more flexible understanding of consonant and dissonant chords, Rimsky-Korsakov introduces seventh and ninth chords immediately following the short discussion of triads in the Introduction to the treatise and in the first three sections of unit 1,[292] thus making it clear that the seventh chords belong to the preliminary notions as much as the triads, since all have a common tertian structure.[293]

After introducing three types of triads, (major, minor and diminished), Tchaikovsky proceeds to list the triads built on all the scale degrees of the major scale. Unlike Rimsky, he does so without first defining the basic scales used in the treatise, which are two in number: the natural major and the harmonic minor.[294] Rimsky-Korsakov devotes a special section of the "Preliminary Notions" chapter to listing the four main scales that will be used later for building his harmonic system: the natural and harmonic majors and the natural and harmonic minors.

Tchaikovsky sorts the triads built on the scale degrees of the major scale into groups by quality, identifying three major, three minor, and one diminished. Then, he ascribes the functions of tonic, dominant, and subdominant to the three major triads, pointing out that they share an "internal relationship"[295] (i.e., their adjacency on the circle of fifths): "The internal relationship of the three major triads of the major key reflects the relationship … of the three keys adjacent on the circle of fifths."[296] Like the major triads, the minor triads are shown to have a relationship on the circle of fifths (in C major: F major to C major to G major; in A minor: d minor to a minor to e minor) and also to function as the relative keys to the major triads of tonic, dominant, and subdominant: "The relationship between them [the minor triads] is as close as that between the major triads, since they represent the three keys adjacent on the circle of fifths. Their relationship to the major triads reflects the relationship between relative keys."[297] We may conclude from the preceding two statements that the three major and three minor triads also represent the tonic triads of the six keys. Finally, Tchaikovsky divides the major and minor triads of the major scale into three groups: the tonic group (triads on I and vi), the dominant group (triads on V and iii), and the subdominant group (triads on IV and ii).

Rimsky-Korsakov introduces all the major and minor triads (excluding the augmented and the diminished triads) built on the scale degrees of his four basic scales.[298] From the nine different triads of the two major scales and the nine different triads of the two minor scales, three main triads of natural major and three main triads of harmonic minor are then listed: the tonic, the dominant, and the subdominant. The introduction of triads is followed by an introduction of seventh chords on the scale degrees of the four basic scales. The dominant seventh chord is categorized as one of the main chords. In conclusion, Rimsky-Korsakov identifies all remaining triads and seventh chords as secondary.

Both composers open their treatises with a functional approach to the chords of the major and minor scales that they adduce. However, a difference can be discerned between their views of function. Tchaikovsky, dealing at first exclusively with triads, identifies the three main triads (the tonic, the dominant, and the subdominant) and links the remaining three minor triads to these functions. Rimsky-Korsakov, considering from the beginning a wider range of chords that includes triads and seventh chords, identifies four of these chords (the I, IV, V, and V7) as "main chords."[299] In the 1884 version of the treatise, Rimsky associates the secondary triads with the tonic, dominant, and subdominant triads,[300] similar to Tchaikovsky's approach. The 1886 edition, however, abandons this association: as previously, Rimsky-Korsakov gives the three main chords, with the remaining chords treated as equal and secondary, without any sign of inclination towards a certain function.[301]

In addition to the "internal" circle-of-fifths relationship of consonant triads explained in the first chapter, Tchaikovsky also mentions another type of relationship between triads: an "external relationship" based on the common tones shared between two chords.[302] A table of triads that are externally related to the three major and three minor triads appears in his second chapter, "Combination of Triads in Major."[303] His last category of chord relationship, "the chords that have no external relationship, discussed in the context of chord-connection techniques, and comprises those chords that have no tones in common.[304]

Rimsky-Korsakov, in his "Preliminary Notions" section, also lists three types of chord correlation, pointing out the number of common tones in each type: correlation by a fourth or fifth (e.g., the tonic and the dominant), with one common tone; correlation by a major or minor third (e.g., the major tonic and the minor sixth chord or the minor tonic and the major sixth), with two common tones; and correlation by a second (e.g., the major tonic and the minor supertonic), with no common tones.[305] Although similar to Tchaikovsky in content, Rimsky's classification applies an intervallic concept that does not imply any hierarchy in the relationship of the triads. This system may have seemed odd to Tchaikovsky, who commented on the third type, correlation by a second, with sarcasm: "As if it's a punishment? What a strange correlation …"[306]

In this regard, Rimsky-Korsakov's approach is strikingly different from that of Tchaikovsky: he simply indicates the number of common tones in each category (one in the first category, two in the second, and none in the third). Considering that Rimsky-Korsakov's criterion of relationship is based on common tones, it may be concluded that his second category displays the closest relationship, while the first category represents a relatively close relationship and the third category's relationship is remote. Indeed, a fundamental difference between the approaches of the two composers to the relationship of chords lies in their identification of which type is the closest: Tchaikovsky's most closely related chords are spaced by the interval of a fifth, while Rimsky-Korsakov's are only a third apart.

The consequences of this difference are numerous. Tchaikovsky emphasizes the important role of modulatory chords at the beginning of his discussion of modulation in unit 3, where he defines modulation as a key change performed with the help of a pivotal chord: "This process of transferring harmony from one key area to another [key area] by means of a chord that clearly signals [this] transfer is called modulation."[307] The short introduction is followed by five sections describing various modulatory chords (the dominant seventh, the VII triad in first inversion, the dominant seventh with added sixth, the diminished seventh, etc.), techniques of modulation, and special cases, including the use of a pedal point. Throughout the unit, Tchaikovsky offers no discussion of the principle of key relationship that can be used as a guide for designing modulations. Instead, a sample list of modulations is given for moving from C major to the other eleven major keys in chromatically ascending order.[308]

The second section of Tchaikovsky's unit on modulation, named "Gradual Modulation" in the manuscript but changed to "Passing Modulation" for the printed edition, clarifies his free approach to the choice of keys in modulations, which he believes should be dictated by the composer's personal preference rather than a set of norms:

> In contrast to direct modulation, modulations of other kinds exist, whereby the given key is reached not directly but by first touching one or several secondary keys. One cannot determine precisely in what particular direction such a deviation should be performed; it can only be said that those keys are chosen which are, if not close to a given key, then at least more or less close to it; and if these keys deviate from the straight path to the opposite direction, then they do so only to get close once again to the goal of modulation. In the same way, one may not determine to what extent the passing keys should be touched; it depends on personal taste and whim, based on the impulse of musical feeling.[309]

At best, a guideline can be extracted from the preceding statement that one should perform modulations by passing through close or relatively close keys. Tchaikovsky, unlike Rimsky-Korsakov, does not specify what particular keys he considers close or what particular keys he considers remote. Only briefly is it mentioned that, for modulating through a series of keys to reach a certain destination key, composers usually use what Tchaikovsky calls "a direct path," which may be deviated from. By "direct path," Tchaikovsky presumably means one that utilizes neighboring keys on the circle of fifths and their relative keys, since these are the only two possible key relationships of which we learn in the opening chapter.[310]

Tchaikovsky also implies that there are three categories of key relationship: close, somewhat close, and distant. However, he does not go into greater detail, due to his empirical, rather than theoretical, approach to the subject. Moreover, throughout the discussion of modulatory chords, modulations to close and (presumably) distant keys are cited side by side (e.g., C major to A minor, C major to A-flat major, C major to D minor, C major to D major, A minor to G-sharp minor, A minor to E minor, C major to B major, etc.),[311] showing the composer's lack of concern for large-scale tonal movement or for mapping a tonal system.

Here again, Rimsky-Korsakov's approach is strikingly different. He not only begins his discussion of modulation within the context of the relationship of keys, but also offers a clear presentation of the three degrees of relationship of keys and lists the keys that belong to each of these degrees. In addition, he offers an extensive discussion about the details of modulation between keys in different degrees of proximity as well as guidelines for creating modulatory plans.

Based on the *Guide*, then, Tchaikovsky's conception of tonal movement and notion of three degrees of proximity for keys bear strong resemblance to Rimsky-Korsakov's. Since there is no specific information in Tchaikovsky's treatise regarding keys which he calls "more or less close" and "distant," it can only be established that the five keys that he considers "close" coincide with five of Rimsky-Korsakov's six first-degree keys, specifically the major key's dominant, subdominant, relative minor, median minor, and supertonic minor. Despite this correspondence between their approaches, a definitive conclusion regarding these similarities cannot be drawn. Moreover, as demonstrated by their written correspondence and Tchaikovsky's annotations, the issue of the minor subdominant's close relation to the major tonic was a point of sore disagreement.

A difference between the two authors' harmonic approaches is also visible in the types of exercises chosen for the treatises. In his manual, Rimsky-Korsakov only provides exercises in the sections on the harmonization of melody, and in them he gives melodies to harmonize from the uppermost voice down rather than bass figures upon which to build the harmony from the lowest voice up. This was a topic of special importance to him, as he states in the preface. The more traditional Tchaikovsky offers figured bass exercises throughout a large part of his manual, and exercises in the harmonization of melody appear only in the second half of his book.[312]

It is a well-known fact that Tchaikovsky despised having to give harmony instruction, seeing it as a dull duty rather than a challenge. Tchaikovsky's marginal comments on Rimsky-Korsakov's text strongly convey the his irritation and impatience. Tchaikovsky explains these feelings in the opening of his cover letter to Rimsky:

> The thing is that … my criticism of your textbook, contrary to my intention, bristles with irritation, rage, pickiness, almost unfriendliness. … Why did this happen (that is, this spitefulness)?—I myself do not understand. It seems to me that my hatred for harmony instruction gives itself away here; hatred generated, on the one hand, by the realization of the incompetence of existing theories, and my inability to invent a new, worthwhile one, and, on the other hand, by the nature of my musical temperament, which has lacked the conditions necessary for conscientious teaching. I taught harmony for ten years and for ten years I hated my lectures, my students, my manual, and myself as a teacher. Reading your manual has revived in me my dormant hatred, and it [the hatred] … directed all its spitefulness and poisonousness at your manual.[313]

This irritable tone colors most of Tchaikovsky's remarks. It may be explained, as Tchaikovsky states, by his "hatred for harmony instruction." But we may also consider another possible reason for such a reaction—Rimsky-Korsakov's different treatment of harmony, which apparently found very little enthusiasm in Tchaikovsky.

As is evident in his own manual, Tchaikovsky's main concern was to introduce the available harmonic means and some very basic rules and then leave the choices to the student. This is demonstrated by the way that he introduces all the chords of the major key right at the very beginning and offers only casual guidance as to the modulatory processes. Rimsky-Korsakov's approach instead focuses on choices available for modulatory processes and reflects a distinctive and integrated system introduced gradually and methodically, beginning with basic scales and chords and leading to a set of complex and well-defined rules for large-scale harmonic processes.

Yet, Tchaikovsky was disappointed at the public's perception of him as "old-fashioned," as he shared in an interview conducted in 1892:

> According to a perception common to the Russian musical public, I am regarded as belonging to a camp inimical to Rimsky-Korsakov, whom I love and value above all other living Russian composers. He is the best adornment of The New Russian School; I am treated as [a representative] of an old, retrogressive school. But why? Rimsky-Korsakov submitted, to a greater or smaller degree, to the influence of modern times—I did as well. He composed program symphonies—I did as well. This did not prevent him from composing symphonies in a traditional form, writing fugues with pleasure, and, generally, working in a polyphonic style—I did that too. He was influenced by Wagnerism, or in any case, by innovative operatic texture—I also, perhaps to a lesser degree, was influenced by these. It did not prevent him from still using old forms of cavatinas, arias, and ensembles in his operas—something that was even truer of me. I was for many years a professor at the Conservatory—also known as an enemy of The New Russian School—but Rimsky-Korsakov was too! In one word, despite all the differences of our musical personalities, we, as it seems, travel the same road; and I ... am proud to have such a fellow traveler.[314]

Perceived outside of Russia as a distinctly Russian composer, Tchaikovsky was regarded at home as moderately conservative, with a Western European orientation. Tchaikovsky's position in Russian musical culture took shape in the context of the growing New Russian School, whose leader Balakirev said of Tchaikovsky that he "took Russian themes and converted them to the Lutheran religion." Balakirev's words imply that Tchaikovsky's adaptation of Russian folklore in his works was superficial and had little effect on his basically "Western" or common-practice mode of expression. Indeed, as one of the first graduates of the St. Petersburg Conservatory, Tchaikovsky was a product of the Rubinstein generation and school. By studying composition with Anton Rubinstein and theory with Nikolai Zaremba, Tchaikovsky received a transplanted German training. In the eyes of the domineering and very influential critic Vladimir Stasov, this training had the disadvantage of ironing out the originality and spontaneity from raw young talent and reshaping it according to foreign or otherwise imposed standards. Indeed, all aspects of teaching at the conservatory during its first decade, from the study of form to harmony instruction, were based on the common-practice models, specifically the German tradition.

The position Rimsky-Korsakov reflects in his treatise—while displaying continuity with the Western academic tradition represented by the theorists of German lineage and by his mentor Tchaikovsky, who was trained in that tradition—is at the same time guided by his "kuchkist" aesthetics. It demonstrates his innovative approach to harmony in both the common practice and the contemporary Russian contexts.

# Chapter 18

# Balakirev and Rimsky-Korsakov

Potential sources shaping the distinctive ideas in Rimsky-Korsakov's harmony treatise can be traced in the most immediate roots of his aesthetics and musical language. As discussed in chapter 1, the most definitive influence on Rimsky-Korsakov during his formative years, as well as on the other members of the "kuchka" or The Five, was exerted by Mily Balakirev.[315] Balakirev never wrote a theoretical treatise, but his impact on Rimsky-Korsakov's musical persona was direct and profound and therefore requires close scrutiny.

Calling Balakirev "a personality of the greatest caliber in his circle [The Five]," Tchaikovsky described not only Balakirev's outstanding talent, but also the magnitude of his influence.[316] This influence, immediately evident in the music of The Five, also had a much greater scope. Indeed, Balakirev played a key role in the development of nineteenth-century Russian musical culture overall. He was directly involved in determining a new path of musical education during the crucial period when the educational system began to form in the country. It was Balakirev who opened the St. Petersburg's Free Music School, a milestone in the musical life of the capital. The Free Music School offered an educational alternative to Rubinstein's Russian Musical

Milii Balakirev (1837–1910). Balakirev, Milii Alekseevich. *Sbornik russkikh narodnykh pesen* (Moskva: Muzgiz), 1957.

Society courses, which were subsequently transformed into the St. Petersburg Conservatory. At the heart of Balakirev's philosophy—a philosophy put into practice at his school—lay the preservation and advancement of the national musical tradition and the expansion of education throughout society. The same values moved Balakirev to form a close musical circle in which, under his inspired and fierce leadership, the most promising young composers could participate in exploring and defining unorthodox musical ideas rooted in the national tradition. Russian music did not escape the development of a national style, an important feature of the Romanticism that swept across Europe throughout the nineteenth century.

Eager to develop a national style and supported by the rhetorical and social influence of the music critic Stasov, Balakirev's position could be described as modernist in the sense of denouncing accepted norms and tradition. In his search for new expression, a search also perfectly in line with the pervasive Romantic cult of the original, Balakirev resisted the limitations imposed by the establishment culture of common-practice repertoire represented by German, French, and Italian music. As did his many contemporaries, Balakirev found the fresh sources and new colors he craved by turning to domestic folklore, both Russian and "Oriental."[317] A large part of his artistic position, as well as some of his other innovative ideas, he inherited from his immediate predecessor and teacher, Mikhail Glinka.

The acquaintance with Glinka, which began in late 1855, determined Balakirev's musical future.[318] A short apprenticeship was followed by Balakirev's life-long study and promotion of Glinka's music, including editing his compositions.[319] Glinka experienced a feeling of kinship with Balakirev's musical taste and views, as conveyed in the memoires of his sister, Ludmila Shestakova: "Balakirev was the first person I [Glinka] found whose views were so similar to mine in everything having to do with music."[320] Balakirev mentored *The Five* in a similar fashion to the way he was mentored by Glinka, handing down values and teaching the craft through close supervision and intense interaction.

Balakirev's tendency toward domination, which was frequently noted by friends and colleagues, was not just a characteristic of his teaching style but remained a part of his personality throughout his life. This sense of power, which caused many problems with people around him, may have stemmed from Balakirev's realization of his prodigious musical gift, as displayed in his phenomenal musical memory and superb talent for improvisation and for reinterpreting (even to the point of spontaneously rewriting) the compositions of others.[321] As reflected in the remarks and memoirs of many friends and colleagues, domination was an integral part of his style of mentorship in his circle. The same tendency extended even further in some unusual ways. Becoming inspired by the musical ideas of others and possessing an explosive creative drive, Balakirev knew no limitations and would often vigorously participate in the creation, or sometimes re-creation, of compositions that touched him. These compositions included published works as well as new works-in-progress by his students. Examples include Balakirev's autograph of several versions of different sections from Borodin's First Symphony, his own versions of parts from Liszt's score *Ce qu'on entend sur la montagne*, and reorchestrations of his favorite works, such as Chopin's First Concerto. Balakirev was even known to reach such extremes in the "interpretation" of his favorite pieces as adding music of his own during some performances![322] Such facts reveal an important side of Balakirev's personality naturally extending to his teaching, which could probably be described as "domineering collaboration."

Balakirev's aesthetic position as an heir to Glinka's heritage and as an immediate predecessor to Rimsky-Korsakov is clearly defined in his especial preoccupation with folklore, both from the region now known as "Russia" as well as from the eastern reaches of the Russian empire. During the 1860s, Balakirev actively pursued his passionate interest in domestic folklore. Due to Russia's enormous territory, domestic folklore included both Russian folk songs and musical traditions from several ethnic groups in the south region including the Caucasus and Crimea. Balakirev's groundbreaking collection of forty Russian folk songs was the result of his trip down the Volga River in 1860, during which he made numerous stops to record songs.[323] One of the collection's most distinctive features was Balakirev's innovative harmonic treatment of folk melodies in ways that complemented them stylistically.

Rimsky-Korsakov, following Balakirev's example, also produced two collections, *100 Russian Folk Songs* in 1876 and *40 Folk Songs* in 1882. In addition, his notebooks contain sketches experimenting with various folk songs that were eventually incorporated into his compositions.[324] Many stylistic features of Rimsky-Korsakov's music manifest a Russian folk song influence, including some of his melodies, his use of modal harmony, and his use of certain timbres and formal structures.

The most striking aspect of Balakirev's harmonizations was that, rather than bending the modal melodies to fit common-practice formulae, they were closely knitted with the harmonic progressions. Cesar Cuï, a member of The Five, identifies some of the qualities that typify Russian folk song in his 1866 review of Balakirev's collection. He describes with admiration how Balakirev's arrangements avoid distorting a Russian folk song's distinctive features, particularly its metrical spontaneity and irregularity, but also the particular modal quality of the folk melodies (which, for lack of better terminology, he identifies as Greek):

> The first specialty of the Russian folk song consists of its complete freedom and even capriciousness of rhythm. …
>
> The second remarkable distinction of Russian folk songs is that many of them are based on the so-called Greek scales. … These scales, new to the contemporary European ear, … serve as a proof of the antiquity of so many of our songs …
>
> The third distinction is that the Russian people are very fond of certain modulations which they like to use in their songs. … very often, even in the shortest of songs, the minor is alternated with its corresponding major (for example, B minor and D major). Also, the song that begins in major has a minor ending and vice versa. These quick shifts, which are not especially prepared, sometimes give the song its warm, soulful character.[325]

One of the most prominent qualities exhibited in Russian folk songs and reflected in Balakirev's sensitive harmonizations is the reduced role of the tonic in the tonal hierarchy.[326] In a Russian folk song, the submediant, mediant, and supertonic scale degrees in a major key tend to be as important as a tonic chord in common-practice music, and Balakirev reflects this in his harmonic choices, allowing the tonal center of gravity to shift from one key to another several times during the course of a composition. This quality is known as "peremennost," or mutability.[327] The harmonic mutability so evident in Balakirev's collection similarly permeates the music of Glinka, Balakirev,[328] and Rimsky-Korsakov.[329]

Among the many different possibilities of key combinations, the mutability of the relative keys stands out as an especially typical feature of Russian folk song,[330] and Balakirev reflects it faithfully in his harmonizations of them:

EXAMPLE 17. Balakirev, Song 34, *Poseiali devki len*

The song contains two sections.[331] The first section begins in the key of B minor, as suggested by the melody moving in thirds and delineating a B minor triad on the downbeats in measures 4, 5, and 6 (the first three measures of the second staff system). Balakirev's harmonization of the melody follows the suggestion of B minor as well. The melody then modulates to its relative key of D major with the pitch of D landing on the downbeats in measures 7, 9, and 10, which remains the key to the end of song. Here, Balakirev's harmonization again follows the melody. Neither B minor nor D major can be specified as the more important tonic center, since both keys are presented with equal clarity and occupy about the same number of measures.

In common-practice repertoire, the usual inclination is to modulate from a major key to its relative minor key rather than vice versa. However, in Balakirev's collection, mutability of relative keys occurs in both directions: from a minor to its relative major key (B minor to D major, as in the example above), and from a major key to its relative minor (D major to B minor, as in the example below):[332]

EXAMPLE 18. Balakirev, Song 19, *Podui, podui, nepogodushka*

In this song, the second section (measures 5 and 6) is half as long as the first. In both sections, the melody begins in D major, as evidenced by the use of pitches D and A, but while in the first section the melody ends on A, the dominant of D major, in the second the melody ends on B, its relative minor. Balakirev's harmonization supports these diverse endings: beginning each section in a key of D major and ending the first section on its dominant A chord while ending the second section in B minor, preceded by its natural dominant triad. He also shares a glimpse of B minor within the first section in measures 2 and 3. Although both the first and second parts begin clearly in D major, the piece ends in B minor, creating the overall impression that the two keys, D major and B minor, are equally important.

The mutability of relative keys occurs in both directions throughout Balakirev's collection: from a major key to its relative minor, as in songs 7, "*Nadoeli nochi*" (G major to E minor), 12, "*Polosa l' moia*" (A-flat major to F minor), and 25, "*Uzh ty, pole*" (A-flat major to F minor), and from a minor key to its relative major, as in songs 4, "*Za dvorom*" (F-sharp minor to A major), and 20, "*Katen'ka veselaia*" (B minor to D major).[333]

In addition to the mutability of relative keys, Balakirev also uses several other tendencies in Russian folk song that contribute to the effect produced by the reduced role of a single tonal center. For example, in some songs other secondary keys have an important harmonic purpose of substituting for the dominant or tonic at structurally significant points. such as modulations to the median key in major, as in songs 9, "*Solntse zakatilos*" (D-flat to F minor in measures 3 and 4), and 31,"*Vyletala bedna ptichka*" (A-flat major to C major in measure 3),[334] and to the submediant key in minor, as in song 14, "*Ekhal pan*" (F-sharp minor to D major in measures 8 through 10).[335]

The song in the next example contains two parts, both ending in C minor (measure 3 and measure 6).[336] It may be argued that the melody begins in the key of A-flat major, and Balakirev harmonizes it as such in the song's first three chords, with a conventional progression from the minor subdominant to the dominant fifth in first inversion and then to the tonic. However, the clearly established A-flat major is undermined in the first part of the song by the cadence's resolution into its mediant key of C minor, the key in which the piece mainly continues and also ends. Thus, beginning in the second part, the tonal center of the song shifts from A-flat major to C minor.

EXAMPLE **19.** Balakirev, Song 31, *Vyletala bedna ptichka*

Another important feature of Russian folk songs that diminishes the effect of one clear tonic center is the frequent use of plagal cadences, which often leads to interchangeability between the tonic major and supertonic minor keys.[337] Plagal cadences and turns can be found throughout the collection:

in songs 1, "*Ne bylo vetru*" (measure 8), 4, "*Za dvorom, dvorom*" (measure 11), 7, "*Nadoeli nochi*" (measures 3–5), 16, "*Na Ivanuchke chapan*" (measures 3–4 and 10), 29, "*Kalinushka s malinushkoi*" (measures 6 and 14), 35, "*U vorot*" (measures 8 and 16), and 36, "*Ei ukhnem*"(measures 8 and 16).[338]

EXAMPLE **20.** Balakirev, Song 7, *Nadoeli nochi*

Each part of the folk song, of which only the first page is shown, begins in G major and ends in E minor in the melody as well as in Balakirev's harmonization (measures 1 and 15).[339] The G major key is supported by the authentic cadences in measures 7–8, and 21–22. However, because of the plagal cadence at the midpoint of each section, progressing in the key of G major from the C major dominant to the A minor subdominant but then landing on the relative E minor rather than the G major tonic in measures 4–5 and 18–19, the key of G major is weakened. The use of plagal cadences helps to build a smoother transition between G major and E minor and create a oscillating effect between the two keys.

The song presents an unusual case of mutability in the interaction between a tonic D minor and the key of its natural seventh degree, C major, the latter of which figures prominently in the cadences in measures 2–3 and measures 6–7.[340] The two keys appear side by side throughout the song without a sense of one center prevailing over the other.

**EXAMPLE 21.** Balakirev, Song 17, *Sobiraites'-ka, bratsy-rebiatushki*

When harmonizing Russian folk songs in the natural minor key, Balakirev usually highlights the natural minor's sonic quality by retaining the natural seventh scale degree rather than raising the leading tone, resulting in chords such as the minor dominant triad and minor dominant seventh. In a great number of instances throughout Balakirev's collection, harmonization using the natural minor thus facilitates the use of authentic cadences without a raised leading tone, as well as other interactions between the minor tonic and its natural dominant, helping to decentralize the sense of a tonic.[341]

EXAMPLE **22.** Balakirev, Song 33, *Chto na svete prezhestokom*

Since song 33 begins and ends in D minor, it may be considered to be in that key.[342] From the second measure, however, the melody and Balakirev's harmonization modulate to its natural seventh, C major. Three out of the four measures of its first part (measures 2–4) may be described as harmonized in the key of C major. The melody of the second part and its harmonization (measures 5–8) begin on the natural dominant, A minor, but, as in the first part, immediately modulate to C major, fluctuating between these two keys until the final cadence, which ends on a D minor chord. As a result, the presence of C major in this song outweighs that of D minor, and the effect of D minor as a tonic is significantly weakened.

Of similar importance to Balakirev's musical language and, consequently, to Rimsky-Korsakov's idiom was the music of what was then considered the "Russian Orient," the areas to the south and east of European Russia. These regions were home to a large variety of ethnic traditions, such as Caucasian ethnicities, Georgian, Kabardino-Balkar, Lezgian, Abkhaz, Chechen, Armenian, Circassian, and the Crimean Tatars. Balakirev's familiarity with these traditions most likely began during his early years in Nizhny Novgorod, with its multinational population and its famous annual summer trade fairs, which were among the largest in Europe and attracted people of various nationalities.[343] His famous mentor Ulybyshev has also "described his experience listening to Turkish and Persian songs from the 'natives.'"[344] Later, after moving in 1853 to Kazan, Balakirev continued to gain exposure to the cultures of Tatars, Persians, Buriats, and Turks as well as other ethnic groups.[345] Balakirev further fed his fascination with the traditions and music of the Russian Orient through travel, in 1862 when he first took cures there and again when he visited the region in 1863 and 1868.

Balakirev's passion for Caucasian music and its effect on the members of The Five is vividly recalled by Rimsky-Korsakov:

> You won't believe what an enormous and important role he played in the education of all of us—this energetic young Balakirev, who just returned from the Caucasus and played the little Eastern songs he had heard there! If they still appeal to you now, you can just imagine what they meant in those days to us, who had never heard anything like that. Those sounds were a revelation to us; we were literally reborn.[346]

Rimsky-Korsakov's other telling reminiscence describes Balakirev's brilliant collection of Caucasian melodies and his imaginative interpretations of them: "At that time [during the early 1860s] Balakirev possessed a great supply of melodies and dances, which he remembered from his trips to the Caucasus. He often played them to me and others with his superb harmonization and arrangement."[347] Balakirev never issued a collection of Caucasian folk songs, but much of his music is colored with features specific to Caucasian folk music or Russian-Oriental folklore more generally. For instance, two of his major compositions, the piano fantasy *Islamei* and the symphonic poem *Tamara*, are based on Caucasian folk themes, some of which were transcribed by ear during his trips to the Caucasus.[348] In addition to melodies, Balakirev brought into his music a variety of other compositional elements idiomatic to music of the Russian Orient, from structure and texture to tone color and, of especial interest in relation to his influence on Rimsky, its distinctly chromatic harmonic idiom.[349]

The following elements are consistently used to recreate the atmosphere of the Russian Orient in the music of nineteenth-century Russian composers, Balakirev and Rimsky-Korsakov in particular: (1) in melody, the characteristic

EXAMPLE 23

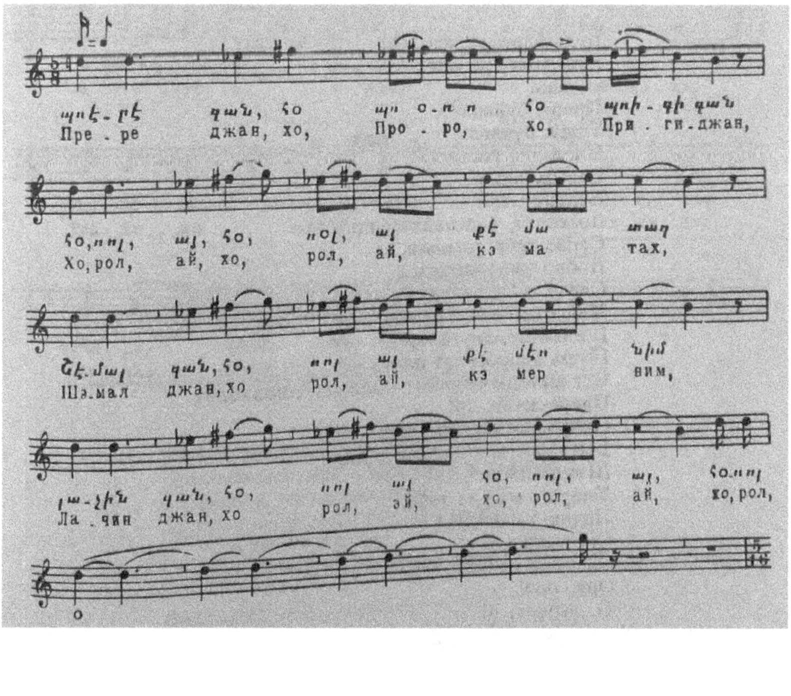

interval of the augmented second, and (2) in harmony, a blend of major keys with the keys of their minor subdominants. The tonal makeup of the repertoire to which Balakirev was exposed is well represented by the following two transcriptions of melodies from the Caucasus region, which were notated by the ethnographer Viktor Beliaev in the mid-twentieth century:

EXAMPLE **24**

The melody begins on the pitch D, ends on G, and contains the following pitches: G, B, C, D, E-flat, F-sharp, and G.[350] All the phrases end on B until the last one, which ends on G. We can read this melody as being in G major with a lowered sixth scale degree, E-flat.

Here, the melody begins on the pitch A, ends on F-sharp and contains the following pitches: D, E, F-sharp, G, A, B-flat, and C-sharp, which are consistent with the D major scale with a lowered sixth scale degree.[351] As demonstrated by the second image taken from the middle of the transcription, the phrase endings often fall on B-flat (see measures 8, 12, and 16), which accentuates the key of G minor, but in many other instances they occur on D (see measures 5 and 9), and F-sharp (see measures 4 and 20). However, the most prominent note of the song overall is D, which is also emphasized as the tonic by the opening of many phrases with the pitches A to D.

In a tonal context, the melodies may be regarded as being in a major key. The augmented second, a pervasive interval in both examples, appears as the lowered sixth and diatonic seventh major scale degrees, corresponding to one of the prevalent modes in folk music of the Caucasian region. Also known as the dual mode, or the augmented second mode, it is a hybrid mode combining both major and minor inclinations, as shown below:[352]

EXAMPLE **25a**

EXAMPLE **25b**

УЧА ДАҒЛАР БАШЫНДА
НА ВЕРШИНЕ ВЫСОКИХ ГОР
Зап. С. Рустамова
11
Умеренно
У_ча дағ_лар ба_шын_да бир сү_ри
го_юн, Бир сү_ри го_юн, ба_лам,
бир сү_ри го_юн. Сә_нә мән
бах_маг и_лә бәс не_чә до_юм.
Бәс не_чә до_юм, ба_лам, бәс не_чә
до_юм. Кү_лүм наз эй_лә,
Эр_ки наз эй_лә. Кәл кир гой-
-ну ма, балам, һа_лым саз эй_лә.
Дур кәл я ны ма, ба_лам,
Ма_нә наз эй_лә.

EXAMPLE 25c

The harmonic implications of the dual mode are demonstrated in the example below, which is a Caucasian melody harmonized by Makar Ekmalian, an Armenian composer who studied with Rimsky-Korsakov:[353]

Here, the melody, harmonized in E-flat major, contains the interval of the augmented second (see, for example, measures 3–4) and therefore may be described as belonging to a dual mode. The harmonies chosen to support this melody exhibit the same inclination as the melody by supporting it in E-flat major at the opening and cadences but also allowing for the strong presence of A-flat minor, which creates an impression of fluctuation between the two keys. The characteristic interval of the

EXAMPLE **26**

augmented second in the melody is complemented in the harmony by a blend of the major key with the key of its minor subdominant. Ekmalian's collection contains many more examples of harmonizations reflecting the implications of the dual mode.[354]

Rimsky-Korsakov's initiation into composition by Balakirev influenced his vocabulary in fundamental ways. Consequently, Rimsky-Korsakov's concept of harmony in his treatise, a reflection of his views on the harmonic aspects of composition, revolved around a number of features peculiar to folk musics of Russia and the Russian Orient as introduced to Rimsky by Balakirev.[355]

One of the most distinctive features of Rimsky-Korsakov's conception of tonal space is that, in addition to such traditional keys as those of the dominant, the relative major or minor, and the subdominant, he also included among the closest or first-degree keys the supertonic and mediant keys in the major key, and the submediant and natural seventh keys in the minor.[356] While in the German treatises discussed in the previous chapter such keys would usually be reached by way of the dominant or subdominant, or by following the circle of fifths,[357] in Rimsky-Korsakov's tonal map they may be approached directly, without mediation by either the dominant or the subdominant.[358] Thus, what for the German theorists were usually secondary keys are in Rimsky-Korsakov's system equally significant to the dominant and subdominant.

In addition to the supertonic and mediant of the major key and the submediant and subtonic of the minor key, Rimsky-Korsakov's harmonic approach identified the relative major and minor keys as closely related to one another, resembling Russian folk idiom's use of the dual mode.[359] The table of modulations given in the 1884 version of the treatise, reproduced in example 11 above, lists the best plans for modulating to all keys from C major (sections A and B) or its relative A minor (sections C and D). If all sections of the table are compared, a symmetry becomes evident. For example, in comparing the first plan of section A, which is a modulation from tonic C major to the D major key located a major second higher and alternates between major and minor (C major to E minor to D major), to the first plan of section D, a modulation from tonic A minor to the B minor key located a major second higher that alternates between minor and major (A minor to G major to B minor), one can see that the intervals between the keys of the latter, which moves first by major second and then by major third, match the intervals of the former, which moves by major third and then major second. A mirror symmetry is displayed between the relative keys on the level of modulatory plans. Comparing similar plans from sections B and C, the inverse intervals appear, in reverse order:

| Plan B1) | C | — | G | — | b |
|---|---|---|---|---|---|
| | | 4/5 | | m6/M3 | |

| Plan C2a) | a | — | F | — | B♭ |
|---|---|---|---|---|---|
| | | M3/m6 | | 5/4 | |

This mirror pattern of the relative keys is maintained throughout the table. Although Rimsky's inclusion of relative keys in the first-degree area in both major and minor is not unusual and may be found in all German models, his approach is distinctive in illuminating their reverse symmetry or mirroring.

Rimsky-Korsakov's conception of tonal space also reproduces other elements characterizing the Russian folk idiom such as plagal cadences.[360] In the *Practical Manual of Harmony*, Rimsky specifically recommends avoiding successive dominant-tonic key relationships in modulatory plans, thereby enhancing the need for the modulatory equivalent of a plagal cadence.[361] Most of the plans found in the table shown in example 11 contain progressions of keys in a major context that exhibit a strong plagal tendency by moving to the major tonic (I) from either the major subdominant (IV) or the minor supertonic (ii).[362] Rimsky-Korsakov shows the same tendency in the minor by preferring modulations to the tonic from the minor subdominant (iv) or the major submediant (VI).[363]

Another feature of Russian folk idiom, the use of the minor key's minor dominant (without the leading tone), is also prominent in Rimsky-Korsakov's harmonic theory.[364] His inclusion of the natural minor scale as one of the four basic scales of the system is in itself quite unusual in comparison to the majority of nineteenth-century German treatises and to that of Tchaikovsky, which use only the harmonic form of the minor scale. Moreover, Rimsky-Korsakov classifies the major subtonic (VII) as a first-degree key.[365] Among the German tonal space models, only Dehn's includes the subtonic, and then only on the basis of its adjacency to the minor dominant, not as a closely related key.

Both tendencies, plagal inclinations and the use of minor dominant in a minor key, reduce the importance of the dominant function in the relationship of tonic and dominant, the cornerstone of common-practice tonality. The influence of folk music of the Russian Orient, via Balakirev's mentorship, on Rimsky-Korsakov's approach to tonal relations can also be discerned in his use of the distinctive color of the dual mode carried over from the Caucasian idiom. In his harmony treatise, Rimsky-Korsakov introduces the harmonic major scale, an exact equivalent of the Caucasian dual mode, as one of the four basic scales of his system. Furthermore, as mentioned above, he outlines the progression of the minor subdominant key to the tonic major key made possible by including the harmonic major in the system.[366]

Yet another aspect of Balakirev's pervasive influence can be traced in the preface to Rimsky-Korsakov's treatise, where Rimsky discusses the harmonization of melody as a main objective in the study of harmony. This angle, faithfully maintained throughout the treatise by the elimination of thorough-bass exercises, shows Rimsky-Korsakov's perception of harmony as a melody-focused process. The musics of both Russian folkways and those of the Russian Orient were traditionally monodic, and the challenge of incorporating them into professional music lay partly in providing harmonizations that would not distort their unique colors.

The distinctive tradition of Russian art music was carefully formed by the guild method or by the handing down of values and craft from master to apprentice: from Glinka to Balakirev, from Balakirev to Rimsky-Korsakov. Balakirev especially vigorously enforced his methods and ideas among his younger colleagues. Rimsky-Korsakov, who at a later stage spent considerable energy expanding his academic background through close study of the German tradition, but who was initiated into art music by Balakirev, was the first of this guild to produce an authoritative harmony treatise in many ways representative of that tradition. Some of the essential premises of the newborn tradition, the New Russian School (another name for The Five), became passively codified into the standard format of a manual, merely as a result of Rimsky-Korsakov's decision to write one. Theoretical speculations were far from, if not against, Rimsky-Korsakov's purpose. The role of the manual was rather to transmit in the most lucid terms possible the composer's conception of harmony in order to guide new students systematically in their study of the subject. The form of practical advice chosen by Rimsky-Korsakov for this purpose, and certainly considered by him as the most efficient and accessible, is reminiscent of that practiced by his teacher not just in essence but even in tone, as seen in his remark about fundamentally practical nature of the treatise: "You will not find here any philosophizing on 'how, what, and why'—one can put as its epigraph: 'Do as I command and all will be fine.'"[367] Indeed, Rimsky-Korsakov's *Practical Manual of Harmony* not only recorded the New Russian School's tradition but laid the groundwork for several decades of compositional training in the St. Petersburg Conservatory, Russia's leading musical institution.

# Conclusions

Written during what is often considered the "golden age" of Russian music, Rimsky-Korsakov's *Practical Manual of Harmony* introduced a distinctive harmonic system. The most prominent feature of this treatise is that Rimsky-Korsakov built his theory systematically around the notions of key relationships and modulation, since, for him, harmonic processes were determined by the underlying relationship of keys. Indeed, in addition to its uniqueness, Rimsky-Korsakov's lucid exposition of the three categories of key relationships is the most explicit among the similar works by other Russian or German authors of the period.

In the *Practical Manual of Harmony*, Rimsky-Korsakov divides all keys into three categories which he treats as degrees of relationship to the tonic. The first degree of relationship includes a set of six keys considered to be the closest to the tonic (in C major: A minor, G major, F major, F minor, E minor, and D minor). The second degree of relationship comprises a set of twelve keys seen as relatively close to the tonic (in C major: C minor, B major, B minor, B-flat, B-flat minor, A major, A-flat, G minor, E major, E-flat major, D major, and D-flat). In thc third degree of relationship there are five keys designated as remote to the tonic (in C major: G-sharp or A-flat minor, F-sharp or G-flat major, D-sharp or E-flat minor, and C-sharp or D-flat minor). As demonstrated in the above analysis using spatial models, Rimsky's system of key relationships exhibits a significant series of symmetrical patterns related to octatonic and whole tone structures.

Investigating the approaches to the key relationships of several nineteenth-century German theorists, with whose work Rimsky-Korsakov was likely familiar, offered a rich field for comparative analysis. Rimsky-Korsakov's system displays important similarities with Moritz Hauptmann's idea of harmonic dualism and also shares elements in common with the theories of Dehn, Weber, Marx, and Lobe. Overall, however, Rimsky-Korsakov's unique tonal map cannot be said to derive from or even closely resemble any of the German models.

The search for the influences that shaped the distinctive elements of Rimsky-Korsakov's harmonic system led also to an examination of the composer's immediate environment when writing the manual, as well as his musical background. His close association and exchange of ideas with Tchaikovsky played the role of a catalyst in the formulation of Rimsky-Korsakov's own harmonic ideas, despite Tchaikovsky's criticism of them. The differences of their approaches to harmony stemmed from the two composers' different schooling and creative paths.

As well, the sound worlds of Russian folk music and folk music of the Russian Orient, originally passed on to him by his teacher Balakirev, also found a reflection in Rimsky's harmonic palette and its structure, even while his theory fluidly provided a continuation of Hauptmann's harmonic ideas taken in a new direction.

# Appendix 1

## Table of Editions in Russia and Soviet Union of Rimsky-Korsakov's *Manual of Harmony* and *Practical Manual of Harmony*

| Date | Place | Edition | Remarks |
|---|---|---|---|
| 1884 | St. Petersburg | Lithograph, vol. 1 | title: Учебник гармонии. Курс придворной капеллы. Выпуск первый: гармонизация аккордами в пределах лада. |
| 1885 | St. Petersburg | Lithograph, vol. 2 | |
| 1886 | St. Petersburg: Büttner | 1st printed edition | title: Практический учебник гармонии, condensed version of the lithograph edition. |
| 1889 | St. Petersburg: Büttner | 2nd | |
| 1893 | St. Petersburg: Beliaev | 3rd | Some changes by Rimsky-Korsakov |
| 1898 | " " | 4th | |
| 1900 | " " | 5th | |
| 1905 | " " | 6th | |
| 1907 | " " | 7th | |
| 1910 | " " | 8th | First posthumous edition |
| 1912 | St. Petersburg | 9th | Edited by I. Vitol and M. Shteinberg |
| 1914 | " " | 10th | " " |
| 1916 | " " | 11th | " " |
| 1918 | " " | 12th | " " |
| 1924 | " " | 13th | Edited by M. Shteinberg |
| 1927 | " " | 14th | " " |

*(Continued)*

**(Continued)**

| Date | Place | Edition | Remarks |
|---|---|---|---|
| 1929 | Moscow | 15th | " " |
| 1937 | " " | 16th | " " |
| 1949 | " " | 17th | " " |
| 1952 | " " | 18th | " " |
| 1956 | Moscow: Muzgiz | 19th | " " |
| 1960 | Moscow: GMI | | v. 4 of Rimsky-Korsakov's *Collected Literary Works and Correspondence* publication |
| 2014 | St. Petersburg: Lan', Planeta muzyki | 20th | |
| 2017 | St. Petersburg: Lan', Planeta muzyki | 21st | |
| 2018 | St. Petersburg: Lan', Planeta muzyki | 22nd | |
| 2019 | St. Petersburg: Lan', Planeta muzyki | 23rd | |
| 2020 | St. Petersburg: Planeta Muzyki | 24th | |

# Appendix 2

## List of Translations of Rimsky-Korsakov's *Practical Manual of Harmony*

**German**
*Praktisches Lehrbuch der Harmonie.*
Translator: Hans Schmidt.
Publication: Leipzig: M. P. Beliaeff, 1895; there are later editions.

**French**
*Traité d'harmonie théorique et pratique.*
Translator: Felix Dorfman.
Publication: Paris: Alphonse Leduc, 1910.

**Italian**
*Trattato pratico d'armonia.*
Translators: G. F. Bucci and A. Zamorski.
Publication: Milan: Sonzogno, 1913; 1932.

**English**
Practical Manual of Harmony.
Translator: Joseph Achron.
Publication: New York: Carl Fischer, [1930], [1943], 2005

# Appendix 3

## Table of Contents of Tchaikovsky's *Manual of harmony* (1872)

TABLE OF CONTENTS


**Introduction**
Intervals

*Harmony*

**Part One**
UNIT I. CONSONANT CHORDS. TRIADS.

| | |
|---|---|
| Chapter I | Triads of the major scale |
| Chapter II | Combination of triads in major |
| Chapter III | Combination of triads with no external connections |
| Chapter IV | Exceptions from the rules of combination of connecting chords |
| Chapter V | Harmonic sequences |
| Chapter VI | Harmony of the minor key |
| Chapter VII | Open chord position |
| Chapter VIII | Inversion of triads |
| Chapter IX | Inversion of diminished and augmented triads |

UNIT II. DISSONANT HARMONIES: SEVENTH AND NINTH CHORDS

| | |
|---|---|
| Chapter X | Dominant seventh chord |
| Chapter XI | Free voice leading |
| Chapter XII | Ninth chord |
| Chapter XIII | Minor and diminished seventh chords |
| Chapter XIV | Combination of dissonant harmonies that resolve into tonic triad |
| Chapter XV | Sequence chords |
| Chapter XVI | Sequence chords in minor |
| Chapter XVII | Harmonization of given melodies |

UNIT III. MODULATION

| | |
|---|---|
| Chapter XVIII | Direct modulations |
| Chapter XIX | Passing modulation |
| Chapter XX | Harmonization of melodies with modulation |
| Chapter XXI | Enharmonicism of the diminished seventh chord |
| Chapter XXII | Pedal point |

**Part Two. Accidental harmonic forms**

UNIT I

| | |
|---|---|
| Chapter XXIII | Suspensions |
| Chapter XXIV | Anticipations |
| Chapter XXV | Passing notes |
| Chapter XXVI | Chords with augmented fifth |
| Chapter XXVII | Chords with augmented sixth |
| Chapter XXVIII | Neighboring notes |

UNIT II. MELODIC DEVELOPMENT OF VOICES

| | |
|---|---|
| Chapter XXIX | Strict style of harmony |
| Chapter XXX | Other development of voice leading |
| Chapter XXXI | Harmonic figuration |
| Chapter XXII | Free preludes |
| Chapter XXXIII | Exceptions from the rules of harmony |
| Chapter XXXIV | Cadences |

# Appendix 4

## Tables of Contents of Rimsky-Korsakov's, *Manual of Harmony* (1884/1885) and *Practical Manual of Harmony* (1886)

TABLE OF CONTENTS

Introduction

UNIT I. HARMONIZATION WITHIN ONE KEY
- Preliminary notions on triads
- Fundamental and secondary triads
- Minor subdominant triad in major
- On the movement of voices
- On the four-part texture

Chapter I. Fundamental triads in major and minor
- Doubling
- Open and close chord position
- Melodic position of a triad
- Connection of triads on I and IV, I and V, and back
- Incorrect voice leading. Forbidden progressions
- Rules for exercises
- On the minor subdominant triad; chromatic passing note; voice crossing
- Introduction of the bass voice and the notes of various note values
- Harmonization of a given bass. Generation of melody. The leading tone.
- Incomplete triad on I
- Independent composition of melody and bass, or short preludes
- Inversion of triads
  - Sixth chords of fundamental scale degrees
  - Full authentic and plagal cadences
  - Complex cadence of 1st order and IV – V progression
  - Connection of $IV^6$ and $V^5_3$
  - Complex cadence of 2nd order with a 64 chord
  - Passing $^6_4$ chord
  - Half cadence
  - Leaps of fourth and fifth in melody and inner voices
  - Leaps of former thirds in bass

Chapter II. Dissonant chords of the dominant harmony

General notions about seventh chords

$V^7$

Inversions of $V^7$

Combination of $V^7$ and its inversions, and of the inversions between themselves

Leaps in melody

Leading $VII^7$: minor and diminished

Ninth chord

Chapter III. Secondary scale degrees in major

Triads

Seventh chords pf the secondary scale-degrees in major

Triads and seventh chord on II

Triads and seventh chord on VI

Deceptive cadence

Triad and seventh chord on III

Minor $VII^6$

Passing $^6_4$ chords of secondary scale degrees

Chapter IV. Secondary triads and seventh chords in minor

General notions

Triad and seventh chord on II

Triad on VI

Deceptive cadence

Triads on II and VII natural and Phrygian cadence

$IV^7$

Diminished $VII^6$ and major triad on IV in minor

Plagal cadence with IV triad in melodic minor

Passing $^6_4$ chords on secondary scale-degrees in minor

Conclusions (I Unit)

UNIT II. MODULATION

Chapter V. Means for gradual modulation

General notions. Close and remote keys

General rules for gradual modulation to close keys

Chromaticism and modulation

Chapter VI. Modulation and deviation to close keys

General notions

Modulation to close keys

The concept of a sentence. Further exercises in modulation

Deviation to close keys

Harmonization of chorale melodies

Chapter VII. Modulation to remote keys

Modulatory plan

Chapter VIII. Pedal point

Three-part texture

Pedal point and pedal in bass

Appendix. Pedal point in upper and middle voices and double pedal point

UNIT III. NONHARMONIC TONES

General notions

Chapter IX. Passing notes and embellishments

Diatonic passing notes

a) Passing notes within single voice, or single passing notes
b) Passing notes in two and three voices, or double and triple passing notes

Diatonic passing notes as a consequence of incorrect voice doubling

Chromatic passing notes

Embellishments

a) Embellishments in a single voice, or simple embellishments
b) Double and triple embellishments, or embellishments in two and three voices

Chapter X. Suspensions

a) Simple nonharmonic descending suspensions
b) Simple nonharmonic ascending suspensions
c) Double and triple suspensions

Appendix. Suspensions of the diminished octave or augmented union

Chapter XI. Melodic figuration

a) Additional harmonic notes
b) Passing notes and embellishments on secondary downbeats
c) Affect of additional harmonic tones and of embellishments on suspension
d) Figured chorale

Appendix. Free use of nonharmonic tones

UNIT IV. COMBINATION CHORDS, ENHARMONICISM, AND DECEPTIVE PROGRESSIONS

Chapter XII. Modified or combination chords

a) Deceptive: $V^7$, diminished and minor; augmented sixth chords
b) Flattening of II scale degree
c) Augmented fifth chords

Chapter XIII. Deceptive progressions within one key and sudden modulation

a) Deceptive progressions within one key

b) Deceptive cadence in major
c) Enharmonicism as means for sudden modulation

<u>Chapter XIV. Deceptive progressions outside one key and circular modulations</u>

Relationship of remote keys
Deceptive progressions on the circle-of-fourths
Deceptive progressions on the circle-of-major-thirds
Deceptive progressions on the circle-of-minor-thirds
Deceptive progressions on the circle-of-major-seconds
Deceptive progressions on the circle-of-minor-seconds
Comments

## Rimsky-Korsakov *Practical Manual of Harmony* (1886)

TABLE OF CONTENTS

UNIT 1. PRELIMINARY NOTIONS
Triads
Seventh chords
Natural and artificial modes. Primary and secondary chords
Relationship of triads
Voice leading

UNIT II. HARMONIZATION BY CHORDS WITHIN ONE KEY
Consonant combinations
Connection of main triads on I and IV, on I and V and back
Connection of main triads on Iand V scale degrees
Connection of sixth chords with triads on I-IV and I-V scale degrees
Connection of $IV^6$ and $V^5_3$
Connection of $IV^5_3$ and $V^6$
Connection of $IV^6$ and $V^6$
Simple full authentic and plagal cadences
Complex cadence with subdominant and dominant
Complex cadence with $I^6_4$
Passing $^6_4$ chord
Half cadence
Leaps of fourth and fifth in melody and middle voices
Leaps of thirds in the melody
Leaps of thirds in the bass
Diminished $VII^6$
Root-position triad on II and its sixth chord
Root-position triad on VI; deceptive cadence
Root-position triad on III in major
Root-position triad on III in natural minor. Phrygian cadence of 1st-order
Root-position triad on VI in natural minor. Phrygian cadence of 2nd-order
Harmonization of chorale (without modulation)
Minor subdominant triad and sixth chord on II in soft or harmonic major
Dissonant combinations
$V^7$ in root position
Inversions of $V^7$
Leading seventh chords on VII: minor and diminished
Root-position seventh chord on II and its inversions

Special kinds of plagal cadences
The use of seventh chords in harmonization of chorale
Ninth chord
Relationship of all triads in a key
a) Sequences with fourths and fifths
b) Sequences with seconds and thirds
Relationship of all seven chords in a key
Sequences with seventh chords
*Appendix.* Free use of all scale degrees

UNIT III. MODULATION
Preliminary notions
Close keys or 1st-degree relationship
Modulation without chromaticism
Complex techniques
The use of IV scale degree of melodic minor
Modulation directly through the tonic triad of the subsequent key
Chromaticism and false progressions. Cross relations
Chromatic modulation
The effect of $IV^5_3$ in melodic minor
Transition modulation and deviation
Perfect modulation
Imperfect modulation
Remote and distant keys
Pedal point

UNIT IV. MELODIC FIGURATION
Passing notes. General notions
Diatonic passing notes
Chromatic passing notes. The notation of chromatic scales
Single, double and other chromatic passing notes
Neighboring and ornamental notes
Suspensions. General notions
Descending suspensions
Ascending and complex suspensions
*Appendix.*
Suspensions of a diminished octave or augmented prime
Strict melodic figuration
Figured chorales and harmonization of melodies containing melodic figuration
Free melodic figuration

UNIT V. ENHARMONIC AND SUDDEN MODULATION
Chromatically altered chords
Deceptive $V^7$ and deceptive diminished $V^7$

Major triad on flat II and $V^7$ with flatted fifth
Chords with augmented fifth
Chords with augmented sixth
Means for enharmonic modulation
Enharmonicism of chords with augmented sixth
Enharmonicism of augmented triad
Deceptive progressions. General notions
Deceptive cadences
Deceptive progressions of triads
Deceptive progressions of $V^7$
The use of deceptive progressions in sudden modulation
Chorale harmonization
*Appendix I.*
The notion of harmonic figuration and pedal point figuration
*Appendix II.*
Certain exceptions in rules of strict voice leading
*Appendix III.*
Sequential use of deceptive progressions
(most commonly used techniques)
Conclusions

# Appendix 5

## Balakirev, *Sbornik Russkikh Narodnykh Pesen*, selected songs

Song no. 1, Не было ветру [*Ne bylo vetru*][368]

# Song no. 4, За двором, двором [*Za dvorom, dvorom*][369]

# Song no. 9, Солнце закатилось [*Solntse zakatilos'*][370]

## Song no. 14, Ехал пан [*Ekhal pan*][371]

(Continued)

**(Continued)**

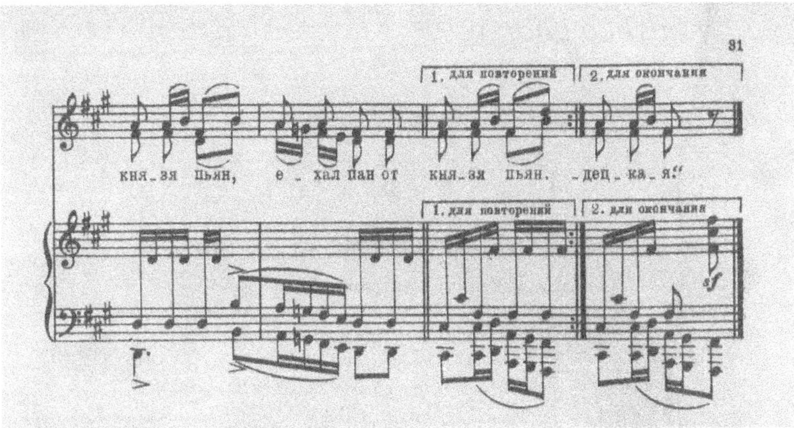
31
1. для повторений
2. для окончания
кня-зя пьян, е-хал пан от кня-зя пьян. -дец-ка-я!"
1. для повторений
2. для окончания
sf

# Song no. 16, На Иванушке чапан [*Na Ivanushke chapan*][372]

*(Continued)*

**(Continued)**

## Song no. 20, Катенька веселая [*Katen'ka veselaia*][373]

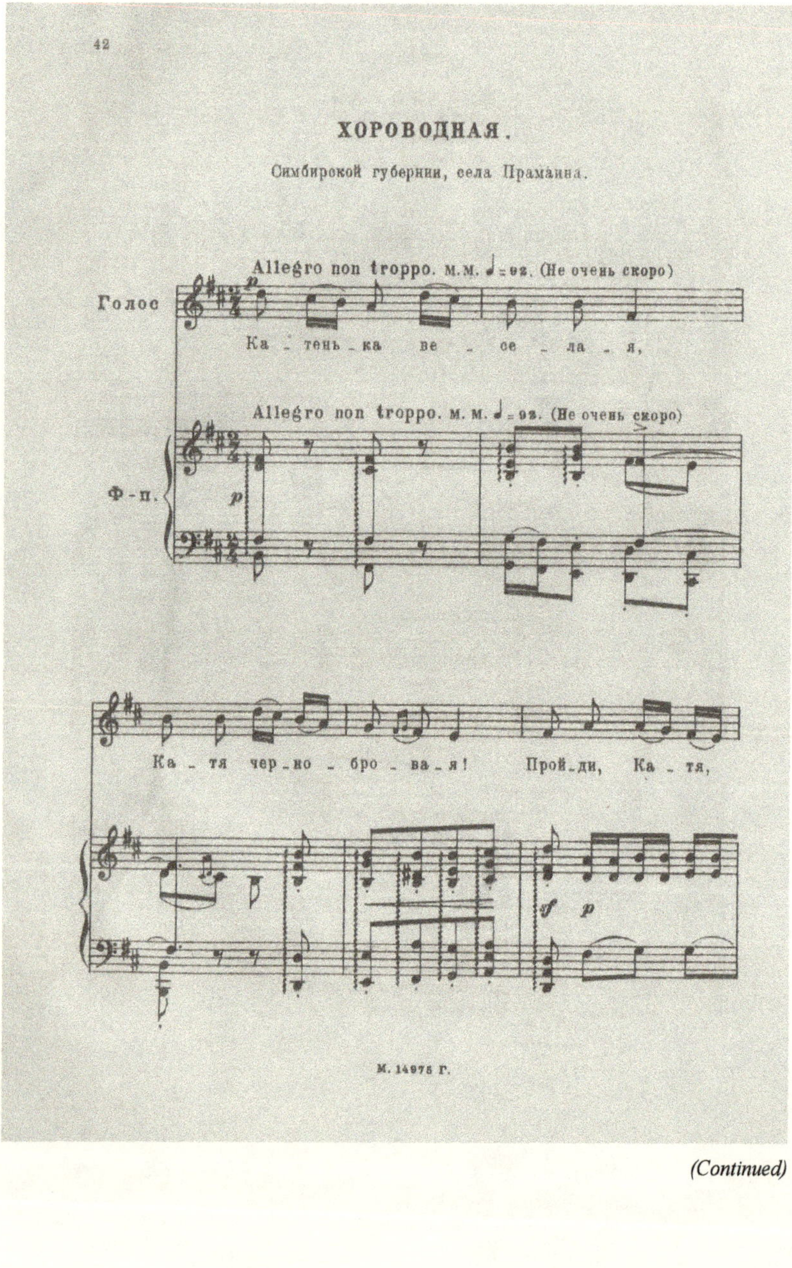


*(Continued)*

**(Continued)**

# Song no. 21, Эко сердце [Eko serdtse][374]

*(Continued)*

**(Continued)**

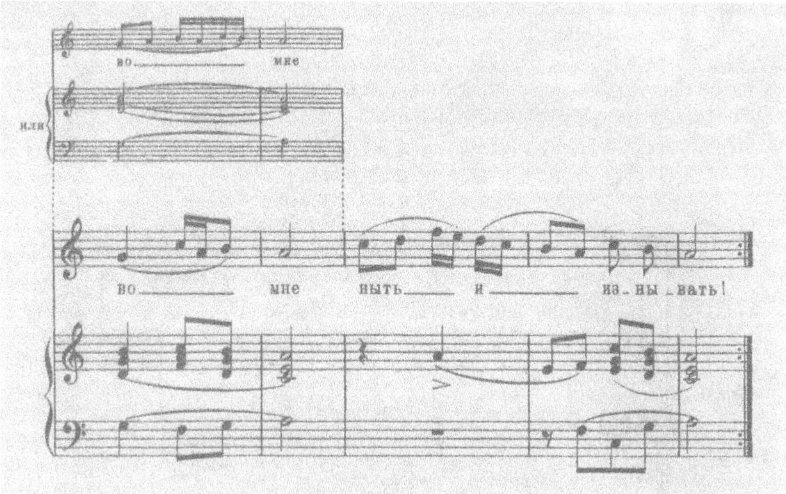

# Song no. 25, Уж ты поле мое [*Uzh ty pole moe*][375]

*(Continued)*

**(Continued)**

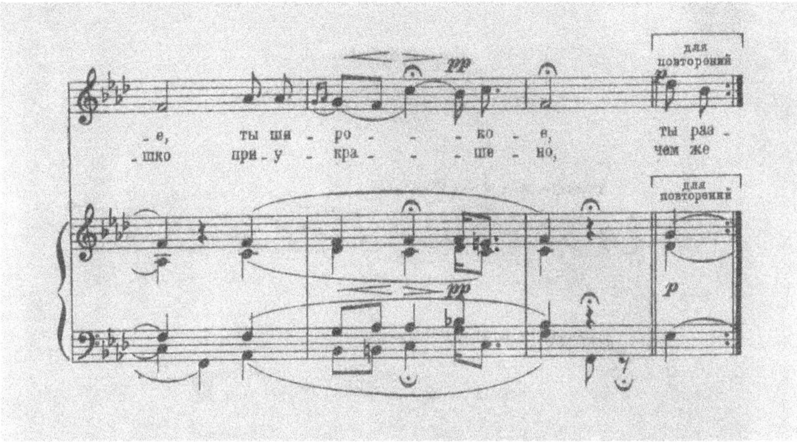
pp
для повторений
- е, ты ши - ро - - - ко - е, ты раз -
- шко при - у - кра - - - ше - но, чем же
для повторений
pp
p

## Song no. 27, Как под лесом [*Kak pod lesom*][376]

# Song no. 29, Калинушка с малинушкой [*Kalinushka s malinushkoi*][377]

*(Continued)*

**(Continued)**

## Song no. 35, У ворот, ворот [*U vorot, vorot*][378]

*(Continued)*

**(Continued)**

Ра - зы - гра - ли - ся ре - бя - та, рас - по - те - - ши - лись.
Ай, Ду - най мой, Ду - най, ай, ве - се - лый Ду - най!

# Song no. 36, Эй, ухнем [*Ei, ukhnem*][379]

(Continued)

**(Continued)**

е - ще ра - зик, е - ще раз! ра - зовьем мы бе - ре - зу,
ff
ра - зовь - ем мы ку - дря - ву! ай - да, да, ай - да,
ай - да, да, ай - да, ра - зовь - ем мы ку - дря - ву!
Цена 7 руб. перепл. 1 руб. 50 коп.
Ред. И. Шишов ГИЗ 6008 Зак. 01164 М616Нр Тех. ред. И. Агапов.
Сдано в произв. 4/V-35 подп. к печ. 10/VI-35 ф 6 82 X 110/16 печ. л. 10
Уполномоченный Главлит №Б-24047 Тир. 10,000 экз. М. 14975 Г.
1-я Образцовая тип. Огиза РСФСР треста „Полиграфкнига" Москва, Валовая 28.

# Appendix 6

## Ekmalian: *Patarag* (liturgical chants for four-part male choir).

*No. 16*[380]

ՄՐԿ. Եւ ևս խաղաղութեան:

ՄՐԿ. Եւ ևս հաւատով:

## *No. 18*[381]

Andante sostenuto.
18.
Tenore Solo.
Tenori II.
Bassi I.
II.
Moderato.
Tenori tutti.

# Ekmalian: *Patarag* (liturgical chants for four-part mixed choir).

*No. 6*[382]

6\. Moderato.

ՍՐԿ. 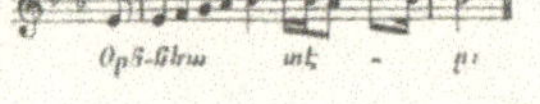

ՔԱՀ. Զի ողորմած և մարդասէր: — Ճաշու գիրք. և յաւարտակն ալէլուիա, առնլով սաղմոս () ըստ պատշաճի աւուրն:

## *No. 16a*[383]

16A.
Moderato.
Դ.Փ.
Քրիս տոս ի մէջ մեր յայ-տնե-ցաւ Որ էնն Աստուած աստ բազ մե-ցաւ.
Ե-կե-ղե-ցիս մի անձն ե-ղե համ-բոյ-րըս յօդ
Խա-ղա-ղու-թեան ձայն հըն-չե-ցաւ սուրբ ող-ջու-նի հրա-ման տը-ւաւ.
Թըշ-նա-մու-թիւ-նըն հե-ռա-ցաւ սէրն յըն-դհա-նու-

# Appendix 7

## List of Early Russian Treatises and Translations of Foreign Treatises

Комендантов, Иван [Komendantov, Ivan].

Начальное основание о гармонии, или Точной порядок происхождения всех постепенно двадцати двух гласов, принадлежащих для одной только октавы [Nachalnoe osnovanie o garmonii, ili Tochnoi poriadok proiskhozhdeniia vsekh postepenno dvadtsati dvukh glasov, prinadlezhashchikh dlia odnoi tolko oktavy].
[The Elementary Principles of Harmony, or the Exact Order of the Origin of All Twenty-Two *Glasy* (modes) Belonging to Only One Octave].
Publication: Moscow: [?], 1801.

Hess de Calvé, Gustav.

Теория музыки, или Рассуждение о сем искусстве, заключающее в себе историю, цель, действие музыки, генерал-бас, правила сочинения (композиции), описание инструментов, разные роды музыки и все, что относятся к ней, в подробности [Teoriia mjzyki, ili Rassuzhdenie o sem iskusstve, zakliuchaiushchee v sebe istoriiu, tsel, deistvie muzyki, general-bas, pravila sochineniia (kompozitsii), opisanie instrumentov, raznye rody muzyki I vse, chto otnositsia k nei, v podrobnosti].
[The Theory of Music, or a Discourse about this Art that Includes the History, Purpose, Effects of Music, Thorough Bass, Rules of Composition, a Description of Instruments, Different Sorts of Music, and All that Is Related to It, in Detail], 2 vols.
Translation: from German [manuscript?] by R. Gonorsky.
Publication: Khar'kov: [?], 1818.

Fuchs, Johann Leopold.

*Praktische Anleitung zur Komposition, sowohl zum Selbstunderricht, wie auch als Hdb. F. Lehrer, nebst einer besondern Anweisung für Kompos. Des Russ. Kirchengsg.*
Publication: St. Petersburg: Karl Kray, 1930.
Translation: Практическое руководство к сочинению музыки, в пользу самоучащихся, и в облегчение учителей с приложением особенных

правил для сочинителей русского церковного пения и двух нотных тетрадей, из которых первая заключает в себе приметы и задачи, а вторая решение задач.
[A Practical Guide to the Composition of Music, for Independent Study and for the Facilitation of Teachers, with a Supplement of Special Rules for the Composition of Russian Church Music, and Two Music Notebooks, of Which the First Includes Examples and Exercises, and the Second the Answers].
Translator: Modest Rezvyi.
Publication: St. Petersburg: Karl Kray, 1930.

Дробиш, Федор [Drobish, Fedor].

Начальное сведение практической музыки [Nachalnoe svedenie praktich-eskoi muzyki].
[Elementary Information on Practical Music].
Publication: St. Petersburg: [?], 1836; 2nd ed. Moscow: [?], 1854.

Габрецеттель, Иван [Gabretsettel, Ivan].

Таблицы всех аккордов, для облегчения учащихся гармонии и сочинения [Tablitsy vsekh akkordov, dlia oblegcheniia uchashchikhsia garmonii I sochineniia].
[Tables of All the Chords, for the Facilitation of Students of Harmony and Composition].
Publication: St. Petersburg: [?], 1940.

Арнольд, Карл [Arnold, Karl].

Краткое руководство к изучению правил композиции [Kratrkoe rukovod-stvo k izucheniiu pravil kompozitsii].
[A Short Guide to the Study of the Rules of Composition].
Publication: St. Petersburg: [?], 1841.

Гебель, Франц [Gebel, Franz].

Руководство к сочинению музыки или теоретико-практическая генерал-басовая школа [Rukovodstvo k sochineniiu muzyki ili teoretiko-prak-ticheskaia general-basovaia shkola].
[A Guide to the Composition of Music, or Theoretical-Practical Thorough-Bass Guide], vol. 1.

Translation: from German by P. Artemov.
Publication: Moscow: [?], [1842].

Фукс, Йоган Леопольд [Fuchs, Johann Leopold].

*Neue Lehrmethode der musikalischen composition, mit besonderer Rücksicht auf die praktische Anwendung der gegeben Regeln.*
Publication: [unpublished?].
Translation: Новая метода, содержащая главныя правила музыкальной композиции и руководство к практическому примемемию их; с кратким изложением оснований двойного контрапункта, канона и фуги.
[A New Method, Containing the Main Rules of Musical Composition and a Guide to Their Practical Application; with a Short Description of the Basics of Double Counterpoint, Canon and Fugue].
Translator: K. Arnold.
Publication: St. Petersburg: Stellovsky, 1843.

Лемох, Викентий [Lemokh, Vikenty].

Общее руководство к изучению музыки [Obshchee rukovodstvo k izucheniiu muzyki].
[A General Guide to the Study of Music].
Publication: Moscow: [?], 1848.

Хунке, Иосиф [Hunke, Joseph].

Руководство к изучению гармонии, приспособленное к самоизучению [Rukovodstvo k izuchrniiu garmonii, prisposoblennoe k samoizucheniiu].
[A Guide to the Study of Harmony, Adapted for Independent Study].
Publication: Moscow: [?], 1852.
Руководство к сочинению музыки [Rukovodstvo k izucheniiu muzyki].
[A Guide to the Composition of Music], 3 vols.
I – Учение о мелодии [A Study of Melody] (1859)
II – О кантрапункте [On Counterpoint] (1861)
III – О формах музыкальных произведений [The Forms of Musical Works] (1863).
Publication: St. Petersburg: [?], 1859–1863.

Одоевский, Владимир [Odoevsky, Vladimir].

Музыкальная грамота, или основания музыки для немузыкантов [Muzykal'naia gramota, ili osnovaniia muzyki dlia nemuzykantov].

[Musical Grammar, or the Elements of Music for Amateurs].
Publication: Moscow [?], 1868.

Аристов, [Г.] [Aristov, [G.]].

Теория диатоническиh гамм [Teoriia diatonicheskikh gamm].
[Theory of Diatonic Scales].
Publication: Kazan': [?], 1871.

Рубец, Александр [Rubets, Alexander].

Краткая музыкальная грамматика [Kratkaia muzykalnaia grammatika].
[Brief Musical Grammar].
Publication: St. Petersburg: [?], 1871.

Арнольд, Юрий [Arnold, Yuri].

"Гармония" [harmony], in *Наука о музыке* [The Science of Music], vol. 1, pt. 1.
Publication: Moscow: Greiner & Bauer, 1875.

Кашкин, Николай [Kashkin, Nikolai].

Учебник элементарной теории музыки [Uchebnik elementarnoi teorii muzyki].
[Elementary Music Theory Manual].
Publication: Moscow: [?], 1875.

Виллуан, Василий [Villoing, Vasily].

Практическое руководство к изучению элементарной теории музыки [Prakticheskoe rukovodstvo k izucheniiu elementarnoi teorii muzyki].
[A Practical Guide toe the Study of Elementary Music Theory].
Publication: Nizhnii Novgorod, [?], 1878.

Казбирюк, Андрей [Kazbiriuk, Andrei].
Руководство к практическому изучению гармонии [Rukovodstvo k prkticheskomu izucheniiu garmonii].
[A Guide to the Practical Study of Harmony].
Publication: St. Petersburg: [?], 1883.

## Russian Translations of Foreign Treatises (chronological order)

Manfredini, Vincenzo.

*Regole armoniche, o sieno Precetti ragionati.*
Publication: Venezia, A. Cesare, 1797.
Translation: Pravila garmonicheskie I melodicheskie dlia obucheniia vsei muzyki.
[The Harmonic and Melodic Rules for the Teaching of All Music], based on the 2nd edition of 1797.
Translator: Stepan Degtiarev.
Publication: St. Petersburg: [?], 1805.

Fétis, François-Joseph.
*A musique mise à la portée de tour le monde.*
Publication: Paris: Alexandre Menier, 1830.
Translation: Muzyka poniatnaia dlia vsekh, ili kratkoe izlozhenie vsego nuzhnogo, chtob sudit' I govorit' ob iskusstve sem, ne uchivshis' onomu.
[Music Accessible to All, or a Short Description of All that is Needed to Judge and Speak about Art for Those Who Have Not Studied It].
Translator: P. Beliakov.
Publication: St. Petersburg, [?], 1833.

Marx, A. B.: *Allgemeine Musiklehre* [1839]
Translation: Obshchee rukovodstvo k izucheniiu muzyki [RMO]
Translator: Lemokh, Vikenty
Publication: Moscow: [?], 1848
Translation: *Всеобщий учебник музыки* [PMO] [*Vseobshchii uchebnik muzyki* (RMS)]
Translator: Famitsyn, Aleksandr
Publication: St. Petersburg: [?], 1860

Richter, E. F.: *Lehrbuch der Harmonie: Praktische Anleitung zu den Studien in derselben* [1853]
Translation: Uchenbnik garmonii: prakticheskoe rukovodstvo k ee izucheniiu [StPCL]
Translator: Famitsyn, Aleksandr
Publication: St. Petersburg: Karl Rikker, 1868

Lobe, J. C.: *Katechismus der Musik* [1851]

Translation: Muzykal'nyi katekhizis [StPCL]
Translator: Tchaikovsky, Peter
Publication: St. Petersburg: [?], 1870

Bussler, Ludwid: *Praktische harmonielehre in vier und fünfzig Aufgaben* [1875]

Translation: Prakticheskii uchebnik garmonii v 54 zadachakh [Rimsky-Korsakov's personal library]
Translator: A. R. Berngard
Publication: St. Petersburg: Bessel, 1885

# Endnotes

A few works mentioned in the notes are identified after the first instance by the following abbreviations:

*PSS/LPP* Protopopov, ed. *Polnoe sobranie sochinenii. Literaturnye proizvedeniia i perepiska*, Moscow: Gosudarstvennoe muzykal'noe izdatel'stvo, 1957.

*PUG* Rimsky-Korsakov, Nikolai Andreevich. *Prakticheskii uchebnik garmonii* (Practical manual of harmony). Saint Petersburg: Biutner, 1886.

1. Yuri N. Tiulin, "Ob istoricheskom znachenii uchebnika garmonii N. A. Rimskogo-Korsakova," in Semen Ginzburg, ed., *Rimskii-Korsakov I muzykal'noe obrazovanie. Stat'I I materialy* (Leningrad: Gosudarstvennoe muzykal'noe izdatel'stvo, 1959), 92.
2. See Matthew Riley, "The 'Harmonic Major' Mode in Nineteenth-Century Theory and Practice," *Music Analysis* 23, no. 1 (2004): 1–26. For further exploration of neo-Riemannian theories and harmonic dualism, see Richard Cohn, "An Introduction to Neo-Riemannian Theory: A Survey and Historical Perspective," *Journal of Music Theory* 42, no. 2 (1998): 167–80; David Lewin, *Generalized Musical Intervals and Transformations* (New Haven: Yale University Press, 1987).
3. See appendix 2.
4. The other harmony manual was Tchaikovsky's *Rukovodstvo k prakticheskomu izucheniiu garmonii*, written in 1872, *PSS/LPP*, 1–162.
5. Notable exceptions include Philip Ewell's work on Rimsky-Korsakov's concept of tonal functions and on the topic of false progressions in Rimsky's treatise. See "Harmonic Functionalism in Russian Music Theory: A Primer," *Theoria* 26 (2020): 61–84; "On Rimsky-Korsakov's False (Hexatonic) Progressions Outside the Limits of a Tonality," *Music Theory Spectrum* 42, no. 1 (Spring 2020): 122–42.
6. See Daniel Werts, "A Theory of Scale References" (dissertation, Princeton University, 1983).
7. Johann David Heinichen, *Der General-Bass in der Composition, oder: Neue und gründliche Anweisung* (Dresden: 1728).
8. Johann Mattheson, *Kleine General-Bass-Schule* (Hamburg: Johann Christoph Kissner, 1735).
9. Johann Philipp Kirnberger, *Die wahren Grundsätze zum Gebrauch der Harmonie* (Berlin: Decker und Hartung, 1773).

10. Heinrich Christoph Koch, *Versuch einer Anleitung zur Composition* (Leipzig: Boehme, 1782–1793).
11. Charles-Simon Catel, *Traité d'harmonie* (Paris: LeRoy, 1802); Jérome Joseph de Momigny, *Cours complet d'harmonie et de composition*, 3 vols. (Paris, 1803–1806); Momigny, *La seule vraie théorie de la musique* (Paris, 1821); Antoine Reicha, *Cours de composition musicale, ou Traité complet et raisonné d'harmonie pratique* (Paris: Gambaro, [1818?]); Reicha, *Traité de haute composition musicale*, 2 vols. (Paris: Zetter, 1824–1826); François-Joseph Fétis, *Traité complet de la théorie et de la pratique de l'harmonie* (Paris: Maurice Schlesinger, 1844); Marie-Gabriel-Augustin Savard, *Cours complet d'harmonie théorique et pratique*, 2 vols. (Paris: Maho, 1853).
12. Emanuel Alois Förster, *Anleitung zum Generalbass* (Vienna: A. Steiner, 1805); August Swoboda, *Harmonielehre* (Vienna, 1828); Simon Sechter, *Die Grundsätze der musikalischen Komposition*, 3 vols. (Leipzig: Breitkopf und Härtel, 1853–1854).
13. Gottfried Weber, *Versuch einer geordneten Theorie der Tonsetzkunst zum Selbstunterricht, mit Anmerkungen für Gelehrtere* (Mainz: B. Schott, 1817–1821); Adolf Bernhard Marx, *Die Lehre von der musikalischen Komposition*, 4 vols. (Leipzig: Breitkopf und Häertel, 1837–1847); Marx, *Allgemeine Musiklehre* (Leipzig: Breitkopf und Härtel, 1839); Siegfried Dehn, *Theoretisch-praktische Harmonielehre mit angefügten Generalbassbeispielen* (Berlin: Wilhelm Thome, 1840); Johann Christian Lobe, *Lehrbuch der musikalischen Komposition*, 4 vols. (Leipzig: Breitkopf und Härtel, 1850–1867); Lobe, *Katechismus der Musik* (Leipzig: J. J. Weber, 1851); Ernst Friedrich Richter, *Die Grundzüge der musikalischen Formen und ihre Analyse* (Leipzig: Georg Wigand, 1852); Richter, *Lehrbuch der Harmonie* (Leipzig: Breitkopf und Härtel, 1853); Moritz Hauptmann, *Die Natur der Harmonik und Metrik* (Leipzig: Breitkopf und Härtel, 1853); Hauptmann, *Die Lehre von der Harmonik* (Leipzig: Breitkopf und Härtel, 1868); Arthur Joachim von Öttingen, *Harmoniesystem in dualer Entwicklung: Studien zur Theorie der Musik* (Dorpat: W. Gläser, 1866); Hugo Riemann, "Die Natur der Harmonik," ed. Paul Graf Waldersee, *Sammlung musikalischer Vorträge: Ein Almanach für die musikalische Welt* 4, no. 40 (1882): 157–90; *Systematische Modulationslehre als Grundlage der musikalischen Formenlehre* (Hamburg: J. F. Richter, 1887); Riemann, *Handbuch der Harmonielehre* (Leipzig, 1887); Riemann, "Das Problem des harmonischen Dualismus: ein Beitrag zur Äesthetik der Musik," *Neue Zeitschrift für Musik* 72, no. 1/4 (1905): 3–5, 23–26, 43–46, 67–70.
14. See Lewin, *Generalized Musical Intervals*; Cohn, "Introduction to Neo-Riemannian Theory," 167–80; Richard Bass, "Harmony and Key Relationships in Romantic Music," in *A-R Online Music Anthology*

(A-R Editions, 2017), http://www.armusicanthology.com/anthology/ViewerPlus.aspx?=1&music_id=757.

15. Heinrich Schenker, *Neue musikalische Theorien und Phantasien*, vols. 1 and 3 (Stuttgart: Cotta, 1906; Vienna: Universal Edition, 1935).
16. Arnold Schoenberg, *Harmonielehre* (Vienna: Universal Edition, 1911); *Structural Functions of Harmony* (New York: W. W. Norton, 1954).
17. Vincent d'Indy, *Cours de composition musicale* (Paris: A. Durand, 1903–1950[?]); Olivier Messiaen, *Technique de mon langage musical* (Paris: A. Leduc, 1944), chapter 16.
18. Boris Yavorsky, *Stroenie muzykal'noi rechi* (Moscow, 1908).
19. Fred Lerdahl and Ray Jackendoff, *A Generative Theory of Tonal Music* (Cambridge: MIT Press, 1983);

    Lewin, *Generalized Musical Intervals*; H. Christopher Longuet-Higgins and Edward R. Lisle, "Two Letters to a Musical Friend," *The Music Review* 23 (1962): 244–48, 271–80; H. Christopher Longuet-Higgins and Edward R. Lisle, "Modeling Musical Cognition," *Contemporary Music Review* 3, no. 1 (1989), 15–27; Fred Lerdahl, "Tonal Pitch Space," *Music Perception* 5, no. 3 (1988): 315–49; Fred Lerdahl, *Tonal Pitch Space* (New York: Oxford University Press, 2001); Leonard Meyer, *Explaining Music: Essays and Explorations* (Chicago: University of Chicago Press, 1973); Carol L. Krumhansl, *Cognitive Foundations of Musical Pitch* (New York: Oxford University Press, 1990).
20. Fétis, *Traité*, XI–XII. The earlier use of the term by Choron in *Methode elementare de composition ... par J.- G. Albrechtsberger* (1814) is discussed by Bryan Simms in "Choron, Fétis, and the Theory of Tonality," *Journal of Music Theory* 19 (1975): 112–38. Its use by Choron and Castil-Blaze in *Dictionnaire de musique moderne* (1821) is also discussed by Renate Groth, *Die französische Kompositionslehre des 19. Jahrhunderts* (Wiesbaden: Franz Steiner, 1983), 58–59.
21. Fétis, *Traité*, 183–84.
22. For a tracing of the lineage of several of Fétis's notions back to Momigny, see Groth, *Die französische Kompositionslehre*, 58–68.
23. Robert W. Wason, *Viennese Harmonic Theory from Albrechtsberger to Schenker and Schoenberg* (Ann Arbor: UMI Research Press, 1985), 3.
24. For a discussion of the Russian chant literature, see Nicholas Shidlovsky, "Sources of Russian Chant Theory," in *Russian Theoretical Thought in Music*, ed. Gordon D. McQuere (Ann Arbor, Michigan: UMI Research Press, 1983), 83–108. For more recent exploration of Russian chant and the concept of mutability in Russian music, see Elena Bakulina, "Tonality and Mutability in Rachmaninoff's 'All-Night Vigil,' Movement 12," *Journal of Music Theory* 59, no. 1 (April 2015): 63–97.

On the concept of mode, see Inessa Bazayev in "The Expansion of the Concept of Mode in Twentieth-Century Russian Theory," *Music Theory Online* 2, no. 3 (2014), https://mtosmt.org/issues/mto.14.20.3/mto.14.20.3.bazayev.pdf.

25. For a brief overview, see Ellon Carpenter, "Russian Music Theory: A Conspectus," in *Russian Theoretical Thought in Music*, ed. Gordon D. McQuere (Ann Arbor: UMI Research Press, 1983), 1–81.
26. Nikolai Rimsky-Korsakov, *My Musical Life*, trans. Judah A. Joffe (New York: Alfred A. Knopf, 1947), 27–28.
27. *Ibid.*, 34.
28. *Ibid.*, 146–47.
29. *Ibid.*, 151.
30. Letter to Kruglikov on June 24, 1884, in Aleksandra Orlova and Vladimir Rimsky-Korsakov, eds., *Stranitsy zhizni N. A. Rimskogo-Korsakova. Letopis'zhizni I tvorchestva*, issue 2, 1876–1893 (Leningrad: Muzyka, 1971), 233.
31. *Ibid.*
32. Aleksandr Olenin, "Moi vospominaniia o M. A. Balakireve," in Frid, *Milii Alekseevich Balakirev*, 321.
33. Rimsky-Korsakov, *My Musical Life*, 286.
34. For a detailed examination of the rivalry between Balakirev and the St. Petersburg Conservatory headed by Rubinstein, see Robert Ridenour, *Nationalism, Modernism, and Personal Rivalry in Nineteenth-Century Russian Music* (Ann Arbor: UMI Research Press, 1981).
35. Nikolai Findeizen, "50-letie S.-Peterburgskoi Konservatorii (1862–1912)," *Russkaia muzykal'naia gazeta* 19, no. 51 (1912): 1129.
36. A. P. Zorina, "Voprosy muzukal'noi pedagogiki …," in Ginzburg, *Rimskii-Korsakov*, 79. Semen Kruglikov (1851–1910), Rimsky-Korsakov's student, was a prominent music critic and professor at the Moscow Conservatory.
37. See N. A. Rimsky-Korsakov, *Polnoe sobranie sochinenii. Literarutnye proizvedeniia i perepiska*, vol. 1 (Moscow: Muzgiz, 1955), 155. Hereafter cited as *PSS/LPP*. The author consulted the copy kept at the Institute of the Theater, Music, and Cinematography in St. Petersburg (N. A. Rimsky-Korsakov's Archive, reference number: A, razd. XXV, no. 45).
38. See Rimsky-Korsakov's letter dated 17 October 1884 and reprinted in *PSS/LPP*, vol. 4 (Moscow: Gosudarstvennoe muzykal'noe izdatel'stvo, 1960), vii.
39. Rimsky-Korsakov, *Uchebnik garmonii*, lithograph ed., 2 vols. (Saint Petersurg, 1884–1885); reprinted in *PSS/LPP*, vol. 4, 5–227.

40. Rimsky-Korsakov, *Prakticheskii uchebnik garmonii*, lithograph ed., (Saint Petersburg, Biutner: 1886); reprinted in *PSS/LPP*, vol. 4, 240–388. Hereafter cited as *PUG*.
41. See appendix 1 for a detailed table of editions.
42. From Rimsky-Korsakov's foreword to the third edition in *PSS/LPP*, vol. 4, 230.
43. Tchaikovsky's manual is the only specific treatise by another author that Rimsky-Korsakov mentions anywhere in his harmony treatise, autobiography, or correspondence.
44. Rimsky-Korsakov, *PSS/LPP*, vol. 4, 237: "V bol'shei chasti sushchestvuiushchikh uchebnikov garmonii my vstrechaem podrobnyj razbor vsevozmozhnykh akkordov i ikh razreshenii, kliuch k chteniiu malo komu nuzhnogo v nastoiashchee vremia tsifrovannogo basa, staratniia obiasnit' vsiakogo roda garmonicheskie iavleniia, kak naprimer, prichiny pochemu zapreshchaiutsia parallel'nye kvinty, no nakhodim malo ili pochti ne nakhodim, prakticheskikh ukazanii i postepennykh pedagogicheskikh priemov dlia garmonizatsii melodii i khoroshego vybora akkordov. To zhe mozhno skazat' kasatel'no ucheniia o moduliatsii. Uchebniki, vystavliaia kak razlichnye moduliatsionnye sredstva raznye dissoniruiushchie akkordy, obkhodiat glavnoe osnovanie moduliatsii—srodstvo stroev i obshchie akkordy."
45. *Ibid.*, 254–308: "Garmonizatsiia akkordami v predelakh odnogo stroia."
46. *Ibid.*, 333–61: "Melodicheskaia figuratsiia."
47. *Ibid.*, 309–32: "Moduliatsiia."
48. *Ibid.*, 362–85: "Engarmonizm i vnezapnaia moduliatsiia."
49. *Ibid.*, 242–53: "Predvaritel'nye poniatiia."
50. *Ibid.*, 246.
51. *Ibid.*, 246–47: "Osnovnye akkkordy."
52. *Ibid.*, 247.
53. *Ibid.*, 309: "Deistvie, posredstvom kotorogo sovershaetsia perekhod iz odnogo stroia v drugoi, nazyvaetsia *moduliatsiei*. Moduliatsiia mozhet byt' *postepennaia* i *vnezapnaia*."
54. *Ibid.*: "Sredstvom dlia postepennoi moduliatsii sluzhit *srodstvo stroev*, sredstvami dlia vnezapnoi moduliatsii sluzhat *lozhnye posledovatel'nosti i engarmonizm*."
55. *Ibid.*, 368–77.
56. *Ibid.*, 309: "Blizkie stroi ili 1-ia stepen' rodstva."
57. *Ibid.*, 309: "Blizkimi stoiami ili nakhodiashchimisia v 1-i stepeni rodstva k dannomu stroiu schitaetsia 6 stroev, kotorykh tonicheskie trezvuchiia zakliuchaiutsia v dannom stroe."
58. *Ibid.*, 310: "Perekhod iz odnogo stroia v drugoi osnovan na akkordakh, obshchikh dannym stroiam."

59. *Ibid.*: "predydushchii stroi" and "posleduiushchii stroi."
60. *Ibid.*, 310–11: "1) Nakhodias' v dannom predydushchem stroe, sleduet vziat' odno iz trezvuchii, obshchikh s posleduiushchim stroem, izbegaia odnako, tonicheskogo trezvuchiia poslednego. 2) Pereimenovat' takoe trezvuchie v sootvetstvuiushchiuiu stupen' posleduiushchego stroia i schitat' moduliatsiiu sovershivsheiusia, pribaviv k nemu odin iz kadansov ili kadansovykh posledovatelnostei posleduiushchego stroia."
61. *Ibid.*, §49, 311.
62. *Ibid.*: "Pri moduliatsii iz dannogo mazhora v stroi mazhornoi i minornoi subdominant (Do – Fa i Do – fa) v bol'shei chasti sluchaev pribegaiut k neskol'ko bolee slozhnomu sposobu, idia predvarietl'no na prervannyi kadans, chtoby imet' vozmozhnost' posle nego poluchit' subdominantovuiu garmoniiu posleduiushchego stroia."
63. *Ibid.*, 312: "Dlia vypolneniia khoroshego perekhoda iz dannogo minora v stroi ego subdominanty (lia-re) pribegaiut k slozhnomu sposobu; perekhodia predvaritel'no v mazhor, parallel'nyi k posleduiushchemu stroiu lia – Fa – re: [example].

    Inogda dlia perekhoda iz dannogo mazhora v stroi mazhornoi subdominanty (Do – Fa) pribegaiut tozhe k slozhnoi moduliatsii Do – re – Fa [example]."
64. *Ibid.*, 324: "Pod stroiami 2-i stepeni rodstva k dannomu stroiu my razumeem stroi, kotorykh tonicheskie trezvuchiia ne zakliuchaiutsia v dannom stroe, no tem ne menee imeiushchie s nim, po krainei mere, odno obshchee trezvuchie."
65. *Ibid.*, 329: "Za iskliucheniem stroev 1-i i 2-i stepeni srodstva k dannomu stroiu, vse prochie stroi, ne imeiushchie s nim obshchikh trezvuchii, schitaiutsia *otdalennymi.*"
66. *Ibid.*: "Engarmonizm i vnezapnaia moduliatsiia."
67. *Ibid.*, 362–64.
68. *Ibid.*, 362, 365–68.
69. *Ibid.*, 368.
70. *Ibid.*, 372: "Vsiakoe sochetanie dvukh akkordov, prinadlezhashchikh porozn' razlichnym stroiam ili ladam, uslovno nazyvaetsia *lozhnoi posledovatel'nost'iu.*"
71. *Ibid.*, 372–76.
72. *Ibid.*, 372.
73. *Ibid.*, 377.
74. *Ibid.*, 134–36, see §175.
75. *Ibid.*, 325.
76. *Ibid.*
77. *Ibid.*, 325: "Sleduet izbegat' trekh mazhornykh ili trekh minornykh stroev podriad."

78. *Ibid.*, 311, 312.
79. *Ibid.*, 326: "Moduliatsiia iz mazhora v minornyi stroi Bolshoi sekundoi nizhe (Do – Si*b*) I iz minora v mazhornyi stroi Bolshoi sekundoi vyshe (lia - Si*b*) trebuet dvukh kvartovykh ili kvintovyhk shagov podrida [example], a potomu predpochtitelnee moduliatsii cherez stroi, parallelnye posleduiushchim stroiam [example], ili cherez stroi, parallel'nye predydushchim [example]."
80. *Ibid.*, 133: "nepriiatnoe odnoobrazie [...], usilivaiushcheesia eshche tem, chto vse tri stroia sut' mazhornye."
81. *Ibid.*, 136: "Perekhod iz stroia Do v stroi si*b* mog by byt' sovershen po bolee korotkomu planu: Do – fa – si*b*, no takim obrazom my poluchaem dva kvintovykh otnosheniia podriad (Do – fa, fa – si*b*), vo izbezhanie chego mezhdu stroiami fa i si*b* luchshe vstavit' odin iz promezhutochnykh stroev Re*b* ili Lia*b*. Podobnoe zhe zamechanie mozhno sdelat' i otnositelno perekhoda iz lia v Si; zdes' naibolee kratkii plan budet: lia – mi – Si, vo izbezhanie zhe dvukh kvintovykh otnoshenii podrida (lia – mi, mi – Si) mezhdu stroiami lia i mi luchshe vstavit' odin iz promezhutochnykh stroev Do ili Sol. To zhe samoe mozhno skazat' i o dvukh drugikh privedennykh planakh moduliatsii iz Do v si*b* i iz lia v Si."
82. *Ibid.*, 326: "napisat' moduliatsionnye plany dlia perekhodov iz stroev Do i lia vo vse stroi 2i stepeni rodstva, izbegaia moduliatsionnykh shagov dva raza podriad na chistye kvarty i kvinty."
83. *Ibid.*, 329.
84. *Ibid.*: "Otpravliaias' iz minornogo stroia, dolzhno srazu modulirovat' na 4 kliuchevykh znaka, a iskhodia iz mazhornogo stroia, delat' eto, predvaritel'no pereidia v parallel'nyi ili odin iz blizkikh minorov, naprimer [example]."
85. Rimsky-Korsakov, *My Musical Life*, 94. By "incoherence" in the first sentence of this passage, Rimsky most likely refers to a second-degree relationship in contrast to the fluent and more desirable first-degree relationships between F-sharp major, C-sharp minor, and B minor.
86. *Ibid.*, 400.
87. Orlova and Rimsky-Korsakov, *Stranitsy zhizni N. A. Rimskogo-Korsakova*, 221: "Potom prikhodilos' mestami delat' moduliatsii. Ved' eto byl chelovek [...] kotoryi, po-vidimomu, nikakikh [...] moduliatsii ne priznaval. Konchit v As i seichas zhe vsled za etim nachinaet v D-dur. Vse takie nerovnosti ia sgladil."
88. *PSS/LPP*, vol. 4, 134: "Itak my vidim, chto otnoshenie minornoi subdominanty, sblizhaiushchee stroi, razniashchiesia mezhdu soboiu chetyr'mia kliuchevymi znakami, predstavliaet soboi odno iz mogushchestvennykh sredstv dlia postepennoi moduliatsii v znachitel'no udalennye drug ot druga stroi."

89. For a short discussion of Rimsky's use of the harmonic major scale, see Riley, "'Harmonic Major,'" 6, 27. This discussion makes characteristically isolated mention of the use of the harmonic major scale in Rimsky's treatise but does not extend to harmonic implications.
90. *PSS/LPP*, vol. 4, 9: "Esli my obratim vnimanie na otnoshenie trezvuchii V i I stupeni minornogo lada, iz kotorykh mazhornoe trezvuchie V stupeni lezhit kvartoiu nizhe minornogo trezvuchiia I stupeni: [example], to my pridem k zakliucheniiu, chto podobnogo otnosheniia mezhdu trezvuchiiami mazhornogo lada my ne vstrechaem; mezhdu tem eta sovershenno estestvennaia dlia ukha posledovatel'nost' zastavliaet zhelat' primenit' ee i k mazhornomu ladu. Deistvitel'no, esli dlia obrazovaniia minornoi garmonicheskoi gammy my pribegaem k izmeneniiu natural'noi minornoi gammy posredstvom sluchainogo znaka, povyshaiushchego ee VII stupen', to poluchitsia sleduiushchii iskustvennyi vid mazhornoi gammy [nazyvaemoi garmonicheskoi mazhornoi gammoi v otlichie ot natural'noi]: [example]. Glavnye zhe trezvuchiia, postroennye na stupeniakh ee, budut sleduiushchie: [example].

    Takim obrazom, posredstvom vvedeniia v mazhornuiu gammu upomianutogo sluchainogo znaka my poluchaem mezhdu trezvuchiiami ee I i IV stupenei tozhe iskomoe otnoshenie, kakoe sushchestvuet v garmonicheskoi minornoi gamme mezhdu trezvuchiiami V i I stupenei: [example]."
91. This remark was added by hand in Rimsky-Korsakov's personal copy of the 1884/1885 edition. In the 1886 edition, the scale was called the "harmonic major" scale.
92. *PSS/LPP*, vol. 4, 309.
93. All of the following diagrams are my own.
94. With the exception of two plans, which are those for the enharmonic duplicates of second-degree keys: A11, C major to C-sharp major, and A12, C major to C-flat major (as compared to D11, A minor to A-sharp minor, and D12, A minor to A-flat minor).
95. *PSS/LPP*, vol. 4, 326.
96. *Ibid.*: "Dlia perekhoda iz mazhora v odnoimennyi minor i obratno (Do – do i lia – Lia), vsledstvie tozhdestva tonik oboikh stroev, prikhoditsia pribegat' k vstavke v eti plany eshche odnogo stroia, a imenno: prezhde sleduet pereiti v stroi parallel'nyi posleduiushchemu: [example]. Sleduet upotrebliat' iskliuchitelno eti sposoby."
97. By way of appropriating the minor subdominant into major and the major dominant into minor as keys related in the first degree.
98. Rimsky-Korsakov, *My Musical Life*, 78, 93.

99. Rimsky-Korsakov, *Uchebnik garmonii*, 222–24. Richard Taruskin discusses these passages in "Chernomor to Kashchei: Harmonic Sorcery; Or, Stravinsky's 'Angle,'" *Journal of the American Musicological Society* 38, no. 1 (1985): 135–38.
100. See Vasilii Yastrebtsev, *Reminiscences of Rimsky-Korsakov*, ed. and trans. Florence Jonas (New York: Columbia University Press, 1985), 326.
101. Among more recent English-language studies of Rimsky-Korsakov's music, a prodigious output by Richard Taruskin stands out as the most comprehensive and rigorous. It includes the topic of Rimsky's use of the octatonic and whole tone scales as well as the history of the composer's music. See "How the Acorn Took Root: A Tale of Russia," *Nineteenth-Century Music* 6, no. 3 (1983): 189–212; "'Entoiling the Falconet': Russian Musical Orientalism in Context," *Cambridge Opera Journal* 4, no. 3 (1992): 253–80; "The Case for Rimsky-Korsakov," in *On Russian Music* (Berkeley: University of California Press, 2009), 166–78; "Catching up with Rimsky-Korsakov," *Music Theory Spectrum* 33, no. 2 (2011): 169–85; "Non-Nationalists, and Other Nationalists," in *Russian Music at Home and Abroad: New Essays* (Berkeley: University of California Press: 2016), 33–51; "Rimskii-Korsakov dogoniaet," in *God za godom. Rimskii-Korsakov – 175. Materialy mezhdunarodnoi nauchnoi konferentsii 18–21 marta 2019* (Saint Petersburg: Sankt-Peterburgskii Gosudarstvennyi Muzei Muzykal'nogo i Teatral'nogo Iskusstva, 2019), 3–21.

    Scholarship in Russian detailing technical accounts of such elements in Rimsky's music as octatonic and whole-tone scales, the Rimsky-Korsakov scale, and modulations by tritone or on circles of minor and major thirds, by tritones may be found in Sergei S. Skrebkov and Marina S. Skrebkova, *Tonalnye struktury v muzyke N. A. Rimskogo-Korsakova* (Moscow: Gosudarstvennyi muzykalno-pedagogicheskii institute im. Gnesinykh, 1986). The implications of symmetrical patterns associated with the octatonic and whole tone scales in Rimsky-Korsakov's music is also discussed in Alexander Dolzhansky, "Aleksandriiskii pentachord i gamma Rimskogo-Korsakova," in Kiui, *Izbrannye stat'i*, 97–99; N. M. Puzei, "Zametki o garmonii N. A. Rimskogo-Korsakova," in *Ural'skaia konservatoriia im. Musorgskogo. Nauchno-metodicheskie zapiski*, vol. 2 (Sverdlovsk: Ural'skaia konservatoriia im. Musorgskogo, 1959), 137–82; I. A. Tiut'manov, "Gamma ton-poluton kak naibolee kharakternyi tip umen'shennogo lada, primeniaemogo v tvorchestve N. A. Rimskogo-Korsakova," in *Saratovskaia konservatoriia im. Sobinova*, vol. 3 (Saratov: Saratovskii universitet, 1959), 109–55; I. A. Tiut'manov, "Nekotorye osobennosti lado-garmonicheskogo stilia N. A. Rimskogo-Korsakova," in *Saratovskaia konservatoriia im.*

*Sobinova. Nauchno-metodicheskie zapiski* (Saratov: Saratovskii universitet, 1957), 39–64.

102. *PSS/LPP*, vol. 4, 134.
103. *Ibid.*, 237.
104. Aleksandr Serov, *Izbrannye stat'i*, vol. 2, ed. Georgii Khubov (Moscow: Gosudarstvennoe Muzykal'noe izdatel'stvo, 1957), 613.
105. *Otchet Russkogo muzykal'nogo obshchestva za 1862–1863 god* (St. Petersburg, 1864), 33–41.
106. A. I. Puzyrevsky and L. A. Sakketti, eds., *Imperatorskoe RMO. Sankt-Peterburgskoe otdelenie. Ocherk piatidesiatiletiia deiatel'nosti S.-Peterburgskoi konservatorii. Sostavili professora S. -Peterburgskoi konservatorii A. I. Puzyrevsky i L. A. Sakketti* (St. Petersburg: Tipografiia Glazunova, 1912), 51–52: "postupaiushchie v etot otdel vybirali dlia spezial'nogo izucheniia igru na fortepiano ili na odnom iz orkestrovykh instrumentov. [...] elementarno-teoreticheskii kurs [...] predstavlial skolok s program dlia germanskikh uchitel'skikh seminarii."
107. *100 let Leningradskoi Konservatorii. Istoricheskii ocherk* (Leningrad: Gosudarstvennoe muzykal'noe izdatel'stvo, 1962), 268. Siegfried Dehn's letter of reference regarding the Rubinstein brothers, Anton and Nikolai, states that they both had completed a full course in music theory. See Liudmila Korabel'nikova, "Stroitel' muzykal'noi Moskvy," *Sovetskaia muzyka* (June 1960), 81.
108. *Muzykal'naia entsiklopediia*, vol. 2 (Moscow: Sovetskaia entsiklopediia, 1974), col. 435. An extensive account of Zaremba's personality and teaching methods may be found in the memoirs of Hermann Laroche, a prominent ninteenth-century critic and one of the first graduates of the St. Petersburg Conservatory. Zaremba is described by Laroche as a fervent follower of his teacher, A. B. Marx, who championed Marx's ideas and espoused a German behavior and frame of mind. See German Larosh, "Iz moikh vospominanii. Chaikovskii v konservatorii," in *Leningradskaia konservatoriia v vospominaniiakh*, 2nd ed., vol. 1 (Leningrad: Muzyka, 1987), 11–13: "The whole makeup of his thoughts and feelings was saturated with the German element to such a degree that it was impossible to take him for a Russian. [...] He settled in Berlin and began to take lessons with the famous Adolf Bernhard Marx, with whom he was utterly infatuated and in whom he believed for the rest of his life. [...] As was expected of a zealous follower of Marx, Nikolai Ivanovich [Zaremba] was a true musical liberal. [...] His only distinction from Marx (whose course he followed literally in everything else) consisted in that after harmony he taught strict counterpoint using Heinrich Bellermann's textbook which had just come out at that time." ("Ves' sklad ego myslei i chuvstv byl do takoi stepeni proniknut nemetskim elementom, chto za russkogo ego vse-taki nel'zia

bylo priznat'. […] On poselilsia v Berline i stal brat' uroki u znamenitogo Adol'fa Berngarda Marska, kotorym uvlekalsia chrezvychaino i v kotorogo uveroval na vsiu zhizn'. […] Kak i sledovalo ubezhdennomu ucheniku Marksa, Nikolai Ivanovich byl muzykal'nyi liberal. […] Edinstvennoe ego otlichie ot Marksa (kursu kotorogo on vo vsem ostal'nom sledoval bukval'no) sostoialo v tom, chto on posle garmonii chital strogii kontrapunkt po tol'ko chto vyshedshemu togda uchebniku Genrikha Bellermana.")

109. Azanchevsky's name appears in a list of Hauptmann's pupils for the year 1862 in Moritz Hauptmann, *The Letters of a Leipzig Cantor*, ed. Alfred Schöne and Ferdinand Hiller (New York: Novello, Ewer & Co., 1892). Reprinted in Dale A. Jorgenson, *Moritz Hauptmann of Leipzig* (Queenston, ON: E. Mellen Press, 1986), 223. The following refers to Azanchevsky's lessons with Richter and Hauptmann during the period from 1861 to 1864: *Muzykal'naia entsiklopediia*, vol. 1, col. 61.
110. For a detailed discussion of Azanchevsky's role in the musical life of St. Petersburg and the important changes he introduced in the conservatory, see Ridenour, *Nationalism*, 212–16.
111. Liudmila Korabel'nikova, "Muzykal'noe obrazovanie," in *Istoriia russkoi muzyki*, vol. 8 (Moscow: Muzyka, 1994), 140. Early in his career, Moritz Hauptmann, who since 1815 had been employed as a music teacher in the household of the Russian Count Repin, visited St. Petersburg, Moscow, Poltava, and Odessa during the time of his service. See also *Muzykal'naia entsiklopediia*, vol. 1., col. 938.
112. Iuly Johansen, *Dvukh, trekh i chetyrekhgolosnyi prostoi, dvoinoi, troinoi i chetvernoi strogii kontrapunkt*. Trans. Nikolai Kazanli (Moscow, [1904?]).
113. Until 1885 the course consisted of a three-year preparatory course, which included harmony, counterpoint, fugue, and canon followed by a final two years that included instrumentation and actual composition. See Puzyrevsky and Sakketti, *Imperatorskoe RMO*, 65.
114. *100 let Leningradskoi Konservatorii*, 244.
115. Rimsky-Korsakov, *My Musical Life*, 272.
116. Rimsky-Korsakov's copy of the Russian translation has an inscription from A. R. Berngard, the translator of Bussler's manual, dated 22 December 1884. It may be found in the Rimsky-Korsakov Archive at the Institute of Theater, Music and Cinematography in St. Petersburg (fond G, razdel III, 1. 1. no. 90).
117. Marx, *Allgemeine Musiklehre*; Richter, *Lehrbuch der Harmonie*; Lobe, *Katechismus der Musik*; Ludwig Bussler, *Praktische harmonielehre in vier und fünfzig Aufgaben* [Практический учебник гармонии в 54 задачах [Prakticheskii uchebnik garmonii v 54 zadachakh], trans. A. R. Berngard (St. Petersburg: Bessel, 1885). First published in 1875 by C.

Habel (Berlin). For details on Russian translations of foreign treatises, see appendix 7.

118. Listed here in chronological order: Gottfried Weber's *Versuch einer geordneten Theorie der Tonsetzkunst* (1817–1821), A. B. Marx's *Allgemeine Musiklehre* (1837–1847), Siegfried Dehn's *Theoretisch-praktische Harmonielehre mit angefügten Generalbassbeispielen* (1840), Johann Christian Lobe's four-volume *Lehrbuch der musikalischen Komposition* (1850–1867) and *Katechismus der Musik* (1851), Ernst Friedrich Richter's *Die Grundzüge der musikalischen Formen und ihre Analyse* (1852) and *Lehrbuch der Harmonie* (1853), Moritz Hauptmann's *Die Natur der Harmonik und der Metrik* (1853) and *Die Lehre von der Harmonik* (1868), and Ludwig Bussler's *Praktische Harmonielehre in vier und fünfzig Aufgaben* (1875).

119. For a more general evaluation of the contributions made by the German theorists discussed in this chapter, see Ian Bent, "History to 1900," in *Analysis* (London: W. W. Norton, 1980), 6–36.

120. An insightful examination of ties between Hegel's philosophy and Hauptmann's music-theoretical concepts is offered by Daniel Harrison in *Harmonic Function in Chromatic Music* (Chicago: University of Chicago Press, 1994), 221–25.

121. Hauptmann, *Die Natur*, §10, 11, 21–22.

122. *Ibid.*, §24, 30: "So kann die Tonart harmonisch sich nur in der Accordfolge darlegen."

123. *Ibid.*, §42, 39.

124. *Ibid.*, §41, 43: "Die Molltonart ist vereinzelt, ohne vermittelten Uebergang in andere."

125. *Ibid.*, §42, 39: "Die Accordreihe des Molltonart-Begriffes geht von einem Momente des Widerspruches aus und bildet nach der einen Richtung eine Kette von Durdreiklängen, nach der andern eine Kette von Molldreiklängen."

126. *Ibid.*, §267, 178.

127. *Ibid.*, §269, 180: "Die Tonarten der Unter- und Oberquint [...] sind es vielmehr wesentlich in dem Sinne, dass der tonische Dreiklang der tonischen als ein Dominantdreiklang in der einen und anderen Dominanttonart, und ebenso der tonische Dreiklang der Dominanttonarten als Dominantdreiklang in der tonischen enthalten ist."

128. *Ibid.*, §272, 181–82.

129. *Ibid.*, §273, 182: "Hiernach tritt zwischen Tonarten des vierten und dritten Grades der Verwandtschaft wieder eine nähere gegenseitige Beziehung ein, als sie die des zweiten Verwandtschaftsgrades gewähren, die wir, sofern sie im tonischen Dreiklange ohne Gemeinschaft sind, als hauptsächlich getrennte sich erweisen sahen."

130. Harrison discusses Hauptmann's concept of dualism in *Harmonic Function*, 226–29. See also Mark McCune, "Moritz Hauptmann: *Ein Haupt Mann* in Nineteenth Century Music Theory," *Indiana Theory Review* 7, no. 2 (1986): 1–28; and Dale A. Jorgenson, "A Résumé of Harmonic Dualism," *Music and Letters* 44, no. 1 (1963): 31–42.
131. Hauptmann, *Die Natur*, §43, 39: "In der Molltonart ist das negative Moment, die Negation des zuerst gesetzen positiven- oder Durdreiklanges, zur Hauptsache, zur Mitte oder **Tonica** bestimmt." Emphasis in original.
132. *Ibid.*: "Wir können den Begriff des Tonartsystemes aber auch so fassen, das er diese Negation, den Molldreiklang, als wesentliche Bestimmung zwar enthalte, ohne jedoch ihn als Hauptmoment hervor zu heben, d. h. in die Mitte des Systemes zu stellen. Dann wird der positive- oder Durdreiklang die Mitte vertreten und dessen Negation, der Molldreiklang, erhält seine Stelle als **Unterdominant** accord." Emphasis in original.
133. *Ibid.*
134. *Ibid.*, §276, 175: "Wir gewinnen durch diese Umdeutung unmittelbar eine nach der Unterdominantseite liegende Region, die in dem successiven Modulationsgange erst in der Fortschreitung durch drei Tonarten erreicht werden würde. Es warden daher überhaupt die nach dieser Seite liegenden ferneren Tonarten auf diesem Wege leicht zugänglich zu erlangen sein."
135. *Ibid.*, §288, 196: "Mit der C-Molltonart würde nur die G-Durtonart mit kleiner Sext, unsere als Moll-Durtonart bezeichnete, verwandt erschein können; wie auch zu dieser, als Haupttonart gesetzt, wieder die C-Molltonart verwandt ist, die zu der G-Durtonart nicht in Verwandtschaft steht."
136. *Ibid.*: "Zu jedem Tonartsysteme wird immer das gleichnamig entgegengesetzte in naher Verwandtschaft stehen; die Molltonart zu gleichnamiger Durtonart, die Moll-Durtonart zu gleichnamiger Moll- oder Durtonart und ebenso auch entgegengesetzt: den die Umwandlung geschieht hier am tonischen Quintintervalle, das aus positiver in negative, oder aus negativer in positive Bedeutung übergeht."
137. *Ibid.*, §274–75, 183–84.
138. *Ibid.*, §275, 183–84.
139. *Ibid.*, §277, 185–86.
140. *Ibid.*, §42, 39.
141. *Ibid.*, §260, 175.
142. *Ibid.*, §288, 195–96.
143. Janna K. Saslaw traces specific influences Weber's ideas had on theorists from Friedrich Schneider to Hugo Riemann. See chapter 7 of her

doctoral dissertation, "Gottfried Weber and the Concept of *Mehrdeutigkeit*" (Columbia University, 1992): 351–403.

144. Weber, *Versuch einer geordneten Theorie*. For bibliographical detail on the French, Danish, and Dutch translations, see Arno Lemke, "Weber, Jacob Gottfried," in *Musik in Geschichte und Gegenwart*, vol. 14, col. 335 (Basel: Bärenreiter Kassel, 1968). Lemke cites two English-language translations: *An Attempt at a Systematically Arranged Theory of Musical Composition, Treated with a View to a Naturally Consecutive Arrangement of Topics*, trans. James F. Warner (Boston: Oliver Ditson, 1846); *Theory of Musical Composition, Treated with a View to a Naturally Consecutive Arrangement of Topics*, trans. James F. Warner, ed. John Bishop (London: Robert Cocks, 1851).
145. Weber, *Versuch einer geordneten Theorie*, §273, 284: "Mit jeder harten Tonart sind also zunächst verwandt diejenigen harten oder weichen Tonarten deren Tonleitern der Ersten am änlichsten sind folglich."
146. *Ibid.*, §272, 284: "nächstverwandte Tonarten."
147. *Ibid.*: "ersten Grade."
148. *Ibid.*, §273, 284; §274, 285; §275, 285–86.
149. *Ibid.*, §280, 290; §283, 292; §284, 293.
150. *Ibid.*, §287, 294: "Die entferntere Verwandtschaft beruht auf dem einfachen Grundsaze: die nächsten Verwandte meiner nächsten Verwandten sind mein Verwandte zweiten Grads. D. h. mit einer Tonart in zweiten Grade verwandt sind diejenigen Tonarten, welche mit den nächsten Verwandten der ersten nächst verwandt sind."
151. *Ibid.*, §287, 294.
152. *Ibid.*, §289, 296.
153. *Ibid.*, §290, 297.
154. *Ibid.*, §290, 298.
155. *Ibid.*, §276.
156. *Ibid.*, §276, 286–87: "die tonische Note von C dur ist auch die von c moll folgich drehen sich beide Tonarten um ein gemeinschaftliches, oder vielmehr um ein und dasselben Vaters, mankönnte sie als Zwillingsschwestern, wiewol von verschiedenen Karakteren, ansehen, wo nicht gar als dieselbe Tonart, nur unter zweierlei Karakter, (Modus.) al seine und dieselbe Person, mer in zweierlei verschiedenen Gemüthsstimmungen.—So wie die tonische Note von C dur auch die von c moll ist, so ist die zweite Stufe von C auch die zweite von c, die fünfte (die Dominante) von C ist auch Dominante von c, das Subsemitonum von C ebenfalls Subsemitonum von c, ja auf der Beiden gemeinschaftlichen fünften Stufe wohnen sogar in beiden Tonarten dieselben Harmonieen, nämlich in C sowol als in c die Harmonieen G und G7. Die Ähnlichkeit dieser Zwillingschwister

ist also so gross, dass sie in einem gewissen Sinn fast aufhört blose Ähnlichkeit zu sein, und beinah Selbigkeit, (Identität) wird,—viel zu grossalso dass man zwei einander in so vielen Stücken so ähnliche Tonarten nicht wenigstens als nächste Verwandte ausehen müsste."

157. *Ibid.*, §277, 287. "Identität im Ganzen."
158. *Ibid.*, §291, 301.
159. *Ibid.*, §278, 288: "und diese Art von Verwandtschaft kann dann im Gegensaz von den unter Ziffer 1). und 2.) angefürten Verwandtschaftsgattungen, mit dem Namen *Seitenverwandtschaft* gelegt werden."
160. Marx, *Die Lehre*, vol. 1, 23.
161. *Ibid.*, 159.
162. Marx's choice of phrase is close to Weber's terminology: "nächstverwandt."
163. Marx, *Die Lehre*, vol. 1, 81: "zwei Durtonarten, die nur in einem einzigen Tone von einander abweichen, nächst-verwandt heissen und sich am engsten an einander schlissen. C- und G dur z. B. [...] sind nur auf der F-Stufe, C- und F dur [...] nur auf der H-Stufe von einander abweichend, folglich nächstverwandt. In Quintenzirkel [...] hat jede Tonart ihre beiden nächstverwandten zu beiden Seiten."
164. *Ibid.*: "Je mehr zwei Tonarten von einander abweichen, desto entfernter ist ihre Verwandtschaft; *D* dur und *B* dur z. B. sind mit C dur im zweiten Grade, unter sich im vierten Grade verwandt, den sie sind von jedem auf zwei Stufen, unter einander aber auf vier Stufen abweichend."
165. *Ibid.*, 158.
166. *Ibid.*, 241.
167. *Ibid.*, 240–41.
168. Marx also mentions the close relationship of a minor key to its relative major. See *Die Lehre*, 211, 214.
169. Marx, *Die Lehre*, vol. 1, 241–42: "trüben, unsichern Karakter der Molltonart."
170. *Ibid.*, 242–43.
171. Here, using the key of minor dominant instead of major dominant, Marx deviates from his intention to employ the harmonic minor scale stated earlier in *Die Lehre* on p. 159.
172. Marx, *Die Lehre*, vol. 1, 159: "gleich der nächste Hauptpunkt nach dem Anfang einem andern Tongeschlechte zugehört, dem Paralleltone des Haupttons. Diesem Parallelton könnte sich zunächst seine Dominante (oder vielmehr der Parallelton von der Dominante des Hauptons), dann die Dominante des Haupttons selbst anschliessen. Nun käme die Tonart der Unterdominante in Gesellschaft ihrer Parallele

[…] die Parallele der Unterdominante sich nicht wohl anschliesst;—man könnte zwischen sie und die vorhergehende Dominantentonart den Hauptton selber eintreten lassen, oder die wiederstrebende Tonart ganz übergehn, oder manchen andern Ausweg finden."

173. Marx, *Allgemeine Musiklehre*, 72–75.
174. *Ibid.*, 75.
175. *Ibid.*: "innige Beziehung."
176. Dehn, *Theoretisch-praktische Harmonielehre*, chap. 1, §7, 58–71.
177. *Ibid.*, 232.
178. *Ibid.*
179. *Ibid.*, 233: "diejenigen Tonarten am nächsten mit einander verwands sind, deren vollkommene Grunddreiklänge (oder Dreiklänge auf dem—Grundton der Tonart) in einer und derselben Tonart als vollkommene Dreiklänge vorkommen."
180. *Ibid.*, 234.
181. *Ibid.*, 233: "Hiernach ist also A moll mit C dur am nächstenverwandt, den der vollkommene Grunddreiklang von A moll kommt als vollkommener Dreiklang auch auf der sechsten Stufe von C dur vor."
182. *Ibid.*, 235.
183. *Ibid.*, 236.
184. *Ibid.*, 236–37.
185. *Ibid.*, 232.
186. *Ibid.*
187. *Ibid.*, 233.
188. Lobe, *Lehrbuch*, 405.
189. *Ibid.*, 413.
190. *Ibid.*
191. Both German terms resemble those used by Weber: close scales (*nächstverwandte Tonleiter*) and first-degree keys (*erster Grad verwandten Tonarten*).
192. Lobe, *Lehrbuch*, 413.
193. *Ibid.*
194. Lobe, *Katechismus*, §113, 31.
195. Lobe, *Lehrbuch*, 413–14.
196. Lobe, *Katechismus*, §§112, 113, 31–33.
197. Richter, *Lehrbuch der Harmonie*, 89: "die Ausweichung von einer Tonart in eine andere."
198. *Ibid.*, 128.: "Die Kunst der Modulation besteht darin, diejenigen Harmonien aufzufinden, die mit zwei oder mehr Tonarten in Verbindung stehen, um vermittelst derselben von einer Tonart in die andere zu gelangen."
199. *Ibid.*: "… erstens: plözlich eintretend, kurz vorüber – und durchgehend, oder zweitens: länger vorbereitet, die neue Tonart als Ziel aufsuchend und für längere Zeit zur Grundlage nehmend."

200. *Ibid.*, 129: "Diese Art der Modulation eignet sich nur für die nächstverwandten Tonarten, und obwohl auch entferntere durch besondere und entschiedene Mittel zu erreichen sind, so müssen in ihrer Entwicklung sehr natürliche und organische Verbindungen herrschen, wenn sie nicht unfasslich und unbeholfen erscheinen sollen."
201. *PUG*, 237.
202. Richter, *Lehrbuch der Harmonie*, 128–37.
203. *Ibid.*, 90.
204. *Ibid.*, 129; see Richter's examples 280 and 281 and text between them.
205. *Ibid.*, 131: "die Harmonieverbindung zunächst am fasslichsten sein wird, welche durch gleiche oder liegenbleibende Töne bewirkt wird."
206. *Ibid.*, 132.
207. *Ibid.*
208. *Ibid.*, 129.
209. Richter, *Die Grundzüge*, 8–12.
210. *Ibid.*, 10: "Der Grund, warum die Tonart der Dominante gewählt wird, liegt darin, weil sie erstens in nächster Bezeihung zur Haupttonart steht, und zweitens als Gipfel der Steigerung zu betrachten ist. Ebenso kann die Dur-Tonart der Dominante bei einem Tonstück in Moll nicht leicht gewählt werden, weil sie in entferntem verwandtschaftlichen Verhältnisse zur Molltonart steht. Man findet daher meistens die Paralleltonart benutzt, oder auch die Molltonart der Dominante."
211. Reinhold Sietz, "Bussler, Ludwig," in *Die Musik in Geschichte*, vol. 15, supplements A–D, cols. 1213–14 (Basel: Bärenreiter Kassel, 1973).
212. *PSS/LPP*, vol. 4, 237.
213. Ludwig Bussler, *Prakticheskii uchebnik garmonii v 54 zadachakh* (Saint Petersburg: 1885); *Praktische Harmonielehre*.
214. This copy is among the few volumes from Rimsky-Korsakov's library that survived. It is preserved in the Rimsky-Korsakov archive at the Institute of Theatre, Music, and Cinematography in St. Petersburg. Rimsky-Korsakov's notes are published in *PPS/LLP*, vol. 4, 436–42.
215. Because the German text was not available, all the references to Bussler's text are given from the English translation, *Elemental Harmony. A Practical and Thorough Course in Fifty-Four Exercises adopted for Public or Private Teaching and Self-instruction.* Trans. Theodore Baker (New York, Schirmer, 1906), §1, 3.
216. *Ibid.*, 1.
217. *Ibid.*, §47, 144–46. Although Bussler lists keys for C minor, these are converted to A minor for easier comparison.
218. *Ibid.*, §47, 147.
219. *Ibid.*, §46, 142.
220. *Ibid.*, §45, 141.

221. The only two authors who offer graphic representation of the relationship of keys are Weber and Lobe. The remaining diagrams are the author's.
222. *PUG*, §48, 309.
223. *PSS/LPP*, vol. 4, 309; Dehn, *Theoretisch-praktische Harmonielehre*, 233.
224. *PSS/LPP*, vol. 4, 324.
225. Tiulin is apparently mistaken in stating that it was Rimsky-Korsakov who first included the key of the minor subdominant among the first-degree keys in major. See "Ob istoricheskom znachenii uchebnika garmonii," 92.
226. *PSS/LPP*, vol. 4, 246; Hauptmann, *Die Natur*, §82, 58.
227. Tchaikovsky, *Rukovodstvo*, 3–163.
228. For a brief account of theoretical treatises in Russia, see Carpenter, "Russian Music Theory."
229. A detailed examination of terminology used in theoretical works before Tchaikovsky and Rimsky is available in I. A. Presniakova, *Stanovlenie russkoiazychnoi muzykal'no-teoreticheskoi terminologii v otechestvennykh muzykal'nykh rukovodstvakh kontsa XVIII – pervoi poloviny XIX vv.: 1773–1862* (master's thesis, Kazanskaia Gosudarstvennaia konservatoriia, 2004).
230. Vincenzo Manfredini, *Regole armoniche, o sieno Precetti ragionati* (Venezia: A. Cesare, 1797); Russian translation: *Pravila garmonicheskie i melodicheskie dlia obucheniia vsei muzyki*, trans. Stepan Degtiarev (Saint Petersburg, 1805). Includes discussion of the musical fundamentals, harmony, figured bass, counterpoint, fugue, vocal ornamentation, and styles. Vincenzo Manfredini (1737–1799), an Italian composer and theorist, lived in Russia from 1758 (1755?) to 1769 and from 1798 until his death.
231. François-Joseph Fétis, *La musique mise à la portée de tour le monde* (Paris: Alexandre Menier, 1830). Russian translation: *Muzyka poniatnaia dlia vsekh, ili kratkoe izlozhenie vsego muzhnogo, chtob sudit' i govorit' ob iskusstve sem, ne uchivshis' onomu*, trans. P. Beliakov (Saint Petersburg, 1833). A popular guide that contains discussions of notation, scales, rhythm, melody, harmony, acoustics, counterpoint, instruments, and both vocal and instrumental performance, as well as the interpretation of music. A prominent Belgian musicologist, critic, composer, and teacher, Fétis (1784–1871) studied with Cherubini and Boieldieu. Boieldieu was a chapel master of the Russian Imperial Court opera in St. Petersburg and an inspector of the St. Petersburg Theatrical School music courses from 1804 to 1810.
232. Ivan Komendantov, *Nachal'noe osnovanie o garmonii* (Moscow, 1901). No biographical information is available.

233. Hesse de Calvé, *Teoriia muzyki, ili Rassuzhdenie o sem iskusstve, zakliuchaiushchee v sebe iztoriiu, tsel', deistvie muzyki, general-bas, pravila sochineniia (kompozitsii), opisanie instrumentov, raznye rody muzyki i vse, chto otnositsia k nei, v podrobnosti.* 2 vols. Trans. R. Gonorsky. (Khar-kov: 1818). Hess de Calvé (1784–1862), a Hungarian pianist, theorist, and composer, moved to Khar'kov in 1812, where he lived until his death. Hesse de Calvé's treatise was never published in German, according to *Musik in Geschichte und Gegenwart*, vol. 16, supplement, col. 678.

234. Johann Leopold Fuchs, *Praktische Anleitung zur Komposition, sowohl zum Selbstunderricht, wie auch als Hdb. F. Lehrer, nebst einer besondern Anweisung für Kompos. Des Russ. Kirchengsg.*, trans. Modest Rezvyi (St. Petersburg: Karl Kray, 1930). A German theorist, Johann Leopold Fuchs (1785–1853) lived in Russia most of his life. He taught harmony and counterpoint in St. Petersburg. Glinka took lessons from him. See also: Johann Leopold Fuchs, *Novaia metoda, soderzhashchaia glavnyia pravila muzykal'noi kompozitsii i rukovodstvo k prakticheskomu primeneniiu ikh, s kratkim izlozheniem osnovanii dvoinogo kontrapunkta, kanona i fugi*, trans. K. Arnold (St. Petersburg: Stellovsky, 1843).

Basically, this was a revised version of the *Practical Guide* in which the author changed the order of the presentation of material in reaction to criticism of his previous treatise and replaced the Russian chant section by a chapter on counterpoint. See Dmitrii Struiskii, "Bibliografiia. Russkie knigi," *Literaturnaia gazeta*, October 29, 1830, 30.

235. Alexander Ulybyshev, review of *Practical Guide to the Composition of Music*, by Johann Leopold Fuchs, *Severnaia pchela*, October 18, 1830.

236. Fedor Drobish, *Nachal'noe svedenie prakticheskoi muzyki*, 2nd ed. (Moscow, 1854). Originally published in 1836. Fedor Drobish was born in the last quarter of the 18th century and died after 1854. He was a conductor of Teplov's orchestra in St. Petersburg. Drobish later lived and taught in Moscow. His other writings include *Noveishaia fortepiannaia metoda* (coauthored with Hunke) (St. Petersburg, 1839), and *Kratkoe nastavlenie, kak dolzhno postupat pri nastraivanii klavishnykh instrumentov* (Moscow, 1854). The treatise was not available for examination.

237. Ivan Gabretsettel, *Tablitsy vsekh akkordov, dlia oblegcheniia uchashchikhsia garmonii i sochineniia* (St. Petersburg, 1840). No biographical information is available.

238. Karl Arnold, *Kratkoe rukovodstvo k izucheniiu pravil kompozitsii.* Publication: St. Petersburg, 1841. No biographical information is

available on Karl Arnold other than the years of his birth and death, 1794–1877. The treatise was not available for examination.

239. Franz Gebel, *Rukovodstvo k sochineniiu muzyki ili teoretiko-prakticheskaia general-basovaia shkola*, vol. 1, trans. P. Artemov (Moscow, 1842). Franz Gebel (Göbel) (1787–1843) was a German composer, pianist, and teacher who studied with Vogler and Albrechtsberger. Gebel moved to Russia in 1817. Gebel's treatise was never published in German, but it was translated from German into Russian by P. Artemov.
240. Vikentii Lemokh, *Obshchee rukovodstvo k izucheniiu muzyki* (Moscow, 1848). No biographical information is available. The treatise was not available for examination.
241. Joseph [Iosef] Hunke, *Rukovodstvo k izucheniiu garmonii, prisposoblennoe k samoizucheniiu* (Moscow, 1852). Joseph Hunke (1802–1883) taught harmony at the Imperial Court Chapel from 1864 until his death and was replaced by Rimsky-Korsakov.
242. Joseph [Iosef] Hunke, *Rukovodstvo k sochineniiu muzyki*, 3 vols. (St. Petersburg, 1859–1863). The three volumes are: I. *Uchenie o melodii* (A Study of Melody) (1859); II. *O kontrapunkte* (On Counterpoint) (1861); III. *O formakh muzykal'nykh proizvedenii* (The Forms of Musical Works) (1863). The treatise was not available for examination.
243. Vladimir Odoevsky, *Muzykal'naia gramota, ili osnovaniia muzyki dlia nemuzykantov* (Moscow: 1868). Prince Vladimir Odoevsky (1804–1869) was a major personality in the musical life of both St. Petersburg and Moscow. A friend of Glinka, he promoted music and laid the foundation for Glinka studies. Odoevsky was also a scientist and a prolific writer on philosophy, music, and music theory, as well as a music critic.
244. The treatise was not available for examination, and hence it is not possible to evaluate the extent of the influence of Helmholtz's ideas as expounded in *Die Lehre von der Tonempfindungen* (Braunschweig: Vieweg, 1863).
245. For example, G. Aristov, *Teoriia diatonicheskikh gamm* (Kazan, 1871). Aristov's short manual explains the formation and transposition of scales and contains a table of the circle of fifths. No biographical information is available. See also Alexander Rubets, *Kratkaia muzykal'naia grammatika* (St. Petersburg, 1871). Alexander Ivanovich Rubets (1838–1913) taught at the St. Petersburg Conservatory from 1866 to 1895. Rubets's treatise was not available for examination.
246. Yuri Arnold, "Garmoniia," in *Nauka o muzyke*, vol. 1, trans. S. S. Iur'ev (Moscow: Greiner & Bauer, 1875), part 1. Yuri (Georgi)

Arnold (1811–1898) was a music theorist, critic, and composer who studied counterpoint with Joseph Hunke and harmony with Johann Leopold Fuchs.

247. Arnold's use of such Hegelian terms as "thesis" and "antithesis" may be found throughout the third lecture, "Dve zvukovye massy. Garmonizirovanie prizvukov v diapazone odnoi oktavy," 28–38.
248. Nikolai Kashkin, *Uchebnik elementarnoi teorii muzyki* (Moscow, 1875). Nikolai Kashkin (1839–1930), a student of Alexander Dubuque, was an important music critic and teacher at the Moscow Conservatory from 1866 to 1906. His manual was very popular and went through numerous editions.
249. Vasily Villoing [Villuan], *Prakticheskoe rukovodstvo k izucheniiu elementarnoi teorii muzyki* (Nizhnii Novgorod: 1878). Vasily Yur'evich Villoing [Villuan] (1850–1922), a conductor, pianist, violinist, composer, and teacher, founded and conducted the Nizhnii Novgorod branch of the Russian Musical Society. He was a nephew of Alexander Villoing (1804–1878), the teacher of Anton and Nikolai Rubinstein. The treatise was not available for examination.
250. Andrei Kazbiriuk [Kazbiryuk], *Rukovodstvo k prakticheskomu izucheniiu garmonii* (St. Petersburg, 1883). Andrei Fedorovich Kazbiriuk (1849–1885), a Ukrainian musicologist, composer, conductor, and teacher, taught at the Kiev music college beginning in 1876. He also conducted the symphony concerts of the Kiev branch of the Russian Musical Society. This treatise was not available for examination. His other writings include *Populiarnoe izlozhenie osnovnykh nachal muzykal'noi teorii* (Kiev, 1885) and *145 Solfedzhio dlia odnogo golosa* (Kiev, 1887).
251. Published by the Beliaeff press for what would have been Glinka's 100th birthday. For details, see *Der Musikverlag M. P. Beliaeff. Eine Stiftung wird Musikgeschichte 1885–1985* (Frankfurt: Beliaeff Musikverlag, 1985).
252. Rimsky-Korsakov, *My Musical Life*, 271–72.
253. *Ibid.*, 272. See also appendix 4.
254. *N. A. Rimsky-Korsakov. Zhizn' i tvorchestvo v 5 vypuskakh*, vol. 3 (Moscow: Muzgiz, 1962), 55.
255. For biographical reference on Iuly Johansen, see chapter 11.
256. See chapter 12.
257. Such as in *Pastoralle*, Op. 33, no. 3, where the major key is integrated with its minor subdominant (the outer sections are in F major, and the middle section in B-flat minor).
258. *PSS/LPP*, vol. 6, 12: "Siuita iz sochinenii Glinki [...] budet sostoiat' iz Mazurki B, Noktiurna f, Tarantelly a, Pol'ki B. Dva srednikh NN po

tonal'nosti ne podkhodiat k B-dur'u- i kak byt'? Esli Noktiurn v g-moll to Tarantellu v kakoi tonalnosti? (I naoborot) Razreshite, radi boga, Nikolai Andreevich!"

259. *Ibid.*, letter of 18 July 1895, 13: "na vtoroi vopros otvetit' trudnee. Dva minora v seredine! [...] Predlagaiu sleduiushchie 4 sposoba [example]."
260. For a brief general overview of both treatises, see Iu. Kholopov, ed., *Muzykalno-teoreticheskie sistemy*, (Moscow: Kompozitor, 2006).
261. Tchaikovsky, *Rukovodstvo*, 3: "Pristupaia k sostavleniiu predlagaemogo rukovodstva, ia vsego menee imel v vidu vnesti v muzykal'nuiu nauku novuiu sistemu, novye vzgliady. [...] Liubiteli teoreticheskikh izyskanii i muzykal'no-filosofskikh umstvovanii ne naidut v moei knige pishchu dlia svoei liuboznatelnosti. [...] Ona ne uglubliaetsia v sushchnost' i prichinu muzykal'no-garmonicheskikh iavlenii, ne tshchitsia otkryt' printsip, sviazuyushchii v nauchnoe edinstvo pravila, obuslavlivaiushchie garmonicheskuiu krasotu, no izlagaet v vozmozhnoi posledovatel'nosti vyvedeny putem empiricheskim ukazaniia. [...] Da pozvoleno budet usomnit'sia v tom, chto oznakomlenie s sushchestvuiushchimi v nastoiashchee vremia, postroennymi na peske, teoriiami garmonii mozhet prinesti sushchestvennuiu pol'zu uchashchimsia."
262. Rimsky-Korsakov, *My Musical Life*, 150. The counterpoint treatises mentioned must have been Luigi Cherubini's *Cours de contrepoint et de fugue* (Paris: Maurice Schlesinger, 1835) and Gottfried Bellerman's *Der Kontrapunkt* (Berlin: Julius Springer, 1862).
263. It is possible that Rimsky-Korsakov used Tchaikovsky's manual up to 1881 or 1882, since a note by one of his students, V. D. Komarova, which can be dated as written between 1881 and 1882, states that Tchaikovsky's book was used during the lessons. See The Stasov Archive at the Institute of Russian Literature, the USSR Academy of Sciences (f. 294, Op. 8, ed. 314, 1. 26). Cited in *PSS/LPP*, vol. 4, 19.
264. Gerald Abraham, "Rimsky-Korsakov, Nikolai Andreevich," in *The New Grove Dictionary of Music and Musicians*, vol. 16 (London: Macmillan, 1980), 29.
265. Neznakomets, "Letopis' moskovskikh kontsertov," *Antrakt* 8 (1868): 3; P. I. Tchaikovsky, "Po povodu 'Serbskoi Fantazii' g. Rimskogo-Korsakova," *Sovremennaia letopis'* 8 (1868): 9–10, reprinted in Tchaikovksy, *Muzykal'no-kriticheskie statii*, ed. A. A. Scherbakova (Leningrad: Muzyka, 1986), 25–27. *Serbian Fantasy* was premiered in Moscow on 16 December 1867, at the third concert of the Russian Musical Society series, with Nikolai Rubinstein conducting.
266. Tchaikovksy, *Muzykal'no-kriticheskie statii*, 27: "Vspomnim, chto g. Rimskii-Korsakov eshche iunosha, chto pered nim tselaia

budushchnost', i net somneniia, chto etomu zamechatel'no darovitomu cheloveku suzhdeno sdelat'sia odnim iz luchshikh ukrashenii nashego iskusstva." Schumann introduced the twenty-one-year-old Chopin to the German public by saying "Hats off, gentleman, a genius," (*Allgemeine Musikalische Zeitung*, 7 December 1831) and debuted a twenty-year-old Brahms as "a young eagle from the North" in the article "Neue Bahnen" (New Paths) in *Neue Zeitschrift für Musik* in 1853.

267. Testified by Tchaikovsky's brother, Modest Il'ich Tchaikovsky, in *Zhizn P. I. Chaikovskogo*, vol. 1 (Moscow: Jurgenson, 1902), 288ff.
268. For correspondence between Rimsky-Korsakov and Tchaikovsky, see *PSS/LPP*, vol. 7.
269. *PSS/LPP*, vol. 14, 604: "V subbotu ia uchastvoval v Russkom simfonicheskom kontserte. Ochen' rad, chto mne prishlos' "publichno dokazat'," chto [...] ia schitaiu dlia sebia lestnym byt' tam, gde glavnym deistvuiushchim litsom Rimskii-Korsakov."
270. *Russkie vedomosti*, January 3, 1874: "preobladanie tekhniki nad kachestvom myslei." Twelve years later, Tchaikovsky wrote in his diary that he liked the new revision of the Third Symphony: see entry for 27 October 1886 in Ippolit Ilyich Tchaikovsky, ed., *Dnevniki P. I. Chaikovskogo* (Moscow: Muzykal'nyi sktor, 1923), 107.
271. *Paraphrases* was received enthusiastically by Franz Liszt, who wrote his own variation on the same theme. Liszt's letter of response about the *Paraphrases* is reprinted in "Semnadtsat' pisem Frantsa Lista," *Muzykal'noe obozrenie*, (1886–1887), 15–17. Originally, it was published in the St. Petersburg newspaper, *Golos*, no. 277 (1879), and then reprinted in Vladimir Stasov, *Sobranie sochinenii*, vol. 3 (St. Petersburg, 1894), 501. See also *PSS/LPP*, vol. 8 (Moscow: Muzyka, 1981), 422.
272. Yastrebtsev, *Reminiscences*, 295.
273. *Ibid.*, 399.
274. Rimsky-Korsakov, *My Musical Life*, 24.
275. Yastrebtsev, *Reminiscences*, 19.
276. Letter of 24 December 1877 in *PSS/LPP*, vol.6, 329: "Ili iz nego vyidet Bolshoi master, ili on okonchatelno pogriaznet v kontrapunkticheskikh shtukakh."
277. Rimsky-Korsakov, *My Musical Life*, 167, 271. Tchaikovsky's second, shorter book on harmony (*Kratkii uchebnik garmonii, PSS/LPP*, vol. 3-A, 165–225) was written at about the same time as his *Guide*, at the suggestion of the Society of Ancient Art, and it was aimed at the musical amateur wishing to learn to write choral music. It did not supersede *The Guide* in popularity, however.

278. The original manuscript is now kept at the Glinka State Museum of Musical Culture in Moscow, archive 88, item no. 168. The four new editions published during the composer's lifetime were in Leipzig in 1876 and 1881 and Moscow in 1885 and 1891, and the last of the four posthumous editions was published in 1909.
279. This letter is published in D. G. Daragan, ed., *Sovetskaia muzyka, tretii sbornik statei* (Moscow: Muzgiz, 1945), 133–34.
280. Tchaikovsky's "Zametki na poliakh uchebnika Rimskogo-Korsakova," are published in *PSS/LPP*, vol. 3-A, 226–49. The original is kept in the archive of the State Tchaikovsky Museum in Klin, Russia.
281. The letter was published in Daragan, *Sovetskaia muzyka*, 134–35.
282. Tchaikovsky, "Zametki," 249.
283. *Ibid.*, 230: "Vsei etoi galimat'i ne ponimaiu. Mozhno li voobshche tolkovat' o blagozvuchnosti posledovatel'nosti, kogda my eshche nichego ne znaem.

    Tochno takzhe mozhno vyvesti vse, chto ugodno, ibo iavnoe blagozvuchie nichego ne oznachaet.

    Otchego zhe ne govoritsia v takom sluchae tut ob iskusstvennom ponizhenii VII stupeni v minore: [example] takzhe estestvennom, kak i vasha ponizhennaia seksta."
284. *Ibid.*, 231: "ob minornom subdominantovom trezvuchii upomianuto v nachale potomu, chto ono prinadlezhit k glavnym trezvuchiiam, a o mazhornom trezvuchii na III stup.[eni] minora budet upomianuto pozzhe, kogda delo doidet do pobochnykh trezvuchii."
285. Rimsky-Korsakov's reply was published in Daragan, *Sovetskaia muzyka*, 133–34, reprinted in *PSS/LPP*, vol. 3-A, 22: "Vse, v chem vy ubedite menia, primu k svedemiiu i po vozmozhnosti ispravliu, no v suti dela vriad li vy menia pokoleblete."
286. For complete tables of contents see Appendices 3 and 4.
287. Tchaikovsky, *Rukovodstvo*, 9: "Sochetaniia muzykal'nykh zvukov byvaiut dvoiakie: takie, v kotorykh zvuki sleduiut odin za drugim, i takie, v kotorykh oni slyshatsia odnovremenno. Sochetaniia pervogo roda nazyvaiutsia melodiei; sochetaniia vtorogo roda—garmoniei."
288. Tchaikovsky, "Zametki," 227.
289. *PSS/LPP*, vol. 4, 241: "Uchenie o sviazi akkordov i sluchainykh sochetanii mezhdu soboiu i ikh upotreblenii dlia muzykal'nogo sochineniia nazyvaiutsia ucheniem o garmonii."
290. Tchaikovsky, *Rukovodstvo*, 10–37.
291. *Ibid.*, 37–73.
292. *PSS/LPP*, vol. 4, 240–46.
293. *Ibid.*, 242–53.
294. Tchaikovsky only cites the two scales, natural major (C) and harmonic minor (a), in the sixth chapter of his manual. See Tchaikovsky, *Rukovodstvo*, 24.

295. Tchaikovsky, *Rukovodstvo*, 11: "vnutrennee rodstvo."
296. *Ibid.*: "vnutrenniaia sviaz' trekh bol'shikh trezvuchii mazhornogo lada est' otrazhenie rodstva [...] trekh riadom lezhashchikh po kvintovomu krugu ladov."
297. *Ibid.*: "Vzaimnaia sviaz' ikh takzhe blizka kak i sviaz' mazhornykh trezvuchii, tak kak i oni predstavliaiut soboiu tri smezhnykh v kvintovom kruge lada [example]. Chto kasaetsia rodstva ikh s bol'shimi trezvuchiiami, to v nem my vidim otrazhenie parallel'nogo rodstva ladov."
298. *PSS/LPP*, vol. 4, 246–47. The four basic scales were previously introduced and discussed in chapter 4.
299. "Main chords" is a translation of "glavnye akkordy."
300. *PSS/LPP*, vol. 4, 66.
301. *Ibid.*, 248.
302. The two terms are also used by Marx. The "external relationship" (vneshniaia sviaz') that describes the relationship based on common tones is cited in *Die Lehre*, 195. The internal relationship, between tonic and dominant and tonic and subdominant, is described in *Allgemeine Musiklehre*, 75.
303. Tchaikovsky, *Rukovodstvo*, 13. See appendix 3 for a complete listing of chapters in Tchaikovsky's *Rukovodstvo.*
304. *Ibid.*, 15–19.
305. *PSS/LPP*, vol. 4, 249.
306. Tchaikovsky, "Zametki," 230–31: "tochno budto v nakazanie? Chto eto za strannoe otnoshenie."
307. Tchaikovsky, *Rukovodstvo*, 73: "Etot process pereneseniia garmonii iz oblasti odnogo tona v drugoi posredstvom iasno ukazyvaiushchego na perekhod akkorda, nazyvaetsia moduliatsiei."
308. *Ibid.*, 77.
309. *Ibid.*, 81: "V protivopolozhnost' moduliatsii neposredstvennoi sushchestvuet drugogo roda moduliatsiia, gde v dannyi ton perekhodiat ne priamo, a snachala kosnuvshis' odnogo ili neskol'kikh pobochnykh ladov. Nel'zia s tochnost'iu opredelit', v kakuiu imenno storonu dolzhno delat'sia podobnoe uklonenie; mozhno tol'ko skazat', chto izbiraiutsia lady, esli ne blizkie k dannomu ladu, to vo vsiakom sluchae bolee ili menee k nemu priblizhaiushchiesia, a esli i ukloniaiutsia ot priamogo puti v protivopolozhnuiu storonu, to s tem, chtoby vnov' priblizit'sia k tseli moduliatsii. Tochno takzhe nel'zia opredelit', naskol'ko sleduet kosnut'sia kazhdoi iz etikh mimokhodnykh tonal'nostei; eto zavisit ot lichnogo vkusa i proizvola, osnovannogo na pobuzhdeniiakh muzykal'nogo chuvstva."
310. *Ibid.*, 11.
311. See these examples in Tchaikovsky, *Rukovodstvo*, 76–77.
312. From chapter 17 to chapter 34.

313. Tchaikovsky's letter in Daragan, *Sovetskaia muzyka*, 133: "Delo v tom, chto kak okazyvaetsia, v moei kritike vashego uchebnika zvuchit, sovershenno nezavisimo ot moei voli, kakaia-to razdrazhitel'nost', zloba, pridirchivost', pochti nedobrozhelatel'stvo. [...] Otchego eto proizoshlo (to est' ekhidstvo),—ia sam ne ponimaiu. Mne kazhetsia, chto v sushchnosti tut daet sebia chuvstvovat' moia nenavist' k prepodavaniiu garmonii, nenavist', proiskhodiashchaia ot soznaniia, s odnoi storony, nesostoiatel'nosti sushchestvuiushchikh teorii i neumeniia izobresti novuiu, sostoiatel'nuiu, a s drugoi storony, ot svoistv moego muzykal'nogo temperamenta, lishennogo uslovii, trebuemykh dlia dobrosovestnogo prepodavaniia. 10 let ia prepodaval garmoniiu i 10 let nenavidel svoi klassy, svoikh uchenikov, svoi uchebnik i sebia samogo, kak prepodavatelia. Chitaia Vashe rukovodstvo, ia ozhivil v sebe ulegshuiu nenavist' i ona-to [. . .] napravila vsiu svoiu edkost' i iadovitost' na Vash uchebnik."

314. Tchaikovsky, "Beseda s Chaikovskim v noiabre 1891 g. v Peterburge," first published in the magazine *Peterburgskaia zhizn* on 12 November 1892 and reprinted in P. I. Tchaikovsky, *Muzykal'no-kriticheskie statii*, 317–23): "Po obshcherasprostranennomu v russkoi muzykal'noi publike predstavleniiu, ia otnesen k partii vrazhdebnoi tomu iz zhivykh russkikh kompozitorov, kotorogo ia liubliu i tseniu vyshe drugikh, - N. A. Rimskomu-Korsakovu. On sostavliaet luchshee ukrashenie "novoi russkoi shkoly"; ia zhe otnesen k staroi, retrogradnoi. No pochemu? N. A. Rimskii-Korsakov podchinialsia v bol'shei ili men'shei stepeni vliianiiam sovremennosti, - i ia takzhe. On sochinial programmnye simfonii, - ia takzhe. Eto ne pomeshalo emu sochiniat' simfonii v traditsionnoi forme, pisat' okhotno fugi i, voobshche, rabotat' v polifonicheskom rode, - i mne takzhe. On v svoikh operakh poddavalsia veeniiam vagnerizma ili inogo, vo vsiakom sluchae, novatorskogo otnosheniia k opernoi fakture, - ia, byt' mozhet v men'shei stepeni, - poddavalsia im takzhe. Eto ne pomeshalo emu vstavliat' v svoi opery kavatiny, arii, ansambli v starykh formakh, - i mne, v bol'shei stepeni, - ne pomeshalo takzhe. Ia mnogo let byl professorom konservatorii – iakoby vrazhdebnoi "novoi russkoi shkole," – i N. A. Rimskii-Korsakov takzhe! Slovom, nesmotria na vsiu raznost' nashikh muzykal'nykh individual'nostei, my, kazalos' by, idem po odnoi doroge, i ia s svoei storony, gorzhus' imet' takogo sputnika."

315. A discussion of Balakirev's impact on Musorgsky is offered by Edward Garden in "Balakirev's Influence on Mussorgsky," in *Musorgsky: in Memoriam 1881–1981*, ed. Malcolm Hamrick Brown (Ann Arbor, Michigan: UMI Research Press, 1982), 11–28.

316. From Tchaikovsky's letter to Nadezhda von Meck, in P.I. Tchaikovsky, *Perepiska s N. F. fon Mekk*, vol. 1. (Leningrad: Akademiia, 1934), 37: "samaia krupnaia lichnost' etogo kruzhka Balakirev."

317. A term mobilized by nineteenth-century intellectuals and politicians, in part to define a Russian national identity distinct from Europe and the West, "Oriental" was used to describe the people of the Caucuses and other areas outside of European Russia, including today's Georgia, Armenia, and Azerbaijan, as well as ethnicities such as Iranian (known as "Persian" in nineteenth-century Russia) and even Spanish because of its links with the Moors. For an in-depth study, see Adalyat Issiyeva's outstanding book, *Representing Russia's Orient* (New York: Oxford University Press, 2020).
318. Balakirev was introduced to Glinka for the first time by his patron, Alexander Ulybyshev, on Christmas Eve 1855. See Sergei Liapunov and Anastasiia Liapunova, "Molodye gody Balakireva," in Frid, *Milii Alekseevich Balakirev*, 48.
319. Findeizen, "50-letie," 1129. Balakirev studied with Glinka intensively until April 1856, by bringing his compositions for criticism. Balakirev wrote in his letter to Findeizen, the editor of *Russkaia muzykal'naia gazeta*, on 3 October 1903: "I was introduced to him [Glinka] by the famous Mozart biographer, Ulybyshev, in December of 1885, right after our arrival in St. Petersburg. Glinka was very friendly with me, and I used to visit him mostly in the mornings, showing my compositions to him ... Glinka liked them and gave me useful advice regarding instrumentation, *Russkaia muzykal'naia gaseta* 41 (St. Petersburg, 1910)." (Menia poznakomil s nim izvestnyi biograf Mozarta Ulybyshev v dekabre 1885 goda vskore po priezde nashem v Peterburg. – Glinka byl ko mne privetliv i ia k nemu prikhodil preimushchestvenno po utram, pokazyvia emu togdashnie svoi sochineniia ... Glinka blagosklonno k nim otnosilsia, daval mne poleznye sovety kasatel'no instrumentovki).
320. Liudmila Shestakova, "Iz moikh vecherov," *Russkaia muzykal'naia gazeta* 41 (1910): 123: "V pervom Balakireve ia [Glinka] nashel vzgliady, tak blizko podkhodiashchie k moim vo vsem, chto kasaetsia muzyki."
321. One of many accounts of Balakirev's outstanding musical talent may be found in Ulybyshev's letter to Mr. Rostislav in the periodical *Severnaia pchela*.
322. Yastrebtsev's manuscript, kept in the Rimsky-Korsakov's archive at the Institute of Theater, Music and Cinematography (ITMC), St. Petersburg, describes Balakirev's own arrangement of Chopin's Scherzo during one of soirees at Pypin's house.
323. Milii Balakirev, *Sbornik russkikh narodnykh pesen* (Moscow: Muzgiz, 1957). Originally published in St. Peterburg by A. Iogansen in 1866.
324. These notebook pages are reprinted in *PSS/LPP*, vol. 6.

325. Tsezar' Kiui (César Cui), "Sbornik russkikh narodnykh pesen, sostavlennyi M. Balakirevym," *Sankt-Peterburgskie vedomosti*, December 31, 1866. The article was reprinted in Kiui, *Izbrannye statii*: "Pervaia osobennost' russkoi narodnoi pesni sostoit v sovershennoi svobode i dazhe kapriznosti ritma …

Vtoraia zamechatel'naia osobennost' russkikh narodnykh pesen sostoit v tom, chto mnogie iz nikh osnovany na tak nazyvaemykh grecheskikh gammakh … Eti tonal'nosti, novye dlia sovremennogo evropeiskogo ukha … sluzhat dokazatel'stvom drevnosti mnogikh nashikh pesen …

Tret'ia osobennost' sostoit v tom, chto russkii narod ves'ma liubit izvestnye moduliatsii, kotorye s okhotoi upotrebliaet v svoikh perniakh. Tak … ves'ma chasto, dazhe v samykh koroten'kikh pesniakh, minor chereduetsia s sootvetsvuiushchim emu mazhorom (naprimer, h-moll i D-dur). Pri etom pesnia s mazhornym ladom imeet minornoe okonchanie, i naoborot. Eti bystrye perekhody, bez osobennogo podgotovleniia, inogda pridaiut pesne samyi teplyi zadushevnyi kharakter …"

326. For an overview of modal qualities of Russian folk songs, see V. A. Vakhromeev, *Ladovaia struktura russkikh narodnykh pesen i ee izuchenie v kurse elementarnoi teorii muzyki* (Moscow: Muzyka, 1968). Among more recent works, see especially T. A. Starostina, "Ladovaia sistematika russkoi narodnoi pesni," *Garmoniia: Problemy nauki i metodiki*, vol. 1 (Rostov-na-Donu, 2002), 85–105.

327. "Переменность" (*peremennost*). The first mention of *peremennyi* (mutable) mode can be found as early as 1681 in the influential *Musikiiskaia grammatika* written by Nikolai Diletskii.

328. This is what Edward Garden erroneously calls the "augmented fifth mannerism," which is just one form of expression in a more general tendency of modulation from major tonic to the relative minor. See Edward Garden, *Balakirev. A Critical Study of His Life and Music* (New York: St. Martin's Press, 1969), 307–8.

329. For a discussion of the use of some Russian folk idioms, see Gerald Seaman, *History of Russian Music* (Oxford: Basil Blackwell, 1967), 17–18. On Balakirev, see Taruskin, "How the Acorn Took Root," 189–213. On Rimsky-Korsakov, see Sergei Evseev, *Rimskii-Korsakov i narodnaia pesnia* (Moscow: Muzyka, 1970); S. O. Grigoriev, *O melodike Rimskogo-Korsakova* (Moscow: Muzgiz, 1961); Viktor Tsukkerman, "Rimskii-Korsakov i narodnaia pesnia," in *Muzykal'no-teoreticheskie ocherki i etiudy* (Moscow: Sovetskii kompozitor, 1970), 311–50; Viktor Tsukkerman, "O siuzhete i muzykal'nom iazyke opery-byliny Rimskogo-Korsakova 'Sadko,'" in *Muzykal'no-teoreticheskie ocherki i etiudy*, 441–504; Viktor Tsukkerman, "Nekotorye voprosy garmonii. Starye lady.

Pobochnaia diatonika," in *Muzykal'no-teoreticheskie ocherki i etiudy*, 150–80.

330. See, for example, on the modality in Russian song, with many examples, Lev Khristiansen, *Ladovaia intonatsionnost' russkoi narodnoi pesni* (Moscow: Sovetskii kompozitor, 1976), 297–310, 336–84.
331. Balakirev, *Sbornik russkikh narodnykh pesen*, 94–95.
332. *Ibid.*, 59.
333. See appendix 5 for selected songs from Balakirev's collection.
334. Balakirev, *Sbornik russkikh narodnykh pesen*, 300, 312.
335. *Ibid.*, 303.
336. *Ibid.*, 86–87.
337. See, for example, a discussion by Sergei Evseev, "Ladogarmonicheskoe stroenie narodnykh pesen," in *Russkaia narodnaia polifoniia* (Moscow: Gosudarstvennoe muzykal'noe izdatel'stvo, 1960), 69–70.
338. See these songs in appendix 5.
339. Balakirev, *Sbornik russkikh narodnykh pesen*, 27–29.
340. *Ibid.*, 53–54.
341. In Song 7, which is in E minor, there is no leading tone in measures 10–11 and 24–25. In Song 19 in B minor, the harmony moves from VII to i in measure 6. In Song 20, which is in B minor, the harmony moves from I to v in measure 1. In Song 21 in A minor, the harmony moves from VII to i in measures 5–6, 11–12, and 14–15. In Song 27 in B-flat minor, there is no leading tone in measures 4 and 5. In Song 29 in G-sharp minor the sequence i – v – VII – v - i occurs in measures 3–5 and the sequence I – v – VII – I occurs in measures 11–13. In Song 31, which is in C minor, the harmony moves from iii to VII to i in measure 6. Song 33 in D minor moves from VII to i in measures 4 and 7. These published songs are reproduced in appendix 5.
342. Balakirev, *Sbornik russkikh narodnykh pesen*, 91–93.
343. For an excellent, exceptionally thorough account of Balakirev's background and relation to the Russian Oriental theme, see Issiyeva, *Representing Russia's Orient*, 163–64.
344. *Ibid.*; T. Zaitseva, ed., *M. A. Balakirev: Lichnost'. Traditsii. Sovremenniki* (Saint Petersburg: Kompozitor, 2004), 96, 145–54.
345. S. M. Mikhailova, "Razvitie orientalistiki v Kazanskom universitete," in Kazan, Moscow, St. Petersburg: Multiple Faces of the Russian Empire, ed. Catherine Evtuhov, Boris Gasparov, Alexander Ospovat, and Mark von Hagen (Moscow: O. G. I., 1997), 275–301.
346. Yastrebtsev, *Reminiscences*, 48.
347. Rimsky-Korsakov, *My Musical Life*, 63.
348. For a comparative analysis of themes from "Tamara" and Balakirev's recording of Caucasian songs preserved at his archive, see Emilia Frid,

"Simfonicheskoe tvorchestvo," in *Balakirev*, 169–73; Emilia Frid, *Balakirev. Issledovaniia i stat'i* (Leningrad: Gosudarstvennoe muzykal'noe izdatel'stvo, 1961), 168–73. For a discussion of folk sources and influence of Caucasian folk music in "Islamei," see Iurii Kremlev, "Fortepiannaia muzyka," in Frid, *Balakirev*, 230–70, also available in Izrail' Nest'ev, "Islamei M. Balakireva," *Sovetskaia muzyka* 3 (1938): 51–67.

349. The various aspects of the chromatic musical language of the Russian Orient in works by composers from Glinka and Balakirev to Rimsky-Korsakov and Borodin have been only sporadically examined. See the following studies regarding the use of elements of Caucasian folklore: Mikhail Ippolotov-Ivanov, "Gruzinskaia narodnaia pesnia i ee sovremennoe sostoianie," *Artist* 45 (1895): 134–46. Taruskin, "'Entoiling the Falconet,'" 253–80; David Brown, "Mikhail Glinka," in *Russian Masters I.* (London: Macmillan, 1986), 30; Gerald Abraham, "Oriental Elements in Russian Music," in *On Russian Music* (New York: Charles Scribner's Sons, 1939), 72–30; Tsukkerman, "Rimskii-Korsakov i narodnaia pesnia," 311–50; Vladimir Protopopov, "Muzykal'nyi iazyk "Zolotogo petushka," in *Izbrannye issledovaniia i statii* (Moscow: Sovetskii kompozitor, 1983), 15–16; *Istoriia russkoi muzyki*, vol. 2, various entries by Alekseii Kandinskii: 231–34, 243–46; Garden, *Balakirev*, 189–93, 220–24, 306–8; Frid, "Simfonicheskoe tvorchestvo," 159–77; and Kremlev, "Fortepiannaia muzyka," 228–39.

Among more recent works, the topic is addressed in Issiyeva, *Representing Russia's Orient*; Marina Frolova-Walker, "Nikolai Rimksy-Korsakov and His Orient" in *Rimsky-Korsakov and His World* (Princeton, NJ: Princeton University Press, 2018), 145–77; A. V. Pronoza, "'Moguchaia kuchka' i orientalism Miliia Alekseevicha Balakireva," *Kul'tura narodov Prichernomor'ia* 174, no. 1. (2009): 170–73; Z. M. Osmanova, "Fenomen orientalizma v russkoi muzykal'noi cul'ture vtoroi poloviny XIX- nachala XX vv," *Sovremennye nauchnye issledovaniia i innovatsii* 7 (2016), http://web.snauka.ru/issues/2016/07/70269.

Despite that this influence is widely recognized in scholarly literature, there have been no recent studies focused on tracing the relationship between the ethnic traditions of the Russian Orient and their interpretations in the music of the leading nineteenth-century Russian composers, with the notable exception of a recent important contribution by Adalyat Issiyeva on the Russian Orient, in which she also examines forgotten historical studies by Ippolitov-Ivanov ("Gruzinskaia narodnaia pesnia"), Koreshchenko ("Nabliudenie nad vostochnoi muzykoi"), and Arakchiev ("Kratkii ocherk razvitiia gruzinskoi kartalino-kakhetinskoi narodnoi pesni") that explored and demonstrated the influence of Arab and Persian music in the Caucasus region since the eighth century.

350. In Viktor Beliaev, *Ocherki po istorii muzyki narodov SSSR, Vypusk 2, Muzykal'naia kultura Azerbaidzhana, Armenii i Gruzii* (Moscow: Gosudarstvennoe Muzykal'noe izdatel'stvo, 1963), 87.
351. *Ibid.*, 154–55.
352. This classification was made by Kristofor Kushnarev in the "Stroenie ladov" chapter of his monumental ethnic study of the Caucasian regions, *Voprosy istorii i teorii Armianskoi monodicheskoi muzyki* (Leningrad: Gosudarstvennoe Muzykal'noe izdatel'stvo, 1958), 381–84, 519ff. This mode is also cited throughout a study by Karine Khudabash'ian, *Armianskaia muzyka na puti ot monodii k mnogogolosiu* (Erevan: Izdatelstvo AN Armianskoi SSR, 1977). A comprehensive survey of the music of different regions of the Caucasus can be found in Beliaev, *Ocherki*. The three melodies are from Beliaev, *Ocherki*, 13, 15–16, 19–20.
353. Makar Ekmalian [Yekmalian, Yekmalyan] (1856–1905) specialized in the sacred Armenian music tradition and produced an important collection of liturgical settings for harmonized chants, *Patarag* (Leipzig: Breitkopf und Härtel, 1896), 187.
354. Ekmalian, *Pataraq*. In Book 1, see No. 16 (120), No. 17 (125), No. 18 (127), and No. 32 (154). In Book 2, see No. 5 (187), No. 6 (188), No. 9 (192), No. 16a (194), No. 17 (196), No. 37 (229), and No. 39 (238). See also appendix 6.
355. For another way of implementing these two core aspects, those of Russian folk music and the folk music of the Russian Orient, by mirroring and parodying each other, see an elegant discussion by Simon Morrison in "The Semiotics of Symmetry, or Rimsky-Korsakov's Operatic History Lesson," *Cambridge Opera Journal* 13, no. 3 (2001), 261–93.
356. See discussion in chapter 5.
357. For example, in a major key of the Weber/Marx/Lobe model (see chapters 12 and 13 above) ii and iii are second-degree keys and, in the context of gradual modulation, can be reached correspondingly through IV and V, and by way of a relative minor subsequently reinterpreted as IV or V. Hauptmann and Dehn include the median minor key among the close keys to a source major. Offering individual interpretations, both however include it on the basis of adjacency to the tonic triad. Dehn is the only one who treats the supertonic minor as closely related to a source major. According to his chart, however, this key is derived by way of the subdominant, F. Regarding the minor key, the same is true: the submediant and subtonic keys are treated as second-degree keys in Weber, Marx, and Lobe. The submediant

major is included by Hauptmann and Dehn among the close keys to a source minor; and the subtonic major is treated as a close key only by Dehn, again on the basis of its adjacency to the dominant.

358. Numerous examples may be found in Rimsky-Korsakov's "Table of modulatory plans," shown in example 11.

359. A theory of "mutable relative major/minor mode" as representative of both Russian folk music and music of the Russian Orient is offered by Nadezhda Dmitriadi in "Stilevye osobennosti russkoi muzyki o Vostoke," *Voprosy teorii i estetiki muzyki* 13 (1974), 119. The term is found in a classical textbook by Igor Sposobin, *Elementarnaia teoriia muzyki* (Moscow: Muzyka, 1951).

360. An extensive analysis of plagal cadences in Russian folk music may be found in Viktor N. Trambitskii, "Plagalnost i rodstvennye ei sviazi v russkoi pesennoi garmonii," in *Voprosy muzykoznaniia*, vol. 2 (Moscow: Gosudarstvennoe Muzykal'noe izdatel'stvo, 1955).

361. *PSS/LPP*, vol. 4, 136, 326.

362. The former (IV to I), is present in plans A10, B1a, B11, and C1, and the latter (ii to I) in A1, A4, B4, B12, C1b, C4, C6b–c, C7a–b, C9, D1, D4, D9a, and D12. Since these can happen in either order, I-IV or I-ii, progressions can be found in plans B2a, C2a, and C12 for the former and plans A2, A3, A11, A12, B2 a–b, B3, B5 a–c, B8 a–b, B10, C3, C11, D2, D3, D10a, and D11 for the latter.

363. The iv-i and VI-i progressions may be found in plans C1b and D9b for the former and plans A1, A7, A10, B1b, B5 b–c, B7 a–b, B9, B11, C7 a–b, C9, D1, D7, and D9 a–b for the latter. Since these can also be reversed, the former progressions (i to iv) are found in plans B2b, C2b, and D10b, and the latter (i to VI) in plans A2, A8, A9, A12, B8a–b, B10, C2a, C6b–c, C8a–b, C10, C12, D2, D8, and D10a–b.

364. Discussions in English of the use of a minor dominant in the minor key in Rimsky-Korsakov's music may be found in John Vincent, *The Diatonic Modes in Modern Music* (Berkeley: University of California Press, 1951), 247–49; and in Richard Taruskin, "How the Acorn Took Root," 198–200.

365. Such progressions (VII to i) can be found in the table of modulatory plans (as in nos. 2, 11, and 12 of section A and nos. 2, 3, 5, 8, and 10 of section B, etc.).

366. Examples may be found in the table of modulatory plans (see plans 3, 5, 6, 10, and 11 in section A; 3, 5 a–c, 7 a–b, 9, and 11 in section B; 3, 7 a–b, 9, and 11 in section C; and 3, 5, 7, 9 a–b, and 11 in section D).

367. From Rimsky's letter to S. N. Kruglikov on 17 October 1884, PSS/LPP, vol. VIIIa (Moscow: Muzyka, 1981), 138.

368. Milii Balakirev. *Sbornik russkikh narodnykh pesen*, 13.

369. *Ibid.*, 20.
370. *Ibid.*, 33.
371. *Ibid.*, 45.
372. *Ibid.*, 50.
373. *Ibid.*, 60.
374. *Ibid.*, 62.
375. *Ibid.*, 72.
376. *Ibid.*, 75.
377. *Ibid.*, 81.
378. *Ibid.*, 94.
379. *Ibid.*, 100.
380. Ekmalian, *Patarag*, 120.
381. *Ibid.*, 127.
382. *Ibid.*, 188.
383. *Ibid.*, 194.

# Bibliography


*100 let Leningradskoi Konservatorii. Istoricheskii ocherk* (100 years of the Lengingrad Conservatory. Historical essay). Leningrad: Gosudarstvennoe muzykal'noe izdatel'stvo, 1962.

Abraham, Gerald. *On Russian Music: Critical and Historical Studies of Glinka's Operas, Balakirev's Works, etc.* New York: Charles Scribner's Sons, 1939.

———. "Rimsky-Korsakov, Nikolai Andreevich," in *The New Grove Dictionary of Music and Musicians*. Vol. 16. London: Macmillan, 1980.

Aldwell, Edward, and Carl Schachter. *Harmony and Voice Leading*. 2nd ed. San Diego: Harcourt Brace Jovanovich, 1989.

Arakchiev, Dmitrii. "Kratkii ocherk razvitiia gruzinskoi, kartalino-kakhetinskoi narodnoi pesni s prilozheniem notnykh primerov i 27 pesen v narodnoi garmonizatsii D. I. Arakchieva." *Trudy MEK sostoiashchei pri etnograficheskom otdele Imperatorskogo Obshchestva Liubitelei Estestvoznaniia, Antropologii, i Etnografii* (Works of MEK at the Ethnographic Department of the Imperial Society of Lovers of Natural Sciences, Anthropology, and Ethnography) 1 (1906): 269–344.

Aristov, G. *Teoriia diatonicheskikh gamm (s tablitsei kvintovykh krugov)* (Diatonic scales theory [with the circle of fifths table]). Kazan, 1871.

Arnold, Karl. *Kratkoe rukovodstvo k izucheniiu pravil kompozitsii* (Short manual for the study of rules of composition). Saint Petersburg, 1841.

Arnold, Yuri. "Garmoniia." In *Nauka o muzyke na osnovanii esteticheskikh i fiziologicheskikh zakonov: chast' 1. Garmoniia* (Science about music on the basis of aesthetic and physiological rules: part 1, harmony). Translated from German by S. S. Iur'ev. Moscow: Greiner & Bauer, 1875.

Bakulina, Elena. "Tonality and Mutability in Rachmaninoff's 'All-Night Vigil,' Movement 12." *Journal of Music Theory* 59, No. 1 (Apr. 2015): 63–97.

Balakirev, Milii Alekseevich. *Sbornik russkikh narodnykh pesen* (Collection of Russian folk songs). 1866. Moscow: Muzgiz, 1957.

Bass, Richard. "Harmony and Key Relationships in Romantic Music." In *A-R Online Music Anthology*. A-R Editions, 2017.

Bazayev, Inessa. "The Expansion of the Concept of Mode in Twentieth-Century Russian Theory." *Music Theory Online* 20, no. 3 (2014).

Beliaev, Viktor. *Ocherki po istorii narodov SSSP. Vypusk 2. Muzykal'naia kul'tura Azerbaidzhana, Armenii i Gruzii* (Essays on the history of peoples of the USSR. Issue 2. Musical culture of Azerbaijan, Armenia, and Georgia). Moscow: Gosudarstvennoe muzykal'noe izdatel'stvo, 1963.

Bellerman, Gottfried. *Der Kontrapunkt* (Counterpoint). Berlin: Julius Springer, 1862.

Bent, Ian. "History to 1900." In *Analysis*, 6–36. New York: W. W. Norton, 1980.

Brown, David. "Mikhail Glinka." In *Russian Masters I*, 1–44. London: Macmillan, 1986.

Bussler, Ludwig. *Elemental Harmony. A Practical and Thorough Course in Fifty-Four Exercises adopted for Public or Private Teaching and Self-instruction.* Translated from second German edition by Theodore Baker. New York: Schirmer, 1906.

———. *Praktische Harmonielehre in vier und fünfzig Aufgaben.* Berlin: C. Habel, 1875.

———. *Prakticheskii uchebnik garmonii v 54 zadachakh.* Saint Petersburg, 1885.

Carpenter, Ellon. "Russian Music Theory: A Conspectus." In *Russian Theoretical Thought in Music*, edited by Gordon D. McQuere, 1–81. Ann Arbor: UMI Research Press, 1983.

Catel, Charles-Simon. *Traité d'harmonie.* Paris: Le Roy, 1802.

Cherubini, Luigi. *Cours de contrepoint et de fugue.* Paris: Maurice Schlesinger, 1835.

Cohn, Richard. "An Introduction to Neo-Riemannian Theory: A Survey and a Historical Perspective." *Journal of Music Theory* 42, no. 2 (1998): 167–80.

Daragan, D. G., ed. *Sovetskaia muzyka, tretii sbornik statei* (Soviet Music, Third Collection of Essays). Moscow: Muzgiz, 1945.

De Calvé, Hess. *Teoriia muzyki, ili Rassuzhdenie o sem iskusstve, zakliuchaiushchee v sebe istoriiu, tsel', deistvie muzyki, general-bas, pravila sochineniia (kompozitsii), opisanie instrumentov, raznye rody muzyki i vse, chto otnositsia k nei, v podrobnosti* (Theory of music, or discussion of this art, including history, goal, effect of music, general bass, compositional rules, description of instruments, different kinds of music and all that is related to it, in detail). 2 vols. Translated from German by R. Gonorsky. Kharkov, 1818.

Dehn, Siegfried. *Theoretisch-praktische Harmonielehre mit angefügten Generalbassbeispielen.* Berlin: Wilhelm Thome, 1840.

D'Indy, Vincent. *Cours de composition musicale.* Paris: A. Durand, 1899–[1950?].

Dmitriadi, Nadezhda. "Stilevye osobennosti russkoi muzyki o Vostoke" (Stylistic features of Russian music about the East). *Voprosy teorii i estetiki muzyki* 13 (1974): 119.

Dolzhansky, Aleksandr. "Aleksandriiskii pentakhord i 'gamma Rimskogo-Korsakova'" (The Alexandrian pentachord and the "Rimsky-Korsakov scale"). In Kiui, *Izbrannye stat'i*, 97–99. Leningrad: Muzyka, 1973.

Drobish, Fedor. *Nachal'noe svedenie prakticheskoi muzyki* (Elementary information of music practice). 1836. 2nd edition. Moscow, 1854.

Ekmalian, Makar. *Patarag*. Leipzig: Breitkopf und Härtel, 1896.

Evseev, Sergei. "Ladogarmonicheskoe stroenie russkikh narodnykh pesen" (Modal-harmonic structure of Russian folk songs). In *Russiaia narodnaia polifoniia* (Russian folk polyphony), 49–79. Moscow: Gosudarstvennoe muzykal'noe izdatel'stvo, 1960.

———. *Rimskii-Korsakov i narodnaia pesnia* (Rimsky-Korsakov and the folk song). Moscow: Muzyka, 1970.

Ewell, Philip. "Harmonic Functionalism in Russian Music Theory: A Primer." *Theoria* 26 (2020): 61–84.

———. "On Rimsky-Korsakov's False (Hexatonic) Progressions Outside the Limits of a Tonality." *Music Theory Spectrum* 42, no. 1 (2020): 122–42.

Fétis, François-Joseph. *La musique mise á la portée de tout le monde* (Music accessible to all). Paris: Alexandre Mesnier, 1830.

———. *Muzyka poniatnaia dlia vsekh, ili kratkoe izlozhenie vsego nuzhnogo, chtob sudit' i govorit' ob iskusstve sem, ne uchivshis' onomu* (Music accessible to all, or a Short description of all that is needed to judge and speak about art for those who have not studied it). Translated by P. Beliakov. Saint Petersburg: 1833.

———. *Traité complet de la théorie et de la pratique de l'harmonie*. Paris: Maurice Schlesinger, 1844.

Findeizen, Nikolai. "50-letie S.-Peterburgskoi konservatorii (1862–1912)" (50th anniversary of the St. Petersburg Conservatory [1862–1912]). *Russkaia muzykal'naia gazeta* 19, no. 51 (1912): 1129.

Förster, Emanuel Alois. *Anleitung zum Generalbass*. Vienna: A. Steiner, 1805.

Frid, Emiliia, ed. *Milii Alekseevich Balakirev: vospominaniia i pis'ma* (Mily Alekseevich Balakirev: memoirs and letters). Leningrad: Gosudarstvennoe muzykal'noe izdatel'stvo, 1962.

———. "Simfonicheskoe tvorchestvo" (Symphonic music). In Frid, *Balakirev*, 169–73.

———. *Balakirev. Issledovaniia i stat'i* (Balakirev. Research and articles). Leningrad: Gosudarstvennoe muzykal'noe izdatel'stvo, 1961.

Frolova-Walker, Marina. "Nikolai Rimksy-Korsakov and His Orient." In *Rimsky-Korsakov and His World*, 145–77. Princeton, NJ: Princeton University Press, 2018.

Fuchs, Johann Leopold. *Novaia metoda, soderzhashchaia glavnyia pravila muzykal'noi kompozitsii i rukovodstvo k prakticheskomu primeneniiu ikh, s kratkim izlozheniem osnovanii dvoinogo kontrapunkta, kanona i fugi* (Neue Lehrmethode der musikalischen Komposition, mit besonderer Rücksicht auf die praktische Anwendung der gegeben

Regeln) (A new method, containing the main rules of musical composition and a guide to their practical application; with a short description of the basics of double counterpoint, canon and fugue). Translated from German by K. Arnol'd. Saint Petersburg: Stellovsky, 1843.

Fuchs, Johann Leopold. *Praktisch Anleitung zur Komposition, sowohl zum Selbstunterricht, wie auch als Hdb. F. Lehrer, nebst einer besondern Anweisung für Komp. Des Russ. Kirchengsg.* (Prakticheskoe rukovodstvo k sochineniiu muzyki, v pol'zu samouchashchikhsia, i v oblegchenie uchitelei s prilozheniem osobennykh pravil dlia sochinitelei russkogo tserkovnogo peniia) (Practical guide to the composition of music, for independent study and for the facilitation of teachers, with a supplement of special rules for the composition of Russian church music). Translated by Modest Rezvyi. St. Petersburg: Karl Kray, 1830.

Gabretsettel, Ivan. *Tablitsy vsekh akkordov, dlia oblegcheniia uchashchikhsia garmonii i sochineniia* (Tables of all chords to aid students of harmony and composition). Saint Petersburg, 1840.

Garden, Edward. *Balakirev. A Critical Study of His Life and Music*. New York: St. Martin's Press, 1969.

———. "Balakirev's Influence on Mussorgsky." In *Mussorgsky: in Memoriam 1881–1981*, edited by Malcolm Hamrick Brown, 11–28. Ann Arbor: UMI Research Press, 1982.

Gebel, Franz. *Rukovodstvo k sochineniiu muzyki ili teoretiko-prakticheskaia general-basovaia shkola* (Music composition manual, or theoretical-practical general bass school). Vol. 1. Translated by P. Artemov. Moscow, 1842.

Ginzburg, Semen, ed. *Rimsky-Korsakov i muzykal'noe obrazovanie. Stat'i i materialy* (Rimsky-Korsakov and music education. Essays and materials). Leningrad: Gosudarstvennoe muzykal'noe izdatel'stvo, 1959.

Grigoriev, S. O. *O melodike Rimskogo-Korsakova* (On Rimsky-Korsakov's melodies). Moscow: Muzgiz, 1961.

Groth, Renate. *Die französische Kompositionslehre des 19. Jahrhunderts*. Wiesbaden: Franz Steiner, 1983.

Harrison, Daniel. *Harmonic Function in Chromatic Music: A Renewed Dualistic Theory and an Account of Its Precedents*. Chicago: University of Chicago Press, 1994.

Hauptmann, Moritz. *Die Lehre von der Harmonik*. Leipzig: Breitkopf und Härtel, 1868.

———. *The Letters of a Leipzig Cantor*. Edited by Alfred Schöne and Ferdinand Hiller. New York: Novello, Ewer and Co., 1892.

———. *Die Natur der Harmonik und der Metrik*. Leipzig: Breitkopf und Härtel, 1853.

Heinichen, Johann David. *Der General-Bass in der Composition, oder: Neue und gründliche Anweisung*. Dresden, 1728.

Helmholtz, Hermann von. *Die Lehre von den Tonempfindungen als physiologische Grundlage für die Theorie der Musik*. Braunschweig: Vieweg, 1863.

Hunke, Joseph [Iosef]. *Rukovodstvo k izucheniiu garmonii, prisposoblennoe k samoizucheniiu* (Manual for the study of harmony, adopted for self-study). Moscow, 1852.

———. *Rukovodstvo k sochineniiu muzyki* (Music composition manual). 3 vols. Saint Petersburg, 1859–1863.

Ippolotov-Ivanov, Mikhail. "Gruzinskaia narodnaia pesnia i ee sovremennoe sostoianie" (Georgian folk song and its contemporary state). *Artist* 45 (1895): 134–46.

Issiyeva, Adalyat. *Representing Russia's Orient*. New York: Oxford University Press, 2020.

*Istoriia russkoi muzyki* (History of Russian music). Vols. 1–10A. Moscow: Muzyka, 1983–97.

Johansen, Iuly. *Dvukh, trekh i chetyrekhgolosnyi prostoi, dvoinoi, troinoi i chetvernoi strogii kontrapunkt* (Two-, three-, and four-voice simple, double, triple, and quadruple strict counterpoint). Translated from German by Nikolaia Kazanli. Moscow, [1904?].

Jorgenson, Dale A. *Moritz Hauptmann of Leipzig*. Queenston, ON: E. Mellen Press, 1986.

———. "A Résumé of Harmonic Dualism." *Music and Letters* 44, no. 1 (1963): 31–42.

Kashkin, Nikolai. *Uchebnik elementarnoi teorii muzyki* (Manual of elementary music theory). Moscow, 1875.

Kazbiriuk, Andrei. *145 sol'fedzhio dlia odnogo golosa* (145 solfège for one voice). Kiev, 1887.

———. *Populiarnoe izlozhenie osnovnykh nachal muzykal'noi teorii* (Popular exposition of the fundamentals of music theory). Kiev, 1885.

———. *Rukovodstvo k prakticheskomu izucheniiu garmonii* (Manual for practical study of harmony). Saint Petersburg, 1883.

Kholopov, Iu., ed. *Muzykal'no-teoreticheskie sistemy* (Music-theoretical systems). Moscow: Kompozitor, 2006.

Khristiansen, Lev. *Ladovaia intonatsionnost' russkoi narodnoi pesni* (Modal intonations of the Russian song). Moscow: Sovetskii kompozitor, 1976.

Khudabash'ian, Karine. *Armianskaia muzyka na puti ot monodii k mnogogolosiiu* (Armenian music on the way from monody to polyphony). Erevan: Izdatel'stvo AN Armianskoi SSR, 1977.

Kirnberger, Johann Philipp. *Die wahren Grundsätze zum Gebrauch der Harmonie*. Berlin: Decker und Hartung, 1773.

Kiui, Tsezar'. *Izbrannye stat'i* (Selected articles). Leningrad: Gosudarstvennoe muzykal'noe izdatel'stvo, 1952.

———. "Sbornik russkikh narodnykh pesen, sostavlennyi M. Balakirevym" (Collection of Russian folk songs, compiled by M. Balakirev). 1860. In Kiui, *Izbrannye stat'i*, 71–83.

Koch, Heinrich Christoph. *Versuch einer Anleitung zur Composition*. Leipzig: Böhme, 1782–1793.

Komendantov, Ivan. *Nachal'noe osnovanie o garmonii, ili Tochnoi poriadok proiskhozhdeniia vsekh postepenno dvadtsati dvukh glasov, prinadlezhashchikh dlia odnoi tol'ko oktavy* (Elementary basis of harmony, or the exact order of the origin of all consequent twenty-two voices belonging to one octave). Moscow, 1901.

Korabel'nikova, Liudmila. "Muzykal'noe obrazovanie" (Musical education). In *Istoriia russkoi muzyki*, Vol. 8, 408–43. Moscow: Muzyka, 1994.

———. "Stroitel' muzykal'noi Moskvy" (The builder of musical Moscow). *Sovetskaia muzyka* (June 1960).

Koreshchenko, Arseny. "Nabliudenie nad vostochnoi muzykoi, preimushchestvenno kavkazskoi" (Observation on Eastern music, predominantly Caucasian). *EO* 1 (1898): 1–22.

Kremlev, Iurii. "Fortpiannaia muzyka" (Piano music). In Frid, *Balakirev*, 230–70.

Krumhansl, Carol L. *Cognitive Foundations of Musical Pitch*. New York: Oxford University Press, 1990.

Kushnarev, Khristofor. *Voprosy istorii i teorii Armianskoi monodicheskoi muzyki* (Issues of history and theory of Armenian monodic music). Leningrad: Gosudarstvennoe muzykal'noe izdatel'stvo, 1958.

Larosh, German. "Iz moikh vospominanii. Chaikovskii v konservatorii" (From my memoirs. Tchaikovsky at the conservatory). In Tigranov, *Leningradskaia konservatoriia v vospominaniiakh*, vol. 1.

Lemke, Arno. "Weber, Jacob Gottfried." In *Musik in Geschichte und Gegenwart*, vol. 14, col. 335.

Lemokh, Vikentii. *Obshchee rukovodstvo k izucheniiu muzyki* (General manual for the study of music). Moscow, 1848.

Lerdahl, Fred, and Ray Jackendoff. *A Generative Theory of Tonal Music*. Cambridge: MIT Press, 1983.

Lerdahl, Fred. "Tonal Pitch Space." *Music Perception* 5, no. 3 (1988): 315–49.

Lerdahl, Fred. *Tonal Pitch Space*. New York: Oxford University Press, 2001.

Lewin, David. *Generalized Musical Intervals and Transformations*. New Haven: Yale University Press, 1987.

Liapunov, Sergei, and Anastasiia Liapunova. "Molodye gody Balakireva" (Balakirev's youth). In Frid, *Milii Alekseevich Balakirev*, 7–71.

Lobe, Johann Christian. *Katechismus der Musik*. Leipzig: J. J. Weber, 1851.

———. *Lehrbuch der musikalischen Komposition*. 4 vols. Leipzig: Breitkopf und Härtel, 1850–1867.

Longuet-Higgins, H. Christopher, and Edward R. Lisle. "Modelling Musical Cognition." *Contemporary Music Review* 3, no. 1 (1989), 15–27.

———. "Two Letters to a Musical Friend." *The Music Review* 23 (1962): 244–80.

Manfredini, Vincenzo. *Regole armoniche, o sieno Precetti ragionati*. Venice, 1775.

———. *Pravila garmonicheskie i melodicheskie dlia obucheniia vsei muzyki* (Harmonic and melodic rules for teaching all music). Translated by Stepan Degtiarev. Saint Petersburg, 1805.

Marx, Adolf Bernhard. *Allgemeine Musiklehre*. Leipzig: Breitkopf und Härtel, 1839.

———. *Die Lehre von der musikalischen Komposition*. 4 vols. Leipzig: Breitkopf und Härtel, 1837–1863.

Mattheson, Johann. *Kleine General-Bass-Schule*. Hamburg: Johann Christoph Kissner, 1735.

McCune, Mark. "Moritz Hauptmann: *Ein Haupt Mann* in Nineteenth Century Music Theory." *Indiana Theory Review* 7, no. 2 (1986): 1–28.

Messiaen, Olivier. *Technique de mon langage musical*. Paris: A. Leduc, 1944.

Meyer, Leonard B. *Explaining Music: Essays and Explorations*. Chicago: University of Chicago Press, 1973.

Mikhailova, S. M. "Razvitie orientalistiki v Kazanskom universitete," in *Kazan, Moscow, St. Petersburg: Multiple Faces of the Russian Empire*, ed. Catherine Evtuhov, Boris Gasparov, Alexander Ospovat, and Mark von Hagen, 275–301 (Moscow: O. G. I., 1997).

Momigny, Jérome Joseph. *Cours complet d'harmonie et de composition*. 3 vols. Paris, 1821.

———. *La seule vraie théorie de la musique*. Paris, 1803–06.

Morrison, Simon. "The Semiotics of Symmetry, or Rimsky-Korsakov's Operatic History Lesson." *Cambridge Opera Journal* 13, no. 3 (2001): 261–93.

*Musik in Geschichte und Gegenwart*. 16 vols. Basel: Bärenreiter Kassel, 1979.

*Musikverlag M. P. Belaieff (der). Eine Stiftung wird Musikgeschichte 1885–1985*. Frankfurt: M. P. Belaieff Musikverlag, 1985.

*Muzykal'naia entsiklopediia* (Music encyclopedia). 6 vols. Moscow: Sovetskaia entsiklopediia, 1973–82.

Nest'ev, Izrail'. "Islamei M. Balakireva" (Balakirev's Islamei). *Sovetskaia muzyka* 3 (1938): 51–67.

Neznakomets. "Letopis' moskovskikh kontsertov" (Chronicle of Moscow concerts). *Antrakt* 8 (1868): 3.

Odoevsky, Vladimir. *Muzykal'naia gramota, ili osnovaniia muzyki dlia nemuzykantov* (Musical grammar, or musical foundations for nonmusicians). Moscow, 1868.

Olenin, Aleksandr. "Moi vospominaniia o M. A. Balakireve" (My memoirs about M. A. Balakirev). In Frid, *Milii Alekseevich Balakirev*.

Orlova, Aleksandra, and Vladimir Rimsky-Korsakov, eds. *Stranitsy zhizni N. A. Rimskogo-Korsakova. Letopis' zhizni i tvorchestva* (Life's pages of N. A. Rimsky-Korsakov. Chronicle of life and works). Issue 2, 1876–1893. Leningrad: Muzyka, 1971.

Osmanova, Z. M. "Fenomen orientalizma v russkoi muzykal'noi kul'ture vtoroi poloviny XIX – nachala XX vv" (Phenomenon of orientalism in Russian musical culture of the second half of the XIX – beginning of XX Century). *Sovremennye nauchnye issledovaniia i innovatsii* (Contemporary scholarly research and innovations) 7 (2016).

*Otchet Russkogo muzykal'nogo obshchestva za 1862–1863 god* (Report of the Russian Musical Society for the 1862–1863 year). Saint Petersburg, 1864.

Öttingen, Arthur Joachim von. *Harmoniesystem in dualer Entwicklung: Studien zur Theorie der Musik*. Dorpat: W. Gläser, 1866.

Presniakova, Inga Aleksandrovna. *Stanovlenie russkoiazychnoi muzykal'no-teoreticheskoi terminologii v otechestvennykh muzykal'nykh rukovodstvakh kontsa XVIII – pervoi poloviny XIX vv.: 1773–1862* (Establishment of the Russian language music-theoretical terminology in domestic musical manuals of the late eighteenth and first half of the nineteenth centuries). Master's thesis, Kazanskaia Gosudarstvennaia konservatoriia, 2004.

Pronoza, A. V. "Moguchaia kuchka" i orientalism Miliia Alekseevicha Balakireva" (The "Mighty Five" and the Orientalism of Mily Alekseevich Balakirev). *Kul'tura narodov Prichernomor'ia* (Culture of Prichenomorye Peoples) 174, no. 1 (2009): 170–73.

Protopopov, Vladimir. "Muzykal'nyi iazyk 'Zolotogo petushka'" (Musical language of "Golden Cockerel"). In *Izbrannye issledovaniia i stat'i*, 4–18. Moscow: Sovetskii kompozitor, 1983.

Protopopov, Vladimir, ed. Rimsky-Korsakov, N. A. *Polnoe sobranie sochinenii. Literaturnye proizvedeniia i perepiska* (Complete edition of works. Literary works and correspondence). Vol. 4. Moscow: Gosudarstvennoe muzykal'noe izdatel'stvo, 1960.

Puzei, Nikolai. "Zametki o garmonii N. A. Rimskogo-Korsakova" (Notes on Rimsky-Korsakov's harmony). In *Ural'skaia Gosudarstvennaia*

*Konservatoriia im. M. P. Musorgskogo. Nauchno-metodicheskie zapiski* (Ural Musorgsky State Conservatory. Scholarly-methodological notes), vol. 2, 137–83. Sverdlovsk: Ural'skaia Gosudarstvennaia Konservatoriia im. M. P. Musorgskogo, 1959.

Puzyrevsky, A. I., and L. A. Sakketti, eds. *Imperatorskoe RMO. Sankt-Peterburgskoe otdelenie. Ocherk piatidesiatiletiia deiatel'nosti S.-Peterburgskoi konservatorii. Sostavili professora S.-Peterburgskoi konservatorii A. I. Puzyrevskii i L. A. Sakketti.* (Imperial RMS. St. Petersburg division. Essays on the 50th anniversary of the St. Petersburg Conservatory. Compiled by St. Petersburg Conservatory Professors A. I. Puzyrevsky and L. A. Sakketti). Saint Petersburg: Tipografiia Glazunova, 1912.

Reicha, Antoine. *Cours de composition musicale, ou Traité complet et raisonné d'harmonie pratique*. Paris: Gambaro, [1818?].

———. *Traité de haute composition musicale*. 2 vols. Paris: Zetter, 1824–1826.

Richter, Ernst Friedrich. *Die Grundzüge der musikalischen Formen und ihre Analyse*. Leipzig: Georg Wigand, 1852.

———. *Lehrbuch der Harmonie*. Leipzig: Breitkopf und Härtel, 1853.

Ridenour, Robert. *Nationalism, Modernism, and Personal Rivalry in Nineteenth-Century Russian Music*. Ann Arbor: UMI Research Press, 1981.

Riemann, Hugo. "Das Problem des harmonischen Dualismus: ein Beitrag zur Ästhetik der Musik." *Neue Zeitschrift für Musik* 72, no. 1/4 (1905): 3–5, 23–26, 43–46, 67–70.

———. "Die Natur der Harmonik." Edited by Paul Graf Waldersee. *Sammlung musikalischer Vorträge: Ein Almanach für die musikalische Welt* 4, no. 40 (1882): 157–90.

———. *Handbuch der Harmonielehre*. Leipzig, 1887.

———. *Systematische Modulationslehre als Grundlage der musikalischen Formenlehre*. Hamburg: J. F. Richter, 1887.

Riley, Matthew. "The 'Harmonic Major' Mode in Nineteenth-Century Theory and Practice." *Music Analysis* 23, no. 1 (2004): 1–26.

Rimsky-Korsakov, Andrei. *N. A. Rimskii-Korsakov. Zhizn' i tvorchestvo v 5 vypuskakh* (N. A. Rimsky-Korsakov. Life and works in 5 issues). Vol. 3. Moscow: Muzgiz, 1962.

Rimsky-Korsakov, N. A. *My Musical Life* (Letopis' moei muzykal'noi zhizni). 1909. Translated from the fifth Russian edition by Judah A. Joffe. New York: Alfred A. Knopf, 1947.

———. *Prakticheskii uchebnik garmonii* (*PUG*) (Practical manual of harmony). Saint Petersburg: Biutner, 1886. Reprinted in his *Polnoe sobranie sochinenii. Literaturnye proizvedeniia i perepiska* (PSS/LPP) [Complete Collected Works. Literary Works and Correspondence], vol. 4, 240–388.

Rimsky-Korsakov, N. A. *Uchebnik garmonii* (Manual of harmony). Lithograph edition. 2 vols. Saint Petersburg, 1884–1885. Reprinted in his *PSS/LPP*, vol. 4, 5–231.

Rubets, Aleksandr. *Kratkaia muzykal'naia grammatika* (Concise musical grammar). Saint Petersburg, 1871.

Saslaw, Janna K. "Gottfried Weber and the Concept of *Mehrdeutigkeit*." PhD diss., Columbia University, 1992. ProQuest document ID 303967575.

Savard, Marie-Gabriel-Augustin. *Cours complet d'harmonie théorique et pratique*. 2 vols. Paris: Maho, 1853.

Schenker, Heinrich. *Neue musikalische Theorien und Phantasien*. Vols. 1 and 3. Stuttgart: Cotta, 1906; Vienna: Universal Edition, 1935.

Schoenberg, Arnold. *Harmonielehre*. Vienna: Universal Edition, 1911.

———. *Structural Functions of Harmony*. New York: W. W. Norton, 1954.

Seaman, Gerald. *History of Russian Music*. Oxford: Basil Blackwell, 1967.

Sechter, Simon. *Die Grundsätze der musikalischen Komposition*, 3 vols. Leipzig: Breitkopf und Härtel, 1853–1854.

Serov, Aleksandr. *Izbrannye stat'I* (Selected essays). 2 vols. Edited by Georgii Khubov. Moscow: Gosudarstvennoe muzykal'noe izdatel'stvo, 1957.

Shestakova, Liudmila. "Iz moikh vecherov" (From my musical evenings). *Russkaia muzykal'naia gazeta* 41 (1910): 123.

Shidlovsky, Nicholas. "Sources of Russian Chant Theory." In *Russian Theoretical Thought in Music*. Edited by Gordon D. McQuere. Ann Arbor, Michigan: UMI Research Press, 1983.

Sietz, Reinhold. "Bussler, Ludwig." *Die Musik in Geschichte und Gegenwart*. Vol. 15, supplements A–D, cols. 1213–14. Basel: Bärenreiter Kassel, 1973.

Simms, Bryan. "Choron, Fétis, and the Theory of Tonality." *Journal of Music Theory* 19 (1975): 112–38.

Skrebkov, Sergei S., and Marina S. Skrebkova. *Tonal'nye struktury v muzyke N. A. Rimskogo-Korsakova* (Tonal structure in music of N. A. Rimsky-Korsakov). Moscow: Gosudarstvennyi muzykal'no-pedagogicheskii institute im. Gnesinykh, 1986.

Starostina, T. A. "Ladovaia sistematika russkoi narodnoi pesni" (Modal systems of Russian folk song). In *Garmoniia. Problemy nauki i metodiki. Sbornik statei* (Harmony. Issues of science and method. Collection of essays). Vol. 1, 85–105. Rostov-na-Donu, 2002.

Stasov, Vladimir. *Sobranie sochinenii* (Collected works). 3 vols. Saint Petersburg, 1894.

Steinpress, Boris. "Der Petersburger Musiker Leopold Fuchs." Translated from Russian by Ernst Stöckl. *Musikforschung* 15 (1962): 39–44.

Struiskii, Dmitrii. "Bibliografiia. Russkie knigi" (Bibliography. Russian books). *Literaturnaia gazeta*, October 29, 1830, 230.

Swoboda, August. *Harmonielehre*. 2 vols. Vienna, 1828.

Taruskin, Richard. "The Case for Rimsky-Korsakov." In *On Russian Music*, 166–78.

———. "Catching up with Rimsky-Korsakov." *Music Theory Spectrum* 33, no. 2 (2011): 169–85.

———. "Chernomor to Kashchei: Harmonic Sorcery; Or, Stravinsky's 'Angle'." *Journal of the American Musicological Society* 38, no. 1 (1985): 72–142.

———. "'Entoiling the Falconet': Russian Musical Orientalism in Context." *Cambridge Opera Journal* 4, no. 3 (1992): 253–80.

———. "How the Acorn Took Root: A Tale of Russia." *Nineteenth-Century Music* 6, no. 3 (1983): 189–212.

———. "Non-Nationalists, and Other Nationalists." *Russian Music at Home and Abroad: New Essays*, 33–51.

———. *On Russian Music*. Berkeley: University of California Press, 2009.

———. "Rimskii-Korsakov dogoniaet" (Rimsky-Korsakov catches up). *God za godom. Rimskii-Korsakov – 175. Materialy mezhdunarodnoi nauchnoi konferentsii 18–21 marta 2019 g* (Year after year: Rimsky-Korsakov – 175, March 18–21, 2019, conference proceedings), 3–21. Saint Petersburg: Sankt Peterburgskii Gosudarstvennyi Muzei Muzykalnogo i Teatralnogo Iskusstva, 2019.

———. *Russian Music at Home and Abroad: New Essays*. Berkeley: University of California Press, 2016.

Tchaikovsky, Ippolit Ilyich, ed. *Dnevniki P. I. Chaikovskogo* (P. I. Tchaikovsky's diaries). Moscow: Muzykal'nyi sktor, 1923.

Tchaikovsky, Modest I. *Zhizn' P. I. Chaikovskogo* (Life of P. I Tchaikovsky). Vol. 1. Moscow: Jurgenson, 1902.

Tchaikovksy, P. I. "Beseda s Chaikovskim v noiabre 1892 g. v Peterburge" (Conversation with Tchaikovsky in November 1892 in St. Petersburg). 1892. In *Muzykal'no-kriticheskie statii*, 317–23.

———. *Kratkii uchebnik garmonii, prisposoblennyi k chteniiu dukhovno-muzykal'nykh sochinenii v Rossii* (Concise manual of harmony, adopted for reading spiritual musical compositions in Russia). Reprinted in his *Polnoe sobranie sochinenii. Literaturnye proizvedeniia i perepiska* (PSS/LPP) [Complete Collected Works. Literary Works and Correspondence], vol. 3-A, 165–225.

———. *Muzykal'no-kriticheskie statii* (Music criticism essays). Edited by Shcherbakova, A. A. Leningrad: Muzyka, 1986.

———. *Perepiska s N. F. fon Mek* (Correspondence with N. F. von Meck). Vol. 1. Leningrad: Akademiia, 1934.

———. "Po povodu "Serbskoi Fantazii" g. Rimskogo-Korsakova" (About the "Serbian Fantasy" of Mr. Rimsky-Korsakov). 1868. In *Muzykal'no-kriticheskie stat'i*, 25–27.

Tchaikovksy, P. I. *Rukovodstvo k prakticheskomu izucheniiu garmonii* (Manual for practical study of harmony). Reprinted in his *PSS/LPP*, vol. 3-A, 1–162.

———. "Zametki na poliakh uchebnika Rimskogo-Korsakova." (Notes on margins of Rimsky-Korsakov's manual). In *PSS/LPP*, vol. 3-A, 226–49.

Tigranov, G. G., ed. *Leningradskaia konservatoriia v vospominaniiakh*. 2 vol. Leningrad: Muzyka, 1987–88.

Tiulin, Yuri N. "Ob istoricheskom znachenii uchebnika garmonii N. A. Rimskogo-Korsakova" (On the historical significance of the harmony manual by N. A. Rimsky-Korsakov). In Ginzburg, *Rimsky-Korsakov*, 81–93.

Tiut'manov, I. A. "Gamma ton-poluton kak naibolee kharakternyi tip umen'shennogo lada, primeniaemogo v tvorchestve N. A. Rimskogo-Korskova" (Octatonic scale as the most characteristic type of diminished mode used in Rimsky-Korsakov's music). In *Saratovskaia Gosudarstvennaia konservatoriia im. Sobinova. Nauchno-metodicheskie zapiski. Sbornik* (Saratov Sobinov State Conservatory. Scholarly-methodological notes. Collection), 109–55. Vol. 3. Saratov: Tipografiia Saratovskogo Universiteta, 1959.

———. "Nekotorye osobennosti lado-garmonicheskogo stilia N. A. Rimskogo-Korsakova" (Select features of Rimsky-Korsakov's modal-harmonic style). In *Saratovskaia konservatoriia im. Sobinova. Nauchno-metodicheskie zapiski* (Saratov Sobinov State Conservatory. Scholarly-methodological notes), 39–64. Saratov: Saratovskii universitet, 1957.

Trambitskii, Viktor N. "Plagal'nost' i rodstvennye ei sviazi v russkoi pesennoi garmonii" (Plagal style and related issues in Russian song harmonies). In *Voprosy muzykoznaniia* (Issues in musicology). Vol. 2. Moscow: Gosudarstvennoe muzykal'noe izdatel'stvo, 1955.

Tsukkerman, Viktor. "Nekotorye voprosy garmonii. Starinnye lady. Pobochnaia diatonika" (Issues in harmony. Older modes. Secondary diatonic). *Muzykal'no-teoreticheskie ocherki i etiudy* (Musical-theoretical essays and etudes). Vol. 2. Moscow: Sovetskii Kompozitor, 1975.

———. "O siuzhete i muzykal'nom iazyke opery-byliny Rimskogo-Korsakova 'Sadko'" (On the plot and musical language of Rimsky-Korsakov's epic opera "Sadko"). In *Muzykal'no-teoreticheskie ocherki i etiudy*, 441–504. Moscow: Sovetskii Kompozitor, 1970.

———. "Rimskii-Korsakov i narodnaia pesnia" (Rimsky-Korsakov and folk song). In *Muzykal'no-teoreticheskie ocherki i etiudy*, 311–50.

Ulybyshev, Alexander. Review of *Practical Guide to the Composition of Music*, by Johann Leopold Fuchs. *Severnaia pchela*, October 18, 1830.

Vakhromeev, V. A. *Ladovaia struktura russkikh narodnykh pesen i ee izuchenie v kurse elementarnoi teorii muzyki* (Modal structure of Russian folk songs and its study in the course of elementary music theory). Moscow: Muzyka, 1968.

Villoing, Vasily. *Prakticheskoe rukovodstvo k izucheniiu elementarnoi teorii muzyki.* (Practical manual for the study of elementary music theory). Nizhnii Novgorod, 1878.

Vincent, John. *The Diatonic Modes in Modern Music.* Berkeley: University of California Press, 1951.

Wason, Robert W. *Viennese Harmonic Theory from Albrechtsberger to Schenker and Schoenberg.* Ann Arbor: UMI Research Press, 1985.

Weber Gottfried. *Versuch einer geordneten Theorie der Tonsetzkunst zum Selbstunterricht, mit Anmerkungen für Gelehrtere.* Mainz: B. Schott, 1817–1821, 1824, 1830–1832.

Werts, Daniel. "A Theory of Scale References." Ph.D diss., Princeton University, 1983. ProQuest document ID 303177824.

Yastrebtsev, Vasilii. *Reminiscences of Rimsky-Korsakov.* Edited and translated by Florence Jonas. New York: Columbia University Press, 1985.

Yavorsky, Boris. *Stroenie muzykal'noi rechi* (Structure of musical language). Moscow, 1908.

Zaitseva, T. A., ed. *M. A. Balakirev: Lichnost'. Traditsii. Sovremenniki: sbornik statej i materialov* (M. A. Balakirev: Personality. Traditions. Contemporaries: Collection of articles and materials). Sankt Peterburg: Kompozitor, 2004.

Zorina, A. P. "Voprosy muzykal'noi pedagogiki v perepiske N. A. Rimskogo-Korsakova s S. N. Kruglikovym" (Issues of musical pedagogy in correspondence of N. A. Rimsky-Korsakov and S. N. Kruglikov). In Ginzburg, *Rimsky-Korsakov*, 71–80.

# Index

## A

Abraham, Gerald, 131
*Allgemeine Musiklehre* (Marx), 63, 120
*Antar* (Rimsky-Korsakov), 5, 44
Arnold, Karl, 122
Arnold, Yuri, *The Science of Music*, 123
    *Short Guide to the Study of the Rules of Composition*, 122
Azanchevsky, Mikhail, 62

## B

Balakirev, 4–8, 125, 127, 132, 143, 145–168, 170
    authentic cadences, use of, 157–158
    Caucasian music features, 160–161
    dual mode, use of, 161–164
    harmonic mutability, 149–155
    influence of folk music, 166
    influence of Russian folk music, 148–149, 156
    life-long study and promotion of Glinka's music, 147–148
    musical language, 158
    passion for Caucasian music, 158–159
    philosophy, 146–147
    tendency toward domination, 147
Beliaev, M. P., 7
Beliaev's circle, 7–9
Beliaev, Viktor, 160
Bellerman, Gottfried, 131
Berliner Musikschule, 59
Bülow, Hans von, 65
Bussler, Ludwig, 63–64, 99, 120
    difference between Rimsky-Korsakov and, 96
    harmony manual, 95–96
    idea of modulation, 96–97
    *Praktische Harmonielehre in vier und fünfzig Aufgaben*, 63
    relationship of keys, 96

## C

*Capriccio Espagnol* (Rimsky-Korsakov), 6
Catel, Charles-Simon, x

Cherubini, Luigi, 131
Cuï, Cesar (Kiui, Tsezar'), 149

## D

Davydov, Karl, 62
De Calvé, *The Theory of Music*, 121
deceptive cadences, 21, 24, 34–35
Dehn, Siegfried, x, 60–61, 63–64, 85–90, 94–95, 100–103, 108–110, 112–113, 166, 169
  circle-of-fifths, 88
  common triads, 85, 87
  concept of first-degree keys, 101
  minor-major key system, 85, 88–90, 103
  relationships between keys, 85–90, 101
  *Theoretisch-praktische Harmonielehre mit angefügten Generalbassbeispielen*, 85
*Die Lehre von der musikalischen Komposition* (Marx), 78, 120
*Die Lehre von der musikalischen Komposition, praktisch-theoretisch* (Marx), 78
*Die Musik in Geschichte und Gegenwart*, x
*Die Natur der Harmonik und der Metrik* (Hauptmann), 65, 121
Drobish, Fedor, *Elementary Information on Practical Music*, 122

## E

Ekmalian, Makar, 163–164
*Elementary Information on Practical Music* (Drobish), 122
*Elementary Music Theory Manual* (Kashkin), 123
*Elementary Principles of Harmony* (Komendantov), 121
Elena Pavlovna, Duchess, 60

## F

*Fantasia on Serbian Themes* (Rimsky-Korsakov), 5
Fétis, François-Joseph, x–xi
  *Music Accessible to All*, 120
  *Traité complet de la theorie et de la pratique de l'harmonie*, 120
The Five (Moguchaia kuchka), 4, 7, 132, 141, 145, 147, 149, 158, 167
Förster, Emanuel, x
Free Music School, 9, 145
Fuch, *Practical Guide to the Composition of Music*, 121–122

## G

Gabretsettel, Ivan, 122
Gebel, *Guide to the Composition of Music*, 122

*General Guide to the Study of Music* (Lemokh), 122
German music theory
  theorists, 65–97
  tonal models, 99–105
*Geschichte der Musiktheorie im IX.–XIX* (Riemann), xi
Glazunov, 7
*Guide to the Composition of Music* (Gebel), 122
*Guide to the Practical Study of Harmony* (Kazbiriuk), 123
*Guide to the Study of Harmony, Adapted for Independent Study* (Hunke), 122

## H

*Harmonic and Melodic Rules for the Teaching of All Music* (Manfredini), 120
harmonic dualism, ix
harmonic major scale, ix, xi
harmonic system, 4–5
  arrangement of chords and triads, 47
  degrees of proximity, 51
  essential elements, 54
  harmonic ("artificial") source major scale, 47
  major and minor keys, 45–46, 48
  octatonic scale, 52
  principal concepts, 43
  relative keys, 48, 53
  symmetry, 49, 52–53
  tonal relationships, 44, 48, 53
  whole-tone scale, 52
harmonic theory, x
*Harmoniesystem in dualer Entwicklung* (Öttingen), 121
Hauptmann, Moritz, ix–x, 62–64, 100, 115, 127, 169–170
  commonality of functions, 71
  concept of *Moll-Durtonart*, (minor-major key system), 65, 67–73, 103, 127
  *Die Natur der Harmonik und der Metrik*, 65, 121
  first degree keys, 108, 110
  harmonic theory, 66, 70
  idea of modulation, 67, 69–72
  tonal system, 67–69, 102
  triads, 67, 70
Hegel's philosophical system, 66
Heinichen, Johann, x
Helmholtz, *Lehre von der Tonempfindungen*, 121, 123
Hunke, *A Guide to the Study of Harmony, Adapted for Independent Study*, 122

## I

Imperial Court Chapel, 8–9, 11, 121, 125
Ivanitsky, G. V., 11

## J

Jackendoff, Ray, xi
Joachim, Joseph, 65
Johansen, Iuly, 60, 62, 127

## K

*Kashchei the Immortal* (Rimsky-Korsakov), 44
Kashkin, *Elementary Music Theory Manual*, 120, 123
*Katechismus der Compositionslehre* (Lobe), 90
*Katechismus der Musik* (Lobe), 63, 90
Kazbiriuk, *Guide to the Practical Study of Harmony*, 123
*Khovanshchina* (Musorgsky), 44
Kirnberger, Johann, x, 121
Komendantov, *Elementary Principles of Harmony*, 121
Kruglikov, Semen, 8
Krumhansl, Carol, xi
Kuchka, Moguchaya (The Five), 4–5, 44
*kuchkists'* philosophy, 8

## L

*Lehrbuch der Harmonie* (Richter), 63, 92, 94, 120
*Lehrbuch der musikalischen Composition* (Lobe), 90
*Lehre von der Tonempfindungen* (Helmholtz), 121
Leipzig Conservatory, 59, 61–62, 65
Lemokh, Vikentii, *General Guide to the Study of Music*, 122
Lerdahl, Fred, xi
Lewin, David, xi
Liadov, Anatoly, 7, 62–63, 132
    impact of *Practical Manual*, 125–126
    methods and system of teaching harmony, 127
    theoretical views, 125–126
    tonal plan, 128
Lisle, Edward, xi
Lobe, Johann Christian, x, 64, 100, 120
    closeness of scales, 91
    horizontal and vertical tonal symmetry, 115–116
    *Katechismus der Compositionslehre*, 90

*Katechismus der Musik*, 63, 90
*Lehrbuch der musikalischen Composition*, 90
minor-major key system, 90
relationship between keys, 90–91
second-degree-related keys, 91–92
tonal systems, 103–105

## M

Manfredini, *Harmonic and Melodic Rules for the Teaching of All Music*, 120
*Manual of Harmony* (Rimsky-Korsakov), 6
Marx, Adolf Bernhard, x, 62–64, 88–92, 100–105, 109, 112–113, 120, 169
*Allgemeine Musiklehre*, 63, 120
common tones, 84
*Die Lehre von der musikalischen Komposition*, 78, 120
*Die Lehre von der musikalischen Komposition, praktisch-theoretisch*, 78
horizontal and vertical tonic lines, 115–116
minor-major key system, 79–85
relationship between keys, 79–85
tonal systems, 83–84, 103–105
Mattheson, Johann, x
*May Night* (Rimsky-Korsakov), 6
Meyer, Darius, xi
modulation, 16, 21, 35, 67. *See also* theory of key relationships and modulations
deceptive and enharmonic progressions, 21, 24, 33–35
between first-degree keys, 23–25
fourths or fifths in, 41
kinship of keys as means, 21
second-degree, 28
tonalities and, 22
modulatory plan, 37–42, 50
alternating between major and minor, 39
common keys, 39
major to major, 38, 49
major to minor, 38
minor to major, 38
minor to minor, 38, 49
to remote keys, 39, 42
use of relative keys, 41
Momigny, Jérôme-Joseph de, x
Moscow Conservatory, 122
*Music Accessible to All* (Fétis), 120

*Musical Grammar, or the Elements of Music for Amateurs* (Odoevsky), 123
Musorgsky, Modest, 4–5, 9
  *Khovanshchina*, 44

## N

*Nachal'noe osnovanie* ("elementary principles"), 119
*Nachal'noe svedenie* ("elementary information"), 119
*New Grove Dictionary of Music and Musicians*, x
New Russian School, 4, 6, 143, 167–168

## O

Odoevsky, *Musical Grammar, or the Elements of Music for Amateurs*, 123
Öttingen, Arthur von, x, 123
  *Harmoniesystem in dualer Entwicklung*, 121
*Overture on Russian Themes* (Rimsky-Korsakov), 5

## P

*Practical Guide to the Composition of Music* (Fuch), 121
*Practical Guide to the Study of Elementary Music Theory* (Villoing), 123
*Practical Manual of Harmony*, ix–x, xii, 6, 11, 43, 52, 59, 95, 116, 123, 125, 127, 168–169
  copy of, 11
  motivation for writing, 15–16
  versions and editions, 11, 13
*Prakticheskii uchebnik garmonii*, xii
*Praktische Harmonielehre in vier und fünfzig Aufgaben* (Bussler), 63
*Pskovitianka* (*The Maid of Pskov*), 5
Purgold, Nadezhda, 60, 62

## R

Reicha, Antoine, x
  *Traité complet de la haute composition musicale*, 120
Richter, Ernst, x, 61–64, 99, 120
  approach to modulation, 92–94
  common tones for modulation, 93
  key relationships, 93
  *Lehrbuch der Harmonie*, 63, 92, 94, 120
  minor-major key system, 93–94
  tonal relationships, 94
Riemann, Hugo, x
  *Geschichte der Musiktheorie im IX.–XIX.*, xi

Rimsky-Korsakov, 65
- *Antar*, 5, 44
- approach to tonal space, 108, 113, 166–167
- basic chords, 18
- basic scales, 17–18
- *Capriccio Espagnol* (*Ispanskoe kaprichio*), 6
- choice of keys, 128
- commonality of functions, 110
- common tones, 139
- criterion of relationship, 139
- education, musical, 5
- *Fantasia on Serbian Themes* (*Fantaziia na serbskie temy*), 5
- harmonic implications of dual mode, 161–163
- harmonic thinking, 4–5, 59, 135–136, 164–167, 170. *See also* harmonic system
- horizontal and vertical tonic lines, 112–114
- idea of modulation, 108, 141, 165
- influence of Balakirev. *See* Balakirev
- *Kashchei the Immortal* (*Kashchei bessmertnyi*), 44
- main scales, 137
- *Manual of Harmony* (*Uchgebnik garmonii*), 6
- *May Night* (*Maiskaia noch'*), 6
- melody, 161
- membership of Balakirev's circle, 7
- Moscow Conservatory professorship, 5
- musical education, 5
- notion of common triads, 109
- *Overture on Russian Themes* (*Uvertiura na russkie temy*), 5
- parallel minor or major keys, 110–112
- perspective on tonal relationships, ix–x
- piano technique, 4–5
- *Practical Manual of Harmony* (*Prakticheskii uchebnik garmonii*), ix–x, xii, 6, 11, 43, 52, 59, 95, 116, 123, 125, 127, 168–169
  - copy of, 11
  - motivation for writing, 15–16
  - versions and editions, 11, 13
- pre-conservatory compositions, 127
- principle of interaction of functions, 113
- *Pskovitianka* (*The Maid of Pskov*), 5
- relationship with Tchaikovsky. *See* Tchaikovsky, P. I.
- role as a leading pedagogue, ix
- Russian folk song influence, 148–149

*Sadko*, 5
six keys, 108, 110–111
*The Snow Maiden* (*Snegurochka*), 6
symphonies, 5–6
theory of relationship of keys. *See* theory of key relationships and modulations
training by Balakirev, 6–7
understandings of first-degree keys, 108–110, 166
Rubinstein, Anton, 60–61, 132, 143, 145
*Rukovodstvo*, 119
Russian folk music, 148–149, 156, 170
Russian Musical Society (RMS), 59, 145–146
Russian music theory, 3
German-to-Russian translations, 120
theoretical works, 119–123

## S

*Sadko* (Rimsky-Korsakov), 5
Savard, Marie Gabriel, x
scales of harmonic system, 17–19
Schenker, Heinrich, xi
Schoenberg, Arnold, xi
*The Science of Music* (Arnold), 123
Sechter, Simon, x
Shestakova, Liudmila, 147
*Short Guide to the Study of the Rules of Composition* (Arnold), 122
*The Snow Maiden* (Rimsky-Korsakov), 6
*Sovremennye Izvestiia*, 8
St. Petersburg Conservatory, 3, 5, 8–9, 15, 59–61, 63, 122–123, 127, 143, 146, 168
directors, 60–63
St. Petersburg Conservatory Library, 61–63
St. Petersburg's Free Music School, 145
Stasov, Vladimir, 6–7, 143, 147
Stern'sches Konservatorium (Stern Conservatory), 62
Sullivan, Arthur, 65
Swoboda, August, x

## T

Tchaikovsky, P. I., 129–144, 170
comments on Rimsky-Korsakov's Third Symphony, 132–134
conception of tonal movement, 141

definition of harmony, 136
*Guide to the Practical Study of Harmony (Rukovodstvo k praktich-eskomu izucheniiu garmonii*, 131, 133
idea of modulation, 140–141
internal relationship of triads, 137
key relationships, 140–141
major and minor triads, 138
margin notes on Rimsky-Korsakov's harmony treatise manuscript, 142
modulatory chords, 137, 139–140
notion of three degrees of proximity for keys, 141
position in Russian musical culture, 143
public's perception of him, 143
relationship between triads, 138–139
treatment of harmony, 135–136, 142
*Theoretisch-praktische Harmonielehre mit angefügten Generalbass-beispielen* (Dehn), 85
theory of key relationships and modulations, xii, 15, 169–170
antecedent key, 23
chords, 16
circle of fifths, 41
in first-degree relationship, 22
harmonic successions of keys, 25
important aspects of, 16
keys' letter-symbols, 29–30
melody harmonization, 16
modulation, 16
remote keys, 27
second- and third-degree key relationships, 27–31
subsequent key, 23
tonal relationships, 107
*The Theory of Music* (De Calvé), 121
tonal system, 51–52, 54
German, 99–105
*Traité complet de la haute composition musicale* (Reicha), 120
*Traité complet de la theorie et de la pratique de l'harmonie* (Fétis), 120
*Traite de l'harmonie* (Rameau), x
triads, 19, 22, 29, 46–47, 67

## U

*Uchebnik*, 120
*Uchebnik Garmonii*, xii, 12f
Ulybyshev, Alexander, 122, 158

## V

*Versuch einer geordneten Theorie der Tonsetzkunst* (Weber), 74, 92, 120
Viennese theory and culture, xii
Villoing, *Practical Guide to the Study of Elementary Music Theory*, 123

## W

Weber, Gottfried, x, 63–64, 79, 84–85, 88–92, 99–101, 109–115, 122, 169
 common-tone relationships, 76
 horizontal and vertical tonic lines, 115–116
 minor-major key system, 75–76
 relationships between keys, 74–78
 tonal systems, 83–84, 99–105
 *Versuch einer geordneten Theorie der Tonsetzkunst*, 74, 92, 120

## Y

Yavorsky, Boris, xi

## Z

Zaremba, Nikolai, 60–62, 143